Now–Tomorrow–Flux
An Anthology on the Museum
of Contemporary Art

Contents

Appendix

Chafing at the Present: The Museum of Contemporary Art between Utopia and Restoration—An Introduction

Museums of contemporary art—of the type that has become a fixture on the cultural scene in the past three decades—are premised on a thorough reconception of the very category of the museum. The historical emphasis that has been characteristic of the traditional museum with its core mission of collecting and conservation is sharply at odds with the idea of the contemporary. Can the contemporary moment be preserved? And what does the present encompass? What were the aspirations that defined a contemporary art institution at the time of its founding, and what are its ambitions today? If we examine the development of many such museums founded since the 1950s, tracing their evolution from scenes of progressive ventures to established institutions, the question arises what the future after this process of institutionalization looks like: Does art even need the fixed venues that museums provide, or do they in the long run become a burden? What are the institution's social and political responsibilities with regard to the values it imparts, and what does it owe its audience? Which form does the relationship between institution and artist take? Museums dedicated to contemporary art often work closely with artists to conceive, design, and implement exhibitions. What is the artist's role as a partner in the production and conservation of art, and what potential does such close collaboration hold? These are questions that ultimately concern the character and operation of a museum of the present and the expectations the public brings to it. They inspired us to take a critical look at our own structures.

With a view to the specific situation of the Migros Museum für Gegenwartskunst, which celebrates its twentieth anniversary in 2016, we thought it was important to recall the conceptual underpinnings of its creation; to examine how they have changed over time; and, on a meta-level, to use our own institution as an example in a critical reflection on the model of the museum of contemporary art. We invited Beatrice von Bismarck of the Academy of Fine Arts Leipzig and Peter J. Schneemann of the Institute of Art History at the University of Bern to help us think about what this book should accomplish and complement our practical experience by contributing their broader perspective as scholars. On the museum's side, Barbara Biedermann, Raphael Gygax, and Judith Welter joined the director, Heike Munder, in conceiving the book and coordinating the various sections.

The Migros Museum für Gegenwartskunst was founded in 1996 in a progressive spirit. A modestly refurbished old factory building became home to a new center of contemporary art, housing the museum as well as a number of other institutions and galleries. The stated objective was to forswear conventional ideas of what a museum should be like and avoid the stuffiness, fixation on the past, and elitism that were associated with many traditional institutions. Instead, interplay between the museum's collection and new productions would put the here and now of contemporary art on stage. Art was something that would be taking place, through participation, discussion, and involvement, lowering the threshold for audiences intimidated by other museums. In the spirit of the "relational aesthetics" of the 1990s, the goal was to create an institution that would be actively engaged with the concerns of the society around it—a stance in some ways modeled on the conception of art that was en vogue at the time. No less importantly, the museum would connect the Zurich scene to the international contemporary art world and explore possible ways of inter-twining the production of art with the programming of exhibitions. These ideas worked well in the 1990s: people cooked, hung out, listened to music, or even simply read the paper. The transitions between art and all these other activities seemed fluid. And the museum attracted a diverse audience; students mingled with middle-class art lovers. However, the thrilling energy of the institution's early years inevitably flagged over time. Like many other comparable institutions, the Migros Museum für Gegenwartskunst underwent a transformation in the early 2000s. Rising prices in the market for contemporary art and its growing popularity reshaped the field around the turn of the millennium and ushered in a period of professionalization. As museums of contemporary art moved into the public spotlight and the art they displayed was increasingly valuable, it became necessary to reorganize their operation, introducing regulations and standardized processes as well as the more rigorous conservational standards that contemporary art had hitherto been exempt from. Meanwhile, a number of new alternative art venues that made no effort to collect work catered to the young independent scene. The Migros Museum für Gegenwartskunst's original fan base disintegrated, and a new audience appeared on the scene.

Bruno Latour's actor-network-theory, which identifies the conjunction of more or less uncoordinated activities on the part of individuals as the fundamental principle of social action, can help us understand this shift. In this view, a museum's audience consists in the "association" of actors who, in the pursuit of their own interests or ideas, form networks, converging in nodes and parting ways again without building stable alliances or initiating sustained collaborative undertakings.[1] If we combine this perspective with a contrary standpoint from critical sociology such as Pierre Bourdieu's theory of social fields that evince relatively little interpenetration, we have an outline of today's art audience. As the surveys of visitors to contemporary art museums that Ulf Wuggenig conducted in Vienna, Hamburg, Paris (1993–1995), and Zurich (2009–2010) have demonstrated, contemporary art continues to be a highly rarefied cultural domain, appealing primarily to visitors who have at least a college degree.[2]

In the history of the Migros Museum für Gegenwartskunst, the professionalization of the contemporary art world also manifested itself in the levels of contents and structures: a venue that resembled a municipal gallery rather than a museum was transformed into an institution dedicated to addressing questions of art history. This transformation was made possible by the recruitment of additional staff and a thorough review of the collection in the mid-2000s. Since then, the museum has made critical awareness of its own role in the ongoing revision of art history a crucial part of its mission, which it pursues through reflections on various relevant discourses such as the debate over sculpture or by producing exhibitions with a focus on performative and process-based art.

---

1   See Bruno Latour, *Reassembling the Social: An Introduction to Actor-Network-Theory* (Oxford: Oxford University Press, 2007).

2   See Heike Munder and Ulf Wuggenig, eds., *Das Kunstfeld: Eine Studie über Akteure und Institutionen der zeitgenössischen Kunst* (Zurich: JRP|Ringier, 2012).

The changes we have sketched point to a phenomenon that can be observed with some frequency in the transition from the abstract utopian idea of reinventing the museum to the gradual process of restoration. Similar trajectories[3] have been documented for numerous important innovative institutions including the Stedelijk Museum, Amsterdam, the Museu de Arte de São Paulo (MASP), the Centre Pompidou, Paris, and the Museu d'Art Contemporani de Barcelona (MACBA).[4] These changes affect the institution's vision of its own role in the writing of art history and its implication in concurrent developments in art and society at large, as well as the process of the revision or affirmation of how the museum works and the premises that sustain its operation. Crucially, these institutions are characterized by a perpetual tension between the impulse to launch new ventures and the hardening of what were initially flexible new structures: while the impact of disruptive innovation guided by ideal visions is central to an institution's exhibition programming or its reputation, it is very difficult to sustain such revolutionary momentum in the long run. Still, for a museum to remain true to the present moment and live up to its ever more complex mission of being a witness to the contemporary world, it must stay in motion.

Manifestly, it is developments in the larger society that offer an institution the opportunity to commit to a social or political ideal. Yet the articulation of the values of freedom and democracy often functions only briefly as an expression of an institution's progressive spirit; as the surrounding social or political environment changes, they solidify into a bald assertion that gestures toward the ideals of another time—the past. Yet audiences rightly expect museums of contemporary art to remain flexible and responsive. So what happens in periods of restoration such as the one we live in today? How can a museum stay in motion? Social mechanisms

---

3   Charles Esche has described it as a pendulum motion in a detailed study of selected examples including the MoMA, the Guggenheim, and the MACBA between the 1960s and today: "Eine Erziehungseinrichtung, eine computerisierte Datenbank der Kulturgeschichte, ein Träger für Aktionen," in Barbara Steiner and Charles Esche, eds., *Mögliche Museen* (Cologne: Verlag der Buchhandlung Walther König, 2007), pp. 21–30.

4   The following institutions and their leaders figure prominently in discussions of this issue: Willem Sandberg, the erstwhile director of the Stedelijk Museum in Amsterdam (1945–1963), who framed the idea of an ideal museum for Europe and, as early as 1959, sought to turn the museum into a "living space" by dispelling the sacred solemnity that sealed the museum off against the outside world. Under his leadership, the Stedelijk implemented his ideas, becoming an unpretentious, open, and popular venue. A no less significant innovation was the involvement of artists, some of whom became close collaborators, in the museum's operation. São Paulo's MASP (the building designed by the architect Lina Bo Bardi opened its doors in 1968) and the Centre Pompidou in Paris (designed by Renzo Piano, inaugurated in 1977) sought to achieve a similar inclusiveness through architectonic innovation: museums were to be open to the cities around them, with transparent walls instead of the imposing and intimidating edifices of traditional museums. The aim was to create venues for art that would be non-elitist and amenable to the citizenry's concerns. Opened in 1995, the MACBA with its spectacular architecture by Richard Meier became a center of activism and civic involvement by accommodating the political unrest brewing in Barcelona and integrating the citizens' concerns into its public programs, gaining a reputation for democratic governance as well as critical potential that remains one of its strengths. Ljubljana's Moderna Galerija (founded in 1948) reinvented itself in the late 1980s with the fall of the Iron Curtain; playing an active role in efforts to revisit the art and history of the region, it has built an unrivaled collection of critical art.

of inclusion and exclusion are one set of issues that has become an
increasingly urgent concern. This ties into how the institution relates to
its different audiences and the forms of art education, participation, and
representation it musters to shape that relationship. It is also closely
connected to an institution's collection-building policies; and this is one
place where museums today have room for maneuver. For example, the
Migros Museum für Gegenwartskunst has steadily increased the representation of women artists in its collection, from virtually nil before 1996
to twenty-one percent in 2002, thirty-six percent today, and rising.
The question, then, is whether genuine change requires a concurrent wave
of social transformation: Might it not take place on a smaller stage as well?
This will be a central issue in Oliver Marchart's contribution to this volume.

What became of the progressive institutions that, in their heyday, sought
to change the ways we see and engage with art? It is interesting to note—
the museums mentioned above can serve as examples—that a recognizable
turn toward a comparatively conservative stance has not dispelled their
reputation for revolutionary energy or progressivism. But how long can
this aura last? The Migros Museum für Gegenwartskunst is exemplary in
that it is one such institution that actively seeks to chart fields for possible
innovation.

The questions the present anthology addresses grew out of a
reflection on our own history. The issues broached in the contributions
are real-world problems that confront institutions of contemporary art.
Contradictions between our aspiration to remain innovators and the
tendency toward restoration that is hard to fend off in the everyday
business of running an institution, the influence of social and political
factors, and the question of which formats will hold potential in the future:
these mark out the thematic spectrum to be examined in the following
pages.

The introductory conversation on "The Paradox of the Contemporary"
sketches the discursive framework in which the museum of contemporary
art finds itself operating today and in which the book seeks to stake out a
position. Yilmaz Dziewior, Francesca von Habsburg, and Lars Nittve joined
Heike Munder to talk about the present-day role of the contemporary
art museum and the expectations of its stakeholders. What is this particular
format capable of, and what should it do? Where does it see its place in
a global art world? With a view to the distinctive exhibition practices and

collection histories of the institutions they directed in the past or direct now, the interlocutors discuss how the understanding of the contemporary art museum's role has changed. Central threads in their conversation—the paradoxical conjunction of the museum's traditional role with the aspiration to contemporariness, the integration of production and exhibition-making, and the museum's relationship with different publics—resurface throughout this anthology. The three chapters under the headwords "Now," "Tomorrow," and "Flux" delve deeper into these issues, with additional conversations scrutinizing specific aspects of the larger themes from the perspective of museum practitioners.

The first chapter, "Now," turns the spotlight on the contemporary moment to address questions of museum practices and artistic techniques that serve to engender presentness. Noting that there is no universally shared definition of the present, Sophia Prinz considers changes in the ways we engage with art in relation to the exhibition as an aesthetic form, before scrutinizing the significance of different perceptions and processes of reception on the part of visitors to the concept of an institution's contemporariness. Pinpointing the crucial role the museum plays in engendering the present, her analysis prods us to reenvision the institution, outlining a fruitful approach to the larger question: In which areas is movement—progression or progress—possible today? Prinz's proposal is that institutions should invest more resources into artistic research or projects that initiate open-ended processes, becoming actively involved in the production of new insights, discourses, and viewpoints. Beat Wyss examines a similar idea in a historical perspective. His contribution traces the conjunction of art and knowledge back to its origins in an early modern idea of the collection-on-display and offers a skeptical take on the implications of a collection—which is to say, the core component of many museums of contemporary art—today. Wyss argues that we have reached the post-museum age, a diagnosis he sketches by analyzing historic formats of the arrangement and presentation of knowledge, identifying three major "epistemic forms" of collecting: the cabinet of curiosities, the encyclopedic library, and the bourgeois museum. The emergence of contemporary art on the stage of broad public interest and an ever more thoroughly globalized art system, he believes, marks the onset of a crisis of the collection. Economic interests and capital investments, he criticizes, are displacing the formerly fruitful alliance of art and knowledge. Is the market indeed becoming the primary source of impulses spurring the activities of museums of contemporary art?

The tendency is real, as Bettina Funcke's essay demonstrates. Using the
Whitney Museum of American Art and the Metropolitan Museum of Art
as examples, she shows how museums, under pressure to increase visitor
figures, have come to cater to their audiences' desire for fun and entertainment, raising the question: To which extent do today's museum visitors
actually still want to learn and understand? Claire Bishop's contribution,
an abridged version of her essay on "Radical Museology," similarly
advocates an institutional practice that defies the advice of trustees and
the interests of market players. What are the implications of our multitemporal present, the projection of a post-museum age, or the tendency in
current museum culture to emphasize branding and the fun factor for the
effort to gain an adequate understanding of the complexities of the present
moment? According to Bishop, we must ask why certain temporal registers
appear in certain works of art at specific historic junctures, an inquiry
for which she proposes the methodology of a "dialectical temporality."

If a museum's analytical and theoretical stance is one characteristic of its
work, the handling of works of art is a no less defining part of its daily
operation. Headlined "Tomorrow," the second chapter discusses the
contemporary art museum as a scene of production as well as conservation.
The focus is on the problem of how to preserve contemporary artistic
production, which is defined by the diversity of media, techniques, and
practices. How does the museum's double role—exhibition venue on the
one hand, commissioner of new creative productions on the other—inform
the ways in which it relates to art? Martha Buskirk's contribution portrays
this duality as a complex ensemble that blurs the lines between formerly
distinct roles such as the artist, the curator, the conservator, the historian,
and even the museum's legal adviser. Focusing on the Migros Museum
für Gegenwartskunst's close dovetailing of collection-building activities
and exhibition programming, she undertakes a detailed analysis of the
production of expansive works of installation art for the museum in order
to shed light on the implications for the institution's collection and conservation policies, and ultimately also on the status of the "author" or creator.
Her findings prompt Buskirk to ask whether the museum of the future,
as a productive conglomerate involving many parties, will in fact still need
artists. What is clear is that traditional categories and role models may
no longer be applicable and need to be rethought.

    Beatriz Colomina shifts the focus from the artist to the work of art:
Might it be that the latter has become irrelevant to the kind of aesthetic

experience museums afford? She considers the architectural shell around art as a space that, as contemporary art became popular, has become "hyper-controlled" and "theatrical." The problem Colomina highlights is that this space dissolves the bounds circumscribing what was once the object of experience in the museum, the contemplative immersion in works of art, and even threatens to supplant it altogether. Another aspect of museum architecture is the subject of Donald Preziosi's epistemic approach in his essay, which examines the various structures and mechanisms—the author's umbrella term is *worlding*—that engender meaning. His contention is that the production of meaning, regardless of its particular modality, is always a multilayered process. Architecture, he argues, is just another expressive modality, whose manifestation in a building or material construction is ultimately not unlike art: a construct materializing functional, social, and political relations. What is interpretation, and where does it begin? Can a museum, a work of art, an architectural shell represent itself as a format? Examining these questions in a broad horizon, Preziosi concludes that architecture—and thus also the museum—turns space into a site precisely by doing nothing and being susceptible to the inscription of meaning. The chapter concludes with a conversation on "Materialities— Physical States of Artworks" that complements Preziosi's philosophical take on the materiality of the work of art with a practice-oriented perspective, bringing the challenges museums face every day in handling perishable and fragile works of art into focus. Nadia Schneider Willen and Judith Welter invited Karla Black, Bruna Casagrande, and Wolfgang Ullrich to discuss the novel and often deliberate uses of ephemeral materials in contemporary art and how they affect museum collecting practices, as well as the associated changes in our understanding of ideas such as the work of art, authenticity, and the original.

The third chapter, "Flux," scrutinizes the contemporary art museum's relationships with its public(s), raising questions concerning the forms of—institutional, curatorial, architectural, or educational—address, transparencies, and possible exclusions. The interface between inside and outside is what Oliver Marchart's analysis homes in on, unfolding the full complexity that looms beneath the black-and-white distinction between art and politics. A simplified breakdown into binary positions of the sort that is often the objective and instrument of political propaganda confronts us with a decision: Am I left or right? In favor or against? The rules governing the art field—which, Marchart writes, is primarily interested in "functioning"—stigmatizes such unequivocal positions as bad art and instead promotes art's fundamental semantic openness. Contrasting the traditional idea of "autonomous" art with the institutional straightjacket in which it takes place, Marchart uses the metaphor of the "crack" introduced by the political scientist John Holloway to ask: To what extent is it the institution itself that is afraid of contingency? Permeability, he proposes, might disrupt its smooth operation. His argument culminates in the challenge to institutions to step outside the neutral zone and do more to facilitate linkages between inside and outside in order to allow new spaces of thinking and substitute publics to come into being and strengthen their engagement with political struggles. If we come back to the question with which we began—what the stability of an institution makes possible and how it can avoid the gravitational pull of restoration and return to an activist vision of the art museum—Marchart's contribution may chart one way for a museum of the present to harness the potential of contingency.

The range of political problems this chapter navigates prompts not only a debate over the possible freedoms the museum affords and the leeway it has, it also raises the question of how constrained institutions are by their traditions. The significance or, to use another word, the weight of this legacy can currently be observed in museums all over the world that confront the need to revise their Western-dominated historiography and increasingly turn their attention to issues of race. Christian Kravagna's contribution shows what such an institutional reassessment can look like in specific terms. Based on a research trip during which he studied the representation of race relations in American museums, his essay discusses the ways in which museums of contemporary art take stances on national and regional race issues and related questions. Noting the political challenges the United States face today, fifty years after the successes of the Civil Rights Movement, he spotlights how museums bring history into perspective and position themselves in the current debate over how to deal with the nation's unresolved race issues. Discussing the inaugural exhibition *America Is Hard to See* at the new Whitney Museum of American Art in relation to separate exhibitions held concurrently in Miami and New Orleans, Kravagna portrays different policies and choices designed to counter the racist and discriminatory practices that were long prevalent in the art world as well. The essay contributed by the Vienna-based collective Büro trafo.K examines these questions from the perspective of art education. The authors present approaches to pedagogical work at the museum that are committed to the aspiration to address "everybody," and draw on examples from their own projects to reflect on the challenges and problems as well as the potential of strategies that aim to open up the institution on the levels of both structure and content. The question "What does 'everybody' mean?" serves the collective as a conceptual starting point, but also as a methodological tool that helps them to analyze and disrupt habits in art education and rethink their approach to their work.

Where the first three contributions to this chapter consider politics of the art field in the institutional perspective, the reprint of Artur Żmijewski's essay "The Applied Social Arts" brings the standpoint of art into the debate. Shame, the author argues, is the element that paralyzes the development of political agency. Like Marchart, he notes that art that takes a clear political stance is easily dismissed as propaganda. The genuine rejection of the imputation of any kind of complicity with power, he writes, is what motivates art's efforts to claim autonomy. The consequence is that art becomes incapable of action, inconsequential, and alienating. To chart a way out of this dilemma, art has developed strategies of evaluation and assessment. Besides shame, Żmijewski believes, art's reliance on images is another cause for its alienation. Unlike a text, it conveys its meaning not through narration but through a web of references. In this respect, his critique takes aim not only at artists, but also at the art system. Art critics, he writes, simply do not know enough, curtailing the work's ability to communicate: "What the critic cannot understand cannot be expressed and never makes it into the circuit of knowledge, is not revealed within the work."

Żmijewski's harsh critique of the art system brings us back to the question of how institutions can counter this illegibility—and thus to the crucial issue that was the point of departure for the present volume: What does the museum of the present aspire to be and what can it actually accomplish, how does it relate to art as well as to the artists, and how capable is it of maneuvering between the impulse to innovate and its public cultural mission? This brings a field into focus that has come to play a vital part: art education. In a conversation with Bernadett Settele, Zachary Bowman, and Sepake Angiama, Alena Nawrotzki explores the actual needs and desires with which visitors approach art educators and asks how the latter can introduce people to contemporary art without becoming spokespeople for the institution's interpretive authority. How much pedagogical assistance, how much participation does the self-determined beholder need? Where does art education start, and to which extent can it help people think for themselves and delve deeper into issues, going beyond a narrowly pedagogical approach? The conversation on "Art Education in Contemporary Art Museums" once again draws our attention to a point that surfaces several times in these pages—the separation between the museum's inside and the world outside it—and grounds it in the interlocutors' experiences, projects, and stances. Breaking the mold of a technical debate among professional art educators, the discussion ultimately turns to the question of the potential art holds for society at large.

The volume concludes with a conversation on "The Age of Ethics?!—Ethics and the Contemporary Art Museum" that envisions the complex set of tensions amid which the contemporary art museum seeks to stake out its place today from the angle of ethical responsibility. Raphael Gygax invited Philipp Kaiser, Kate Fowle, and Andrea Fraser to take a personal stand on issues including financing models, transparency, and ethical guidelines. Their conversation sheds light on possible interdependencies between materiality and acquisitions policies and questions the contemporary relevance of ethics codes that often focus on aspects of collection-building. Topics addressed elsewhere in the book such as the role of privately financed collections, art handling, and the relationships between institutions and artists on the one hand and the art market on the other are discussed with a view to the various stakeholders' ethical obligations, adding another important perspective on the significance and intricacy of the questions museums of contemporary art face today.

What becomes clear is that the contemporary art museum operates in a complex environment in which conceptual ambitions, institutional practices, and ideological commitments are not infrequently at odds. Noticeably, the embrace of innovation and the new—what we have described as the museum in motion—sometimes puts institutions maneuvering between the poles of utopian aspiration and restorative tendencies to minor or major tests, or as we might say with the metaphor Oliver Marchart has introduced into the debate: the museum is under constant stress and prone to crack.

Seeking to identify new ideas that can help us understand the causes of the current trend toward restoration and chart ways out of it, we conceived this book as an encounter between theoretical positions and conversations among art-world practitioners. We hope that it will sketch novel approaches for the institutional context that can set the museum in motion again—and refresh our sense of urgency and our appetite for change.

The Paradox of the Contemporary
Heike Munder in conversation with Yilmaz Dziewior,
Francesca von Habsburg, and Lars Nittve

HEIKE MUNDER   The term "museum of contemporary art" contains a contradiction: What do "present" and "future" mean for a collecting museum? The concept of the art museum traditionally places a focus on the past, its preservation and protection. How can the contemporary be preserved, and what is its value? I am referring to a discourse that emerged together with the institutionalization of contemporary art. We also have to consider the entry of cultural studies into the art-historical discussion in the 1990s, initiating a union of content and form in theory. Through this new approach, not only contemporary art but also historical works became embedded in actual contexts, receiving various layers of reading. Institutions such as MACBA in Barcelona, the Serralves in Porto, the MAMCO in Geneva and the Migros Museum für Gegenwartskunst in Zurich, mark this shift in their approach to art.

Some other institutions were forerunners in this field, such as the Museum für Moderne Kunst in Frankfurt (founded in 1981) and the Museum Ludwig in Cologne (1976). In my opinion, these two programmatically oriented institutions mark the shift from an art-historical view to a contemporary perspective. Yilmaz, can you tell us about the initial ideas behind the Ludwig?

YILMAZ DZIEWIOR   The foundation of the Museum Ludwig forty years ago was quite a struggle. There was a lot of criticism of Peter Ludwig: in exchange for donating a large portion of his collection, he insisted that the museum bear his name, which was seen by some as blackmail. From today's perspective, we can be happy that he was successful, because the Ludwig collection forms the basis of our museum. The influence of private collectors on public institutions, a topic of much discussion today, emerged back then but was not as virulent as it is now.

Ludwig's idea of a museum was traditional and advanced at the same time: traditional in that he still believed in the idea of the artist as genius—he wrote his dissertation on Picasso, whom he always preferred to Duchamp—but advanced because he trusted in the political and social function of art. He and his wife, Irene, began quite early on to collect art that did not belong to the canon of the time. There was much heated discussion in West Germany because of his strong interest in art from the GDR; his collection became the biggest outside East Germany.

For me today, his interest in art from Latin America, especially Cuba (where he established a foundation bearing his name), and from Asia, especially China, are key points of departure for my own activities, acquisitions, projects, and exhibitions; they are my way to broaden our perspective far beyond North America and Europe. For Peter and Irene Ludwig, "world art," as they called it, was a crucial part of their understanding of cultural production. Their belief in the social and cultural impact of art can also be traced back to the original name of their foundation, which translates as "The Ludwig Foundation for Art and International Understanding."

HM   I really like their idea of "world art"; that's something the Migros Museum für Gegenwartskunst—which was founded in 1996, twenty years after the Ludwig and four years before London's Tate Modern—is lacking. In the nineties, the biggest break was with the traditional activity of the art museum—transcending the division between collection and production (that is, exhibition practice). The museum was testing its boundaries, becoming a place of production as well as collection and at the same time a living room for the art lover, with music, food, and drink. The presentation of the collection was combined with and complemented by exhibitions of newly commissioned artworks.

Since the turn of the millennium, exhibition programming has returned to a more classical approach, and the concept of a "new contemporary" has found expression in a focus on large-scale commissions that are produced in collaboration with the artists and incorporated into the collection. And since 2002, when I took over at the Migros Museum für Gegenwartskunst, the 1990s-era emphasis on participatory art has been extended to include performative and process-based artworks from the 1960s to the present. In the last decade the Migros Museum für Gegenwartskunst has been particularly interested in reviewing established lines of (art) history. This approach has been crucial to the character of the museum's collection, which has a long history of incorporating works that were ignored by the canon at the time but have since been vindicated: for example, works by Heidi Bucher, Marc Camille Chaimowicz, Gustav Metzger, and Stephen Willats.

Lars, you've directed many museums, including two where you were the founding director. It would be interesting to get your view of the idea laid out above: Where do you see the shift in the manifestation of the contemporary?

LARS NITTVE   I've always been interested in—and amused by—the way institutions that call themselves museums of "modern" or "contemporary" art have struggled with what seems to be a paradox manifest in the very name (and I should say here that I have come more and more to believe that the distinction between "modern" and "contemporary" is actually a modernist construct). There have been a number of instances where museums have tried—for periods of time, under certain directors—to repress their "museum" side, sometimes going so far as to essentially put the collection in storage in an attempt to turn the museum into a contemporary arena—an art gallery or Kunsthalle. And then there have been many other cases where museums have focused completely on their role as "museums"—as institutions working with, constructing, and preserving history—and have almost completely abandoned representing and discussing whatever was happening in the present. But to me this "paradox," if you like, is the key to a lively, energetic, and meaningful art museum. The friction between the two positions—being a place for history as well as a contemporary arena—is, to me, the key to successful museums. Friction creates energy. The contemporary rewrites history in an infinite process, and history gives the present something to resonate off.

Also, the shifts you outline, relating to the move toward commissioning and production—or toward the time-based and performative— do not have such a short history. If you study what Pontus Hultén did at the Moderna Museet in Stockholm in the 1960s, for example (and possibly

Willem Sandberg at the Stedelijk in Amsterdam as well), you'll notice that all these aspects were already part of his arsenal at that time. Just think of the exhibition *Hon* (She) in 1966: it had all these aspects, in a museum with an extraordinary twentieth-century collection.

When it comes to Tate Modern, for example, and the Moderna Museet—and also M+ in Hong Kong—I would say that keeping the "paradox" alive was a central task. Another key approach was to always try to look at history—and, in a way, tell it—from the perspective of "now." And of course, philosophically speaking, you can do nothing else.

HM   On the question of how to construct history from today's perspective, your most recent job, setting up M+ (which is scheduled to open in 2019), is a very interesting example. You've faced a completely different cultural and social context. I'm interested in the way the museum is constructing a national narrative and how it locates itself in a global art world.

LN   To put it very simply, we're trying to do the same thing as other museums around the world that think of themselves as "international" or "global." We look at the world from where we are. In a very simplified way you can think of our collection as concentric circles, with Hong Kong at the center, followed by mainland China, "Greater China," East Asia, Asia, and then the West and the rest. That means that we collect art (and design, architecture, and moving-image work) from Hong Kong and China quite "generously" while making more strategic choices farther from the core of the story.

Of course it's more complex than that, but I imagine that when you walk through the display of the collection in 2019, while you will never doubt that you're in Hong Kong, China, or Asia, you'll also be in the world—just as you never doubt that you're in London, the United Kingdom, or Europe when you walk through the Tate Modern collection, but you're also in the world. Some stories will be similar, others will have a different weight and emphasis, and still others will be totally different.

The interesting thing with the Hong Kong project is that it's probably the only place in Asia where you can, to a large extent, escape the nationalist trap. The Japanese narrative is very Japanese—and then a bit "international." The Korean is Korean, the Singaporean is Singaporean, and the mainland Chinese is definitely nationalistic. Due to the unique and, in many ways, peculiar status of Hong Kong, you can tell what you might call a more pan-Asian story—and then inscribe that narrative into a larger global story. That's something that makes the M+ project unique and extremely exciting.

HM   Since the beginning, the production of art and, with it, participation in the process of creation, have been central for the Migros Museum für Gegenwartskunst. That hasn't changed to this day. It goes hand in hand with trusting in an artist and his or her ideas, and with finding pleasure in realization. Time and again, this approach has enabled us to produce complex installations, such as Ragnar Kjartansson's *The Visitors*, Stephen G. Rhodes' *The Law of the Unknown Neighbor: Inferno Romanticized*, Geoffrey Farmer's *Let's Make the Water Turn Black*, or the Robert Kusmirowski exhibition.

Francesca, I know that this interest in commissioning and following up the process is something that you share with the rest of us.

FRANCESCA VON HABSBURG   In 2001 I fell in love with Janet Cardiff and George Bures Miller's work *Dark Pool* at PS1. I wanted to buy it, but it was not for sale, and I understood, since it was a very personal piece. Another of their personal works that I was interested in was *To Touch* at Luhring Augustine, but the gallery didn't want to sell to a private individual; they wanted the work to be shown. So in 2002 I created an institution— TBA21, in Vienna—to satisfy their demands that an institution acquire the work.

It always amused me that they thought a private collector would somehow be different if they had an institution, not just a private office. I suppose in the long run they were right. Since then I've commissioned ambitious projects that defy traditional classification, in terms of both artistic media and disciplines in general. I might not have had the infra- structure or the professional support to do so if I hadn't created TBA21 all those years ago. So I'm grateful to Janet and George, and to Roland Augustine, for making that condition a prerequisite for owning the work. A few years later we ventured into a much more complex work called *The Murder of Crows*, probably the largest single piece in the whole collection. A few summers ago it filled the Armory in New York and the main hall of the Hamburger Bahnhof.

I'm a private collector with a private foundation. I have the freedom to do whatever I want to do, backed by the great support of my team of curators and project managers in Vienna. So, if you have all the freedom in the world—aside from practical and financial realities—to do something completely different, why would you try to emulate an institutional museum structure? Since TBA21 was founded, I've commissioned incredible, complex works by artists such as Kutluğ Ataman, Candice Breitz, Olafur Eliasson, Carsten Höller, Superflex, and Cerith Wyn Evans, as well as a younger generation of artists such as the Propeller Group. But more interestingly, I have come to realize that artists are accessible people who enjoy dialogue. They don't simply want to fill commercial spaces with salable artworks; they have a need to engage beyond the confines of the art market.

HM   In the past you took a very cosmopolitan approach, with your idea of building pavilions in different time zones. You wanted to present your collection in different contexts, to expose it to a wider range of perceptions. I saw that as a grassroots idea as well. But you gave that up before it happened and have been shifting more and more toward collaborations between the arts and the sciences. Can you tell us something about your visions and how they are linked (or not linked) to institutional ideas?

FH   Well, I didn't give up on it entirely. We toured *The Morning Line* from Seville to Istanbul to Vienna to the ZKM in Karlsruhe, where it now resides. I'm working on an Oceans Pavilion in Venice, and the more I think about what I'd like to do with the collection in the long term, the more I struggle with the idea of putting it all in one place, under one umbrella. I'm thinking of adopting numerous spaces with one common architectural design, an idea I'm working on with Hani Rashid and his partner Lise Anne Couture (Asymptote). The aim of this new partnership is to look for new solutions for us as a deeply personal private collection that is constantly in flux and would face extinction if it tried to conform to the norms of museum building.

Artists are also extremely resourceful in communicating important issues of our time. As the world's image makers, they can propose new solutions without sacrificing complexity or succumbing to reductionist politics. So, after many years of commissioning ambitious projects that defy categorization in terms of art, I decided to expand this notion to knowledge production as well. To my mind, art and knowledge production are not separate, but art can create particular forms of knowledge and engagement. I decided to direct the focus of TBA21 to this type of interdisciplinary production, to tackle some of the most pressing issues of our time, particularly with regard to the oceans and how they are affected by climate change. We develop the commissions in close dialogue with the artists and curators at the foundation. It's important to me that I feel they are projects that need to be made, that they come out of an understanding that we need new ideas, that they are challenging and complex.

HM   Francesca, what is the complexity you expect from your collection? Whom do you want to address with it, today and in the future?

FH   I see myself as an explorer, a producer, and an experimentalist. My vision for TBA21 is closely connected to this. I am passionate and courageous, and I want my foundation to be the same. We've worked with some of the most important and challenging artists today to develop a new language extensively informed by social and environmental issues, science, and sound. We need to understand that the next ten years are going to be the most important in the next ten thousand years of the planet. For me, working with and supporting the work of artists like Armin Linke, from whom I have learned a great deal about the Anthropocene, connects to the idea of being an agent of change rather than a traditional art institution. I don't want to get stuck in institutional infrastructure; I want to adapt and respond to the world that surrounds us, which is complex, moving, and ever-changing.

In terms of location, we're based in Vienna, and I think it's important to continue engaging with the audience we've built up, to create a bastion of free thought and experimentation, especially at a time when politics are closing down rather than opening up. With Olafur Eliasson's *Green Light* project, we turned the exhibition space into an art studio and offered German classes for refugees and asylum seekers who had recently arrived in Vienna. The most we could do for them was to integrate them into our creative force. It was so healing for them. Mario García Torres's exhibition *An Arrival Tale* is a continuation of this, and we worked with the refugees from *Green Light* to collect, describe, and complicate narratives of translation in the artist's films, thereby adding another layer of interpretation to the works.

With the TBA21 Academy, and particularly our exploratory fellowship program *The Current*, which takes place in the South Pacific, we seek to expand the boundaries of disciplines and create new knowledge through synergies between different fields, always starting from an artistic core. Here we've begun to integrate the creative process with science, with a focus on marine biology, all the way to ancient wisdom and shamanism. I want my foundation to act as a catalyst and instigate others to become agents of change. For this, we need new ways of engaging and thinking that bring hope and new solutions to old problems.

HM   To come back to the common thread of this conversation, the paradox of the contemporary: When acquiring new artworks, is the stability of their value part of the decision-making process—that is, is it a topic in your discussions? At the Migros Museum für Gegenwartskunst we have such discussions about conservational aspects, but not about a work's canonical value. So sometimes we take big risks—for example, from a conservational point of view, with Gustav Metzger's *Liquid Crystal Environment*, with its modified projectors and used liquid crystals, or the poor paper and printing quality of Henrik Olesen's *Some Gay-Lesbian Artists and/or Artists Relevant to Homo-Social Culture Born between c. 1300–1870*.

YD   We very seldom buy art from artists who've just started their careers, although recently we made an exception for a work by Anne Imhof: though relatively new in the art field, she seems to me very mature in her work, and we felt we had to acquire it now rather than wait until it was—as has happened on so many other occasions—too expensive. In general, our decisions are less related to the prospective stability of a work's value than to what we think is needed and makes sense for our collection. One of my first acquisitions was two works by the Peruvian artist Teresa Burga, which were a nice addition to our Pop Art collection and are now on view next to Marisol Escobar.

It's much more difficult to broaden the narrative of modernity than it is that of the present. For example, we're very interested in art by the Gutai group from the 1950s in Japan, by the Dansaekhwa group from the mid-1970s in Korea, and by the Tropicália movement from the 1960s in Brazil, but the prices of these positions are already so high that it's almost impossible for us to expand our collection in these necessary directions. But I won't give up—and there's also the possibility that we'll get donations.

HM   Do you claim to be continuously updating art history, and how important is that for you? How do you deal with that in the museum? How is it represented in the exhibitions and, above all, in the collection?

FH   I think the collection that does that at the highest level is the Thyssen-Bornemisza Museum in Madrid. No other private collector had gone to those lengths before.

Working in contemporary art does not—at least to me—define art history! However, moving into a new generation of artists and methodologies does beg the question: How long do we have to remain "contemporary"? It seems like such a dated term! "Modern practice" would be more appropriate. Where do we go from here and now?

YD   At the Museum Ludwig there's a group of supporters called the Perlensucher (pearl seekers) who specialize in acquiring works by artists that have been "forgotten" or overlooked in the history of our collection. They've bought works by Teresa Burga, Valie Export, Charlotte Posenenske, and Ed Ruscha, for example.

In general, it's less about the "newness" of the discussions than about how relevant a discourse is. For example, I think that "old" topics like the emancipation of so-called minority groups are still valid issues. Feminism and the visibility of artists not usually included in the canon are still extremely valid. That's part of why we mounted our Joan Mitchell retrospective: we own works by Jackson Pollock, Franz Kline, and some of her other male contemporaries, but there's nothing by her in our collection. The same goes for Gabriele Münter, whose work we're planning to exhibit together with the Lenbachhaus in Munich and the Louisiana Museum in Humlebæk. We're also planning an exhibition of Japanese photography from the 1970s, to mention just a few of the ways we're trying to rewrite or broaden art history.

LN   I think that engagement with the present—for example, through temporary exhibitions and acquisitions—continuously rewrites the historical narrative. And as a natural consequence, I would say that a properly functioning museum reinstalls its collection so that it makes sense and is productive, so to speak, in relation to contemporary practice. After all, the collection is a great tool for giving the public clues to their reading of the present.

When collecting, I've always underlined the importance of not abstaining from acquisitions just because the work is big or difficult to store or install, or because the materials are fragile and may not last forever. I think one has to accept fluidity in terms of the material aspects— just as one may have to accept it in relation to a work's meaning, importance, and relevance. But remember, too, that works can be "reborn" again thanks to the activities of new generations of artists—or simply shifts in society.

HM   A thought experiment: If you were not constrained by anything and had total freedom, where would you focus your efforts to make a contemporary art museum experimental? What role should it play in society? What would you want to represent with your ideal museum?

I ask this because, for the most part, the rise of art museums coincides with cities' attempts to distinguish themselves from competing cities; investment in culture and leisure is meant to attract creativity and international attention. And of course this is easier to achieve with outstanding architecture and easily accessible shows. But this does not necessarily leave space for social or political experiments, such as the decolonialization discussions currently taking place in Latin America (for example, at the Museo de Arte de Lima under its new director, Natalia Majluf) or the way MSUM in Ljubljana and the Museo Reina Sofía in Madrid have been able to critically reflect on their countries' recent political histories.

LN   Fundamentally, art museums exist because there is, in our society, something we call art. They are not there for their own sake. This means that a museum focused on art made in the present needs to be, in a sense, a consequence of that art, while constantly remembering that its role is also to be the meeting place between that art and the public—the beholders or, perhaps, participants. An ideal museum, then, is a museum that, using its best judgment, without making any type of compromise, follows the lead of the art it finds most important and tries to optimize the way it engages with the public. How experimental this will be is ultimately defined by the artists—and the public. I've often been quoted as saying that the museum should be a good dancer, and that the art/artist should lead in that dance. Perhaps an even better metaphor (or not?) would be that the museum is like a dance coach, pairing the art/artist with the public...?

We all know that museums, and collections, come into the world for all sorts of reasons, some of them of the type you mention above. These aspirations are often something that frames and may sometimes limit what the museum can do. At the same time we have numerous examples of museums that exist for one reason—municipal or national pride, corporate brand-building, personal vanity, etc.—yet their openness to experimentation remains unaffected.

YD   To be honest, I'm skeptical of your question's implication that museums are fully part of what we call the culture industry. While I am aware of the economic and political pressure on museums in general, including the Museum Ludwig, I still fundamentally believe in the freedom of our institution's actions. I think it's often less a question of broad political issues than what I would call micropolitics.

To give you an example: up to now no Turkish artists have been represented in our collection, even though Cologne has one of the biggest Turkish populations in Germany. To change this situation, we're currently in the process of acquiring a relatively large piece by Nil Yalter. We're also collaborating with a social-housing organization to bring people into our museum who would not normally come. With our team, we're working on contextualizing the works in our permanent presentation to help our audience understand the cultural, economical, and political situation the art was created in. So there will be more archival material, films, and other source material to make our visitors aware of the context art is produced, distributed, and presented in. None of these activities will change the world, but I hope they do have effects.

FH   Well, we're having a conversation about our practice here, but we're completely forgetting to talk about the public. Museums are somehow polarized between those that are economically dependent on large visitor numbers and those that aren't. Ticket sales account for a large part of some institutions' budgets.

That's certainly true for the Thyssen-Bornemisza in Madrid. There, the curator has stooped so low as to organize fashion exhibitions after seeing the enormous success of the Met's Costume Institute in New York and the Victoria and Albert in London. The huge difference is that those museums have teams of people dedicated to organizing brilliant exhibitions that fill an important gap in understanding the world we live in, such as the recent David Bowie exhibition at the V&A and the Alexander McQueen and punk shows at the Met. However, these traditional art museums are merely flirting with these topics, as indeed they are with photography and contemporary art. They constitute another superficial layer of crowd-pleasers and are not taken seriously by anyone.

At the Thyssen, I've been blocked from creating an ongoing commitment to contemporary art on the grounds that nobody is interested, no one will come. It's sad but true. So, while we are practitioners of bringing new directions and disciplines to cultural practice, I would be grateful for new arguments to give to the museum, which is already crying about dwindling attendance figures, on how to take a more serious view of their future programming. As for the Migros Museum für Gegenwartskunst, the tragedy lies in the fact that the programming is brilliant but the audience is simply not there!

HM   You were recently considering bringing TBA21 to Zurich.

FH   The idea of making Zurich the final resting place of my collection —as so many have done before me, with gestures far greater and also far more modest that what I've had in mind—has become a huge stumbling block for me. My main concern has been not the collection itself but the investment in energy, skill, and funding that would be required to maintain the energy levels I would need to coerce out of my team if we knew in advance that the audience was simply not there. It's strange, but until now I've never cared about audience numbers that much out in Augarten away from the centralized art scene in Vienna: I would never attract huge numbers and never catered to the crowd I had anyway. That's what kept our program unpredictable and exciting, whatever attendance figures we had. But that's not a luxury I can imagine the Migros Museum für Gegenwartskunst being able to afford.

So what's the solution? I think it's to break things up. For attendance and visibility, go to a location where there is a public, like Venice. Look at the Prada Foundation: two venues, Milan and Venice. Then let's go back to the Swiss national railway and look at the venues they have scattered all over Switzerland, their collaborations on pop-ups and temporary projects, sometimes with residencies that engage local communities as well. Bring the art to the communities, and forget the old central location struggling with endless budget cuts and a lack of support from a conservative board. It's not worth the uphill struggle. The larger Löwenbräu space was destroyed by the complicated investment strategies real estate companies were pursuing in the whole Löwenbräu area, as well as financial restrictions—and in some areas the architecture was falling apart as well. No one wants to be there anymore. If it were me I would completely rethink the future of Migros Museum für Gegenwartskunst and spread yourself thin over a greater area. And let Zurich know that it's slipping away from being a meaningful art center...

HM   In your view, are there any notable differences between public institutions and private museums such as the Migros Museum für Gegenwartskunst, TBA21, the Garage in Moscow, and the Jumex in Mexico City? Among the private institutions, which are the most interesting to you, and why? What role do private institutions play in the contemporary art field, compared to the big state-run institutions? Are the private institutions more flexible and faster in establishing a strong or independent profile?

LN   I don't necessarily think, in light of the above, and as history has also shown, that where the funding comes from is as decisive a factor as one might think. (On the other hand, I'm certain money always has some impact on the directions institutions take, so it's good to have more than one source of support.) It's more about how the museum defines its role: as a public service, a status marker for the owner, a major institution's vanity project, a national/political project, etc. We should remember that most US museums started out as private museums and are still private foundations. And that in Russia and mainland China the most advanced museums, in terms of museological practice, are privately funded. To put it simply, it seems—sadly—that just because a museum is funded by the public, it does not necessarily serve either the public or the artists/art. And it should serve both.

YD   In our anniversary exhibition, *We Call It Ludwig*, the Guerrilla Girls will present a film that answers this question the following way: "Kings, queens, and emperors have always had a lot of stuff. When they ran out of space in their palaces and churches, they founded museums to show how great it all was. Today, it's the super-rich who start museums—all over the world. That's the story of the Museum Ludwig. Now, decades later, more and more billionaire art collectors are setting up their own vanity museums. But instead of donating their collections to the public like the Ludwigs, these collectors are operating their own private museums." My personal opinion is that all the interesting private museums will become public as time goes by, and the other ones will vanish the same way they appeared.

The conversation was realized via e-mail in June 2016.

Archives
Bringing the paradox of the present into focus, this image series
presents works that scrutinize the museum as a scene of preservation.

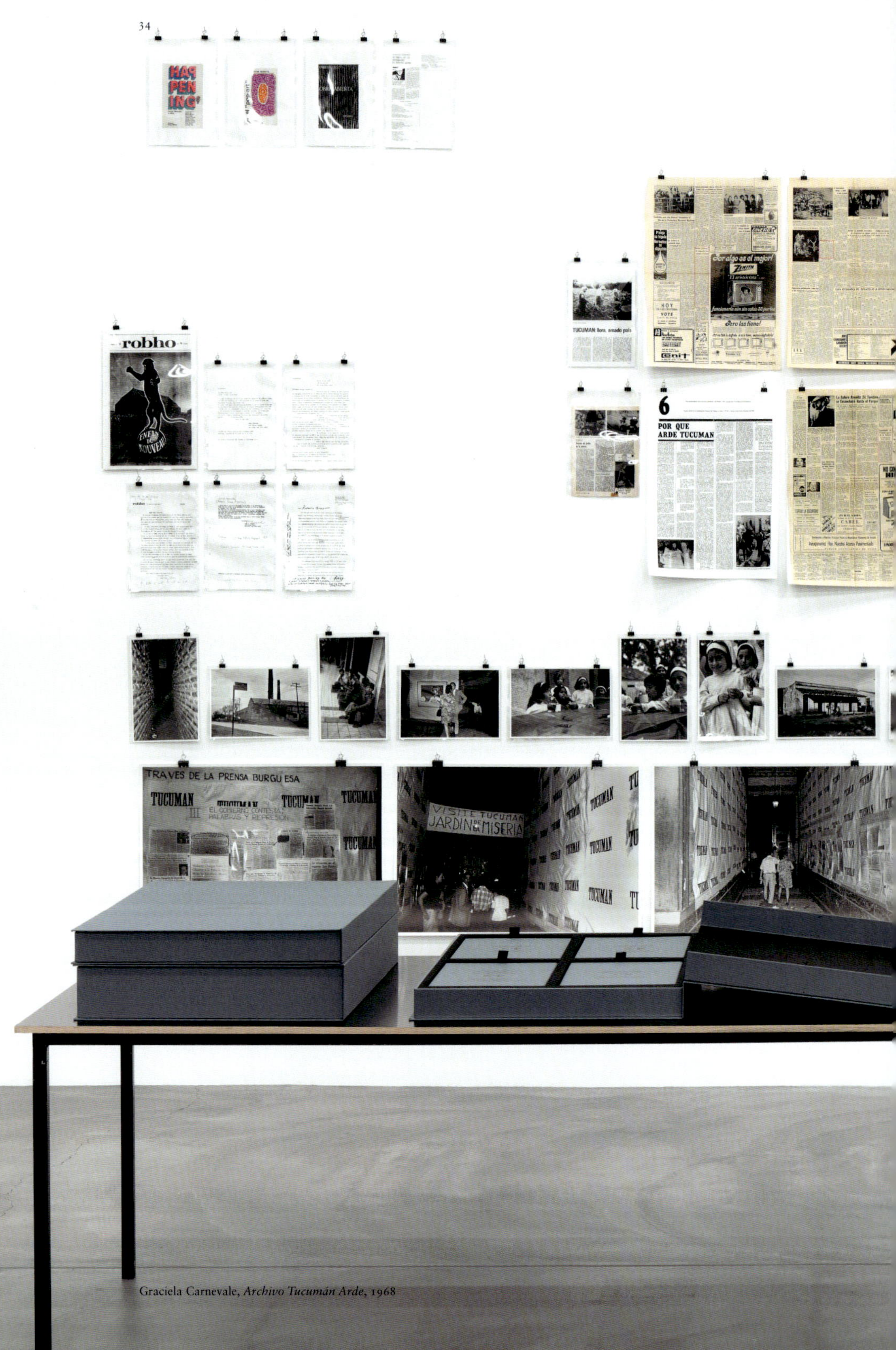

Graciela Carnevale, *Archivo Tucumán Arde*, 1968

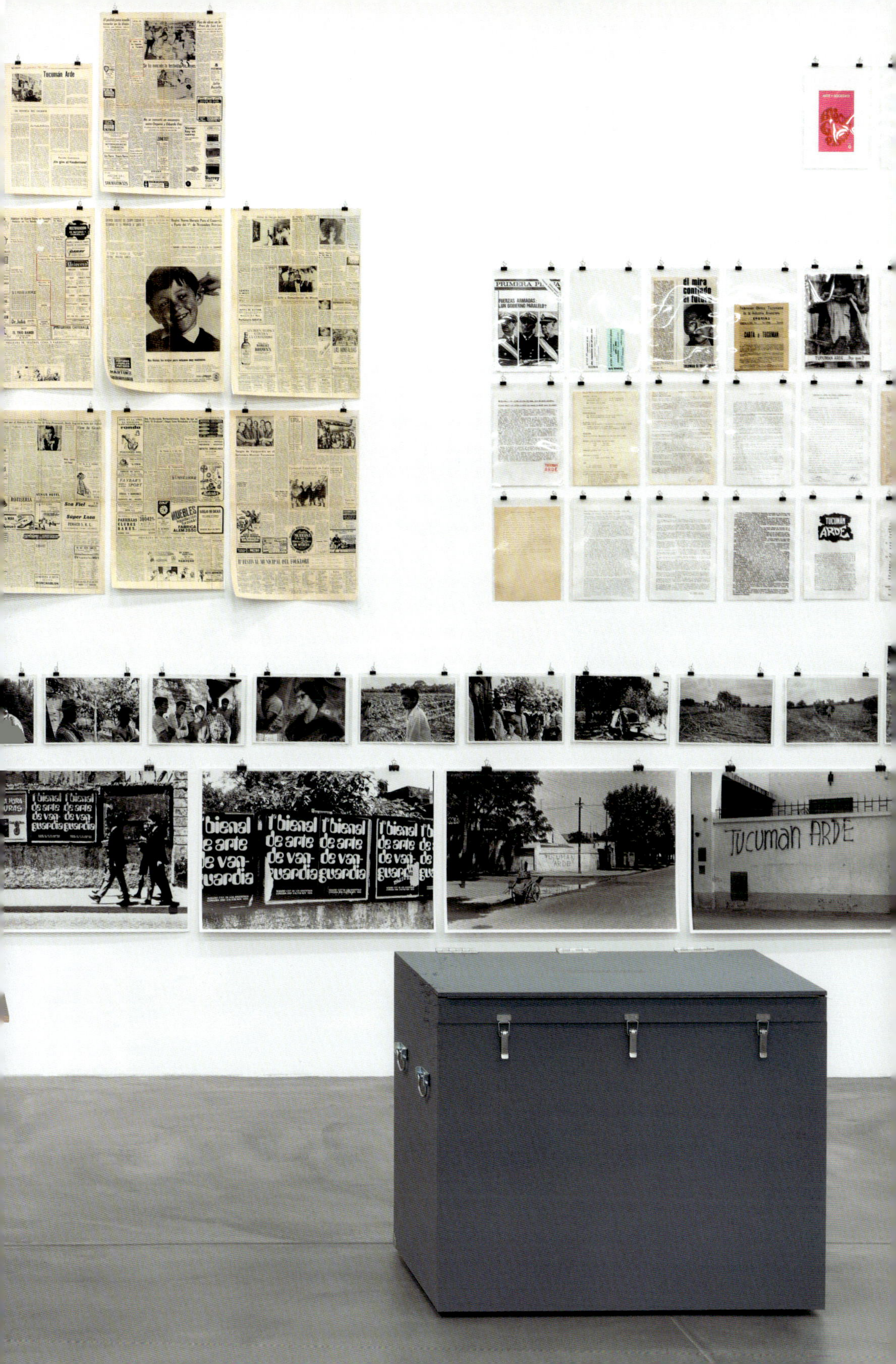

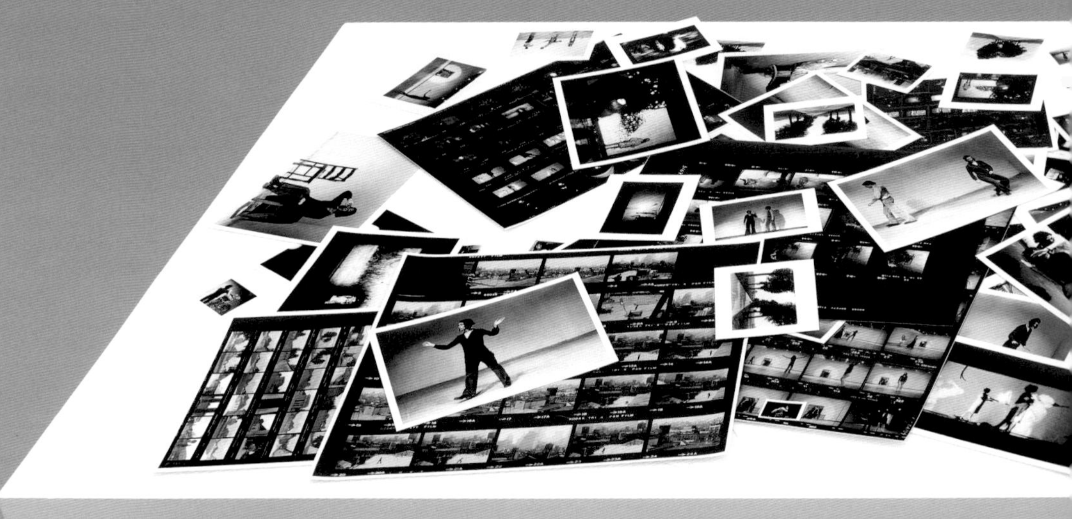

Babette Mangolte, *Touching II & Collage 2, 2008–2010*

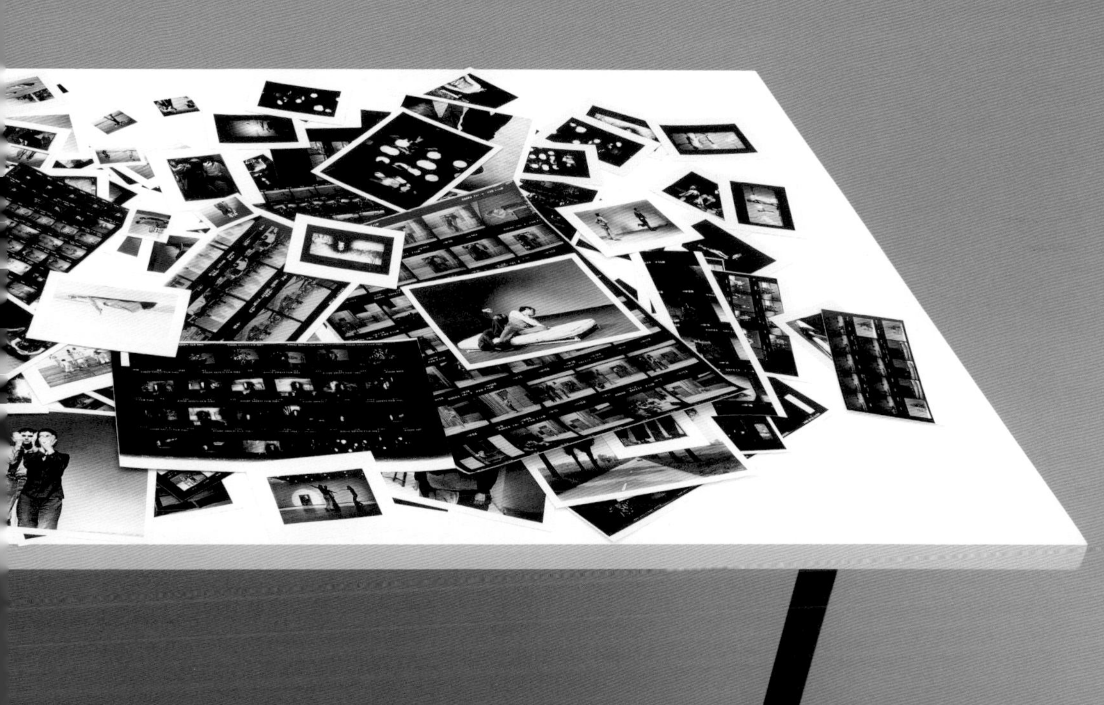

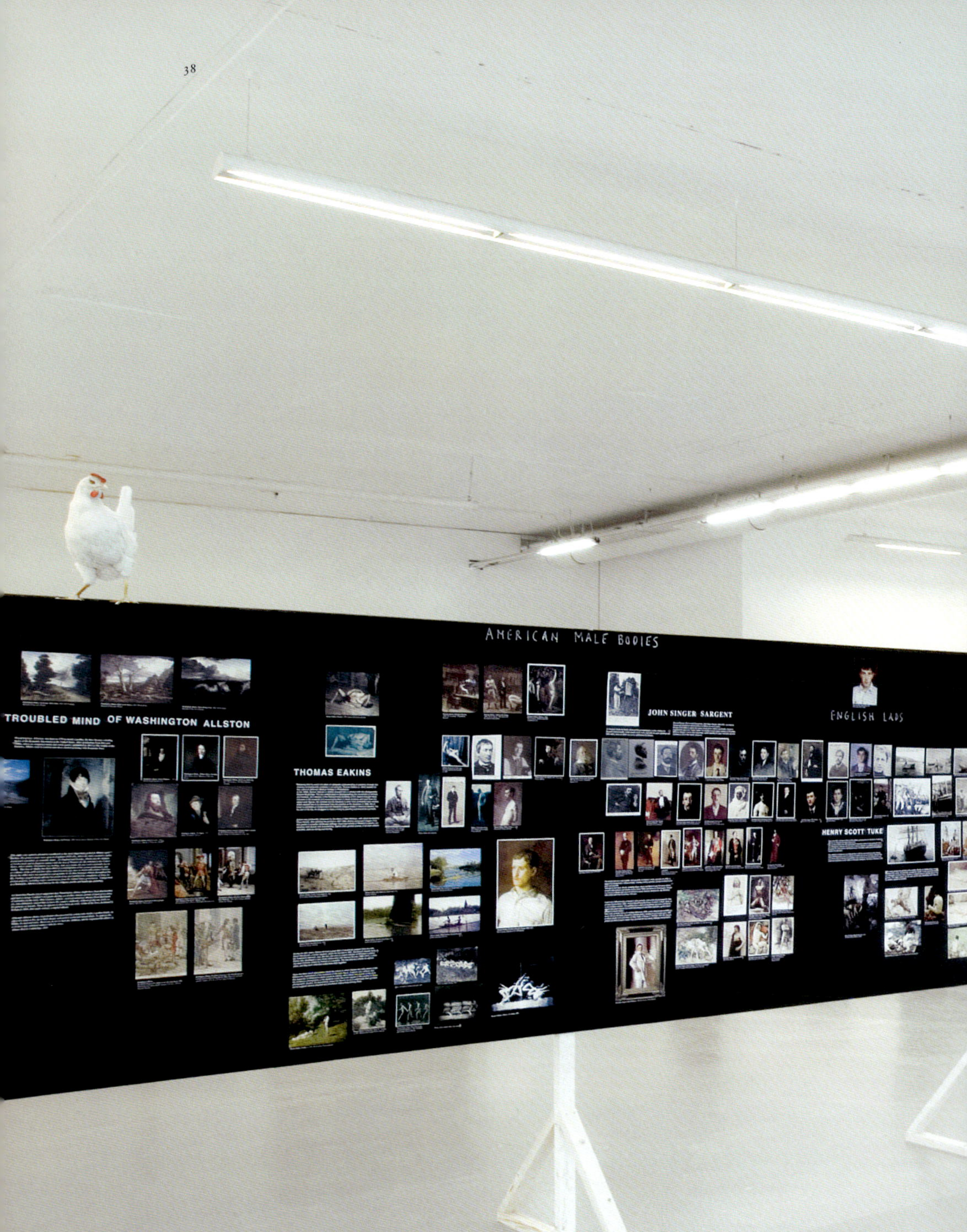

Henrik Olesen, *Some Gay-Lesbian Artists and/or Artists Relevant to Homo-Social Culture Born between c. 1300–1870, 2007*

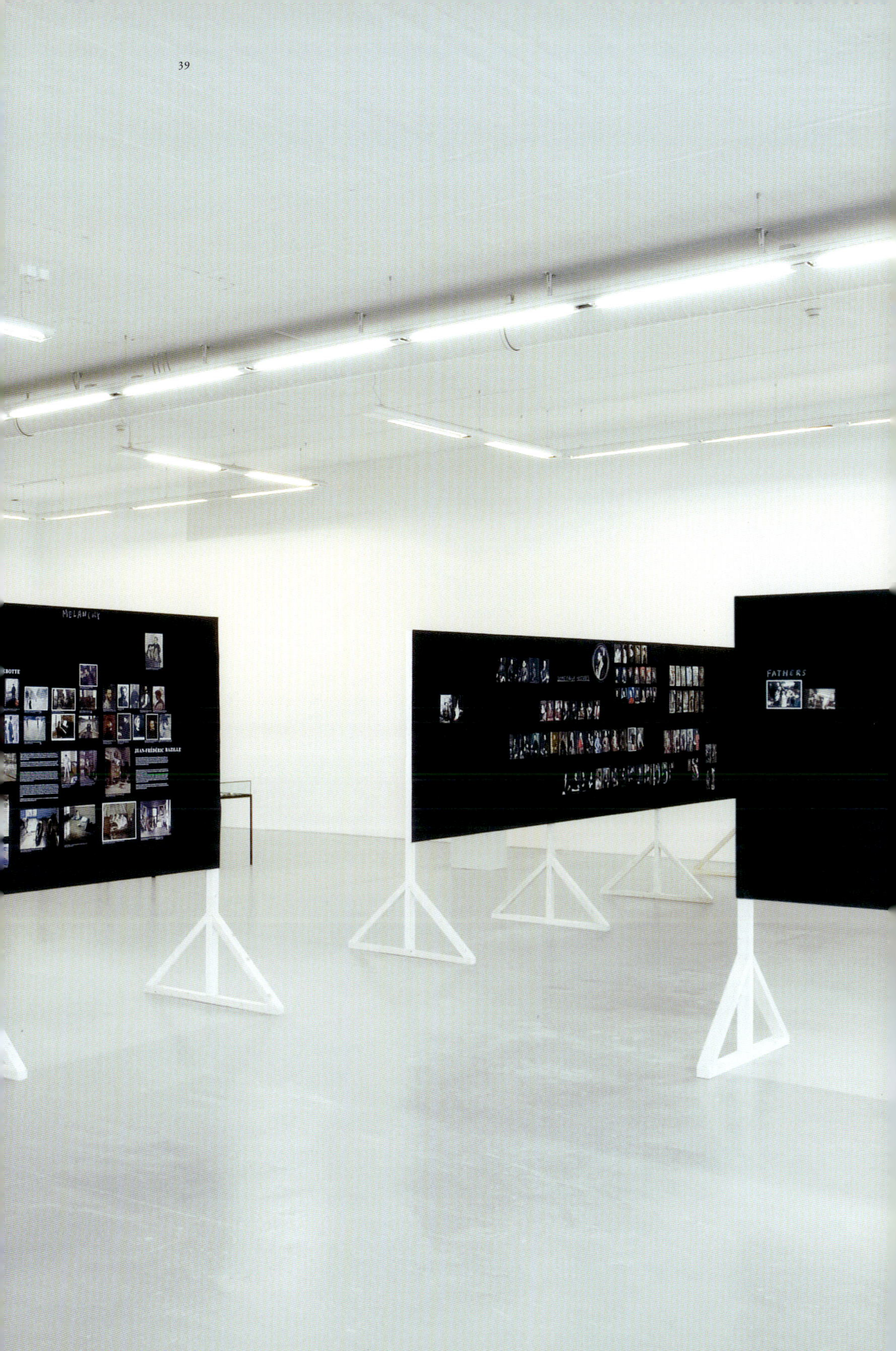

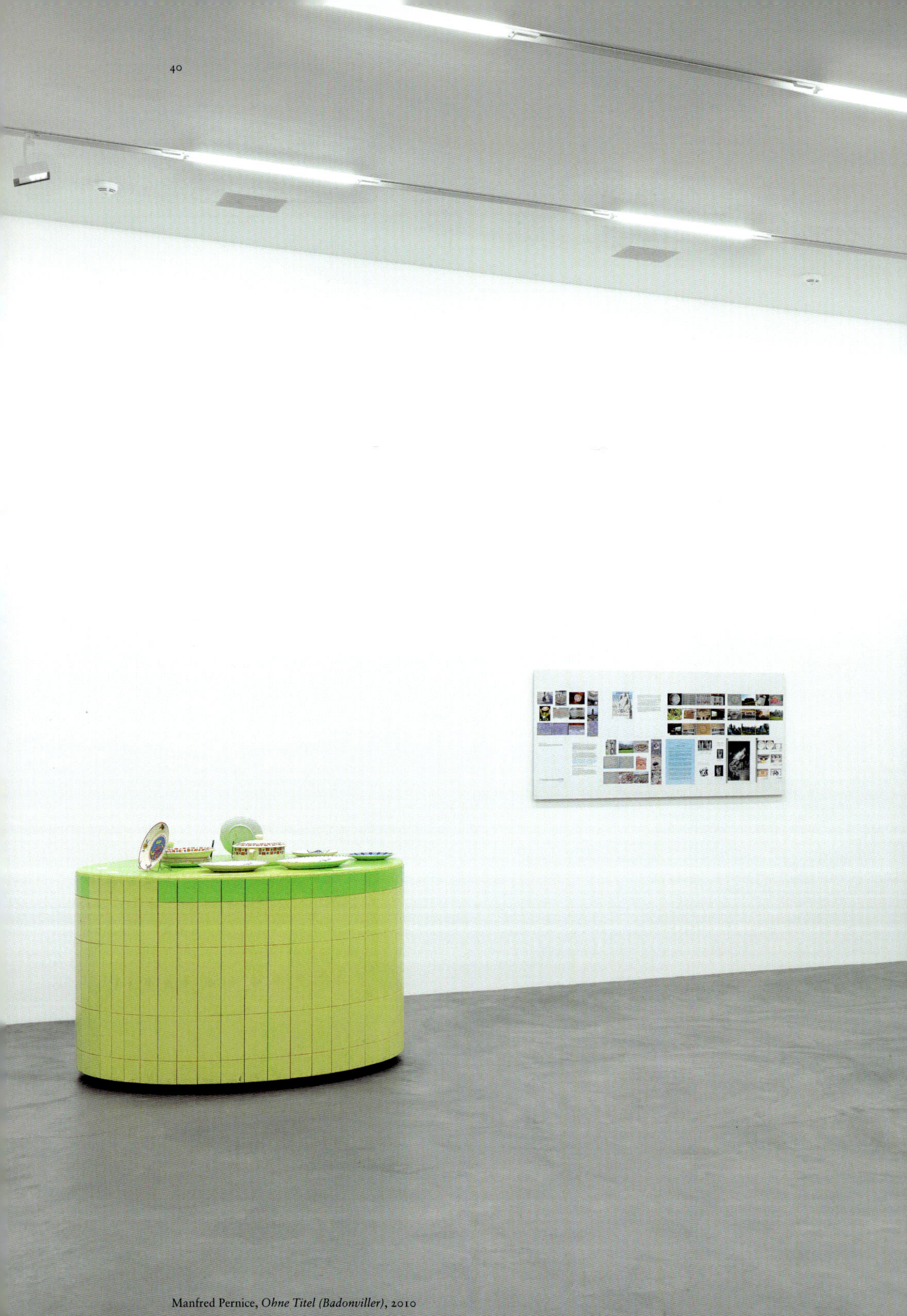

Manfred Pernice, *Ohne Titel (Badonviller)*, 2010

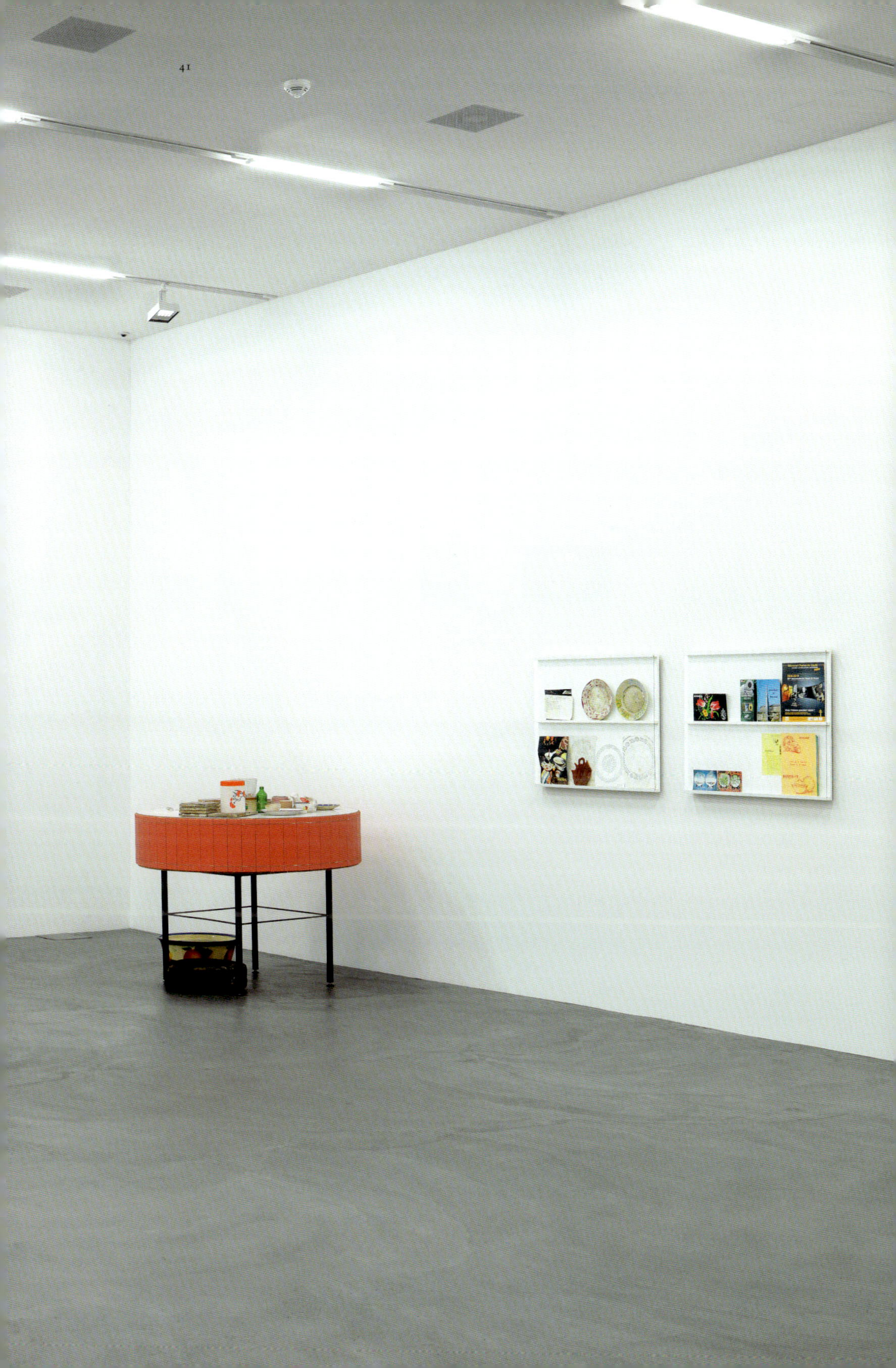

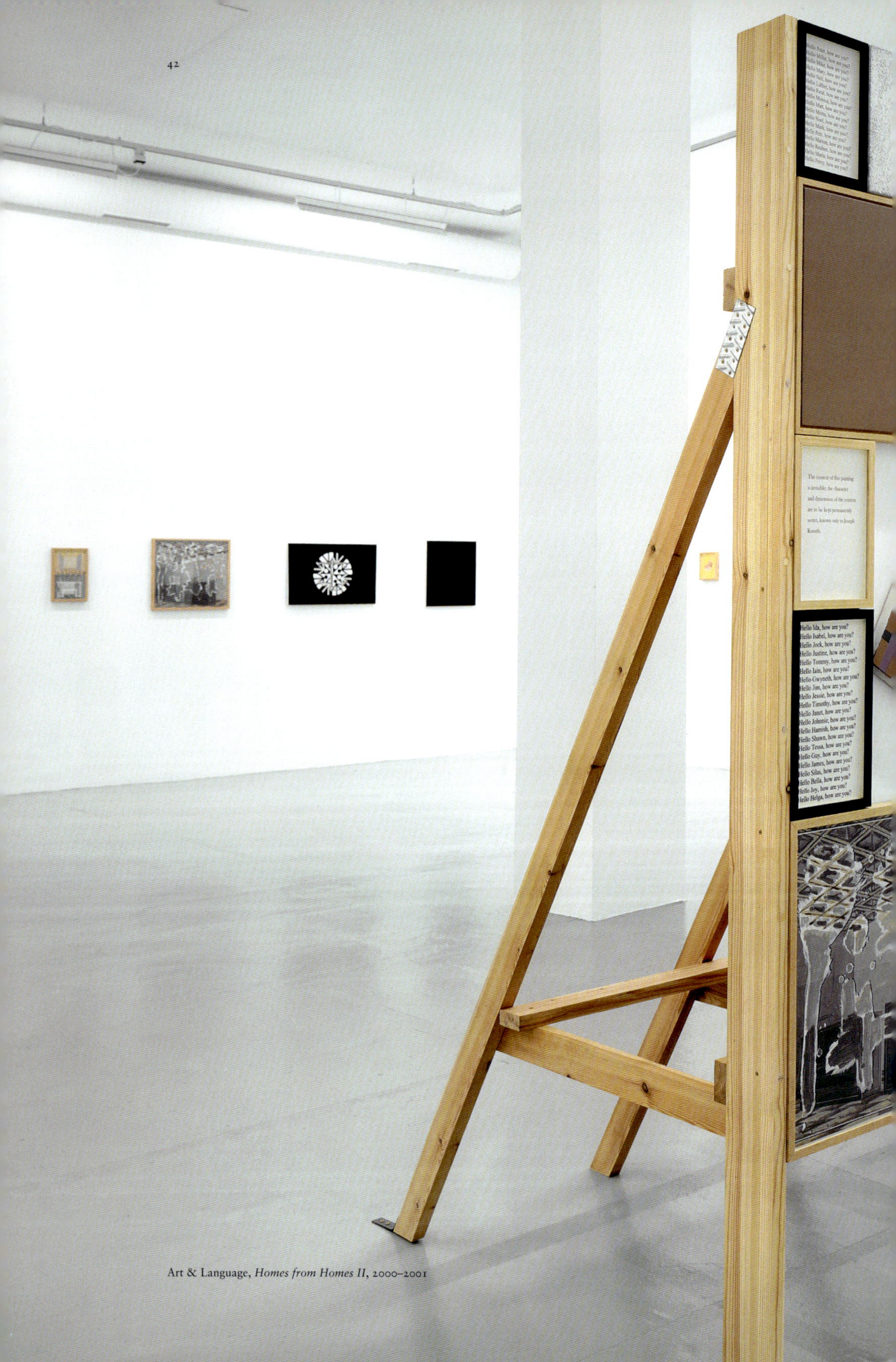

Art & Language, *Homes from Homes II*, 2000–2001

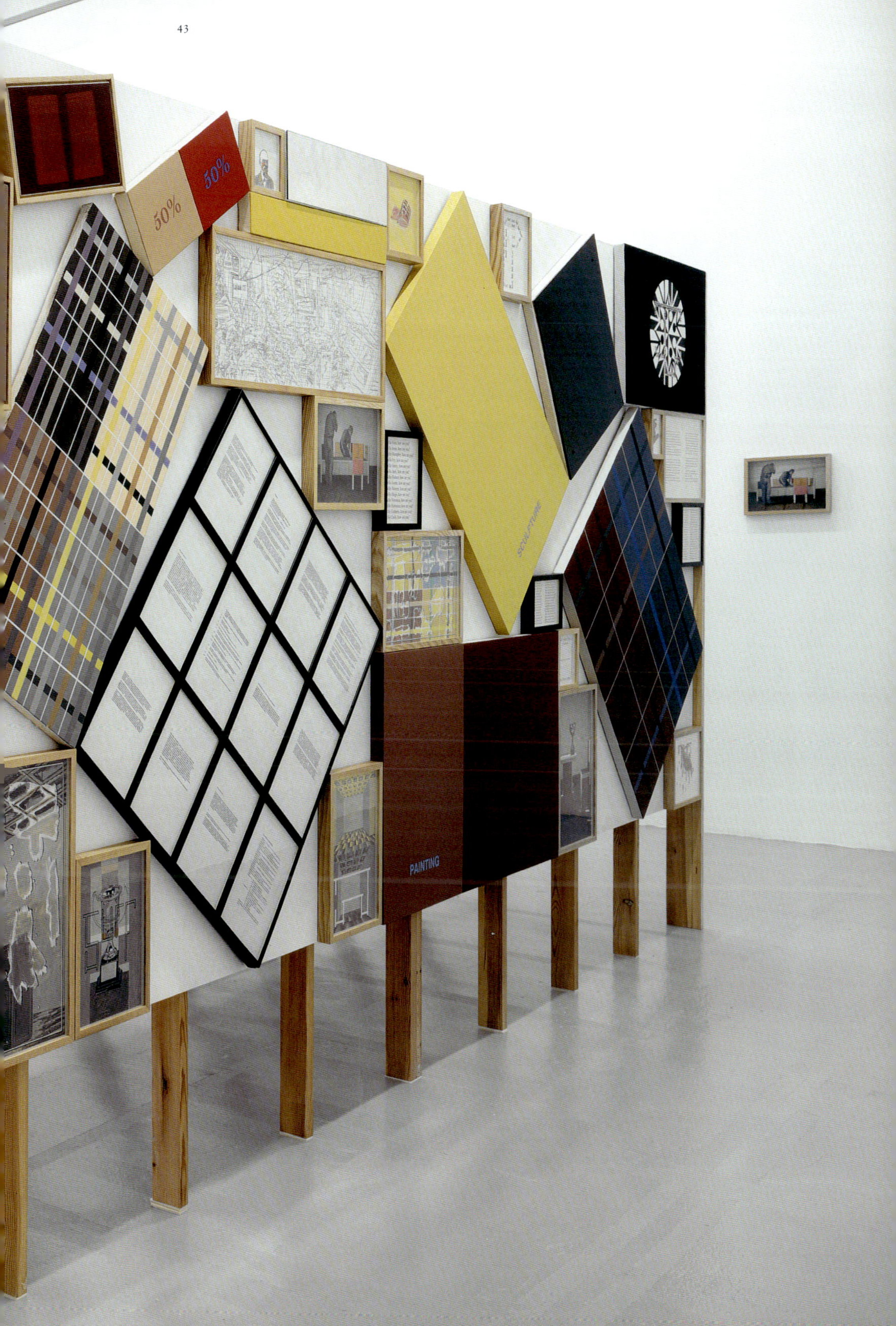
50%
50%
PAINTING
SCULPTURE

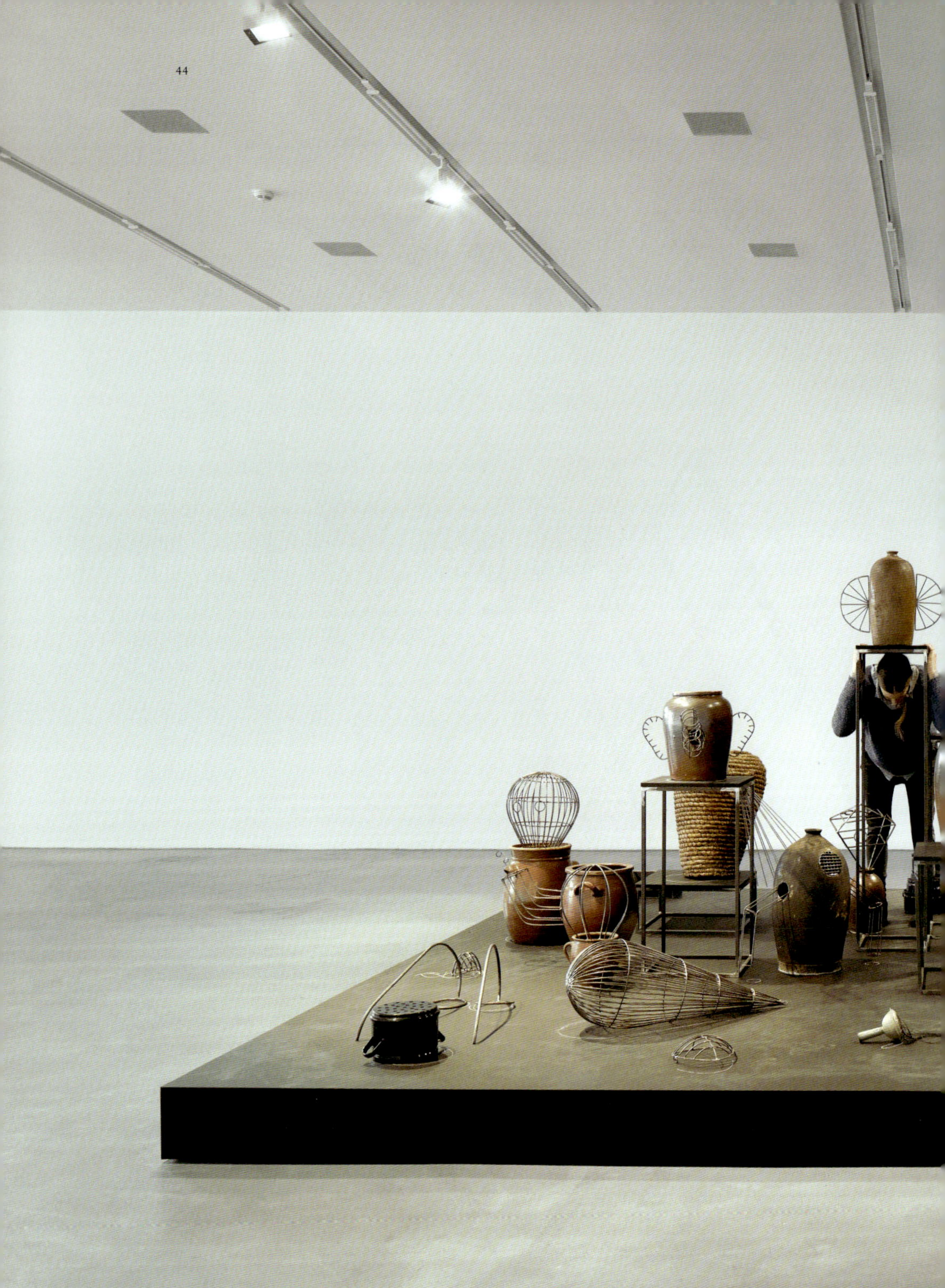

Eva Kot'átková, *Collection of Suppressed Voices*, 2014

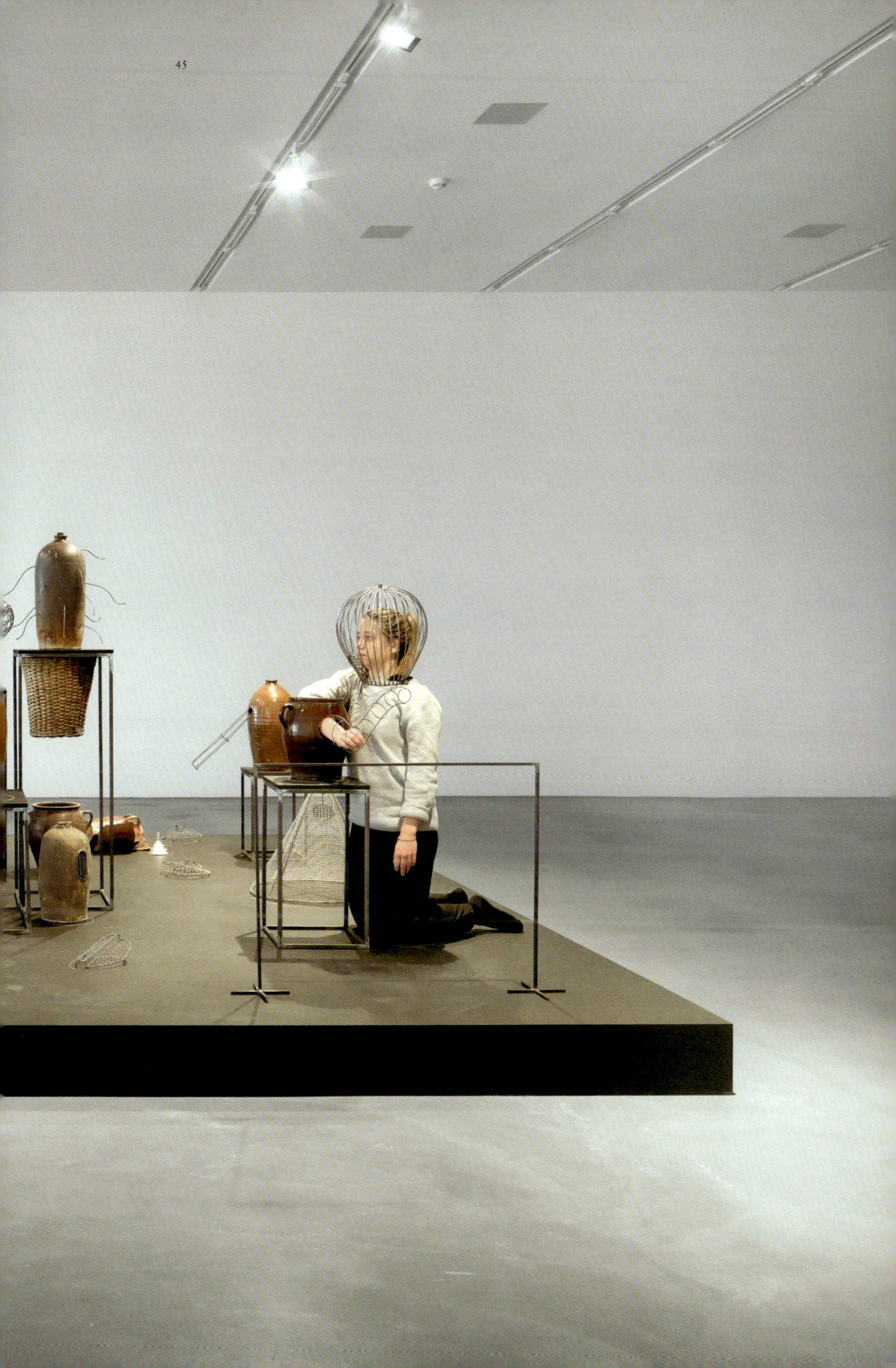

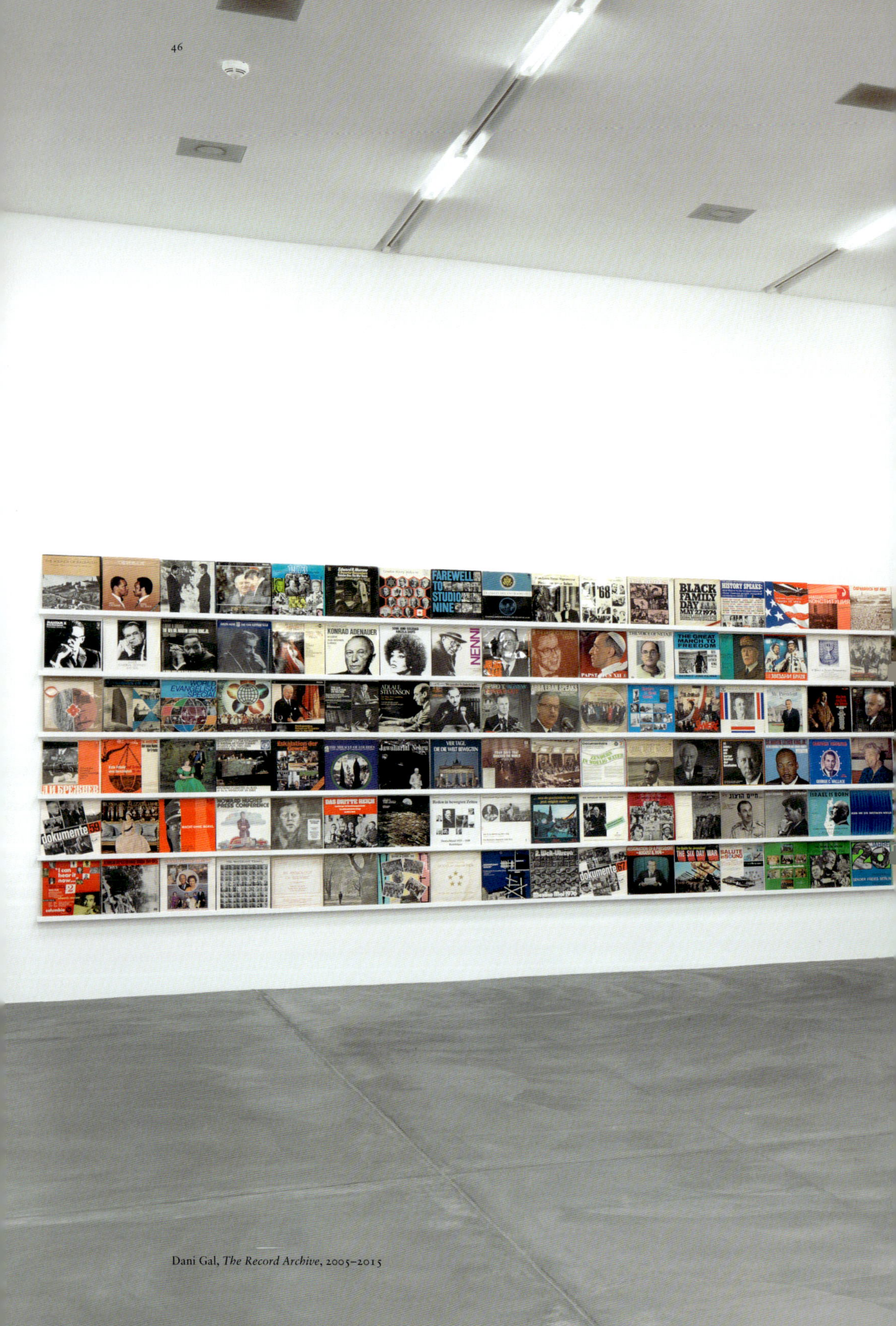

Dani Gal, *The Record Archive*, 2005–2015

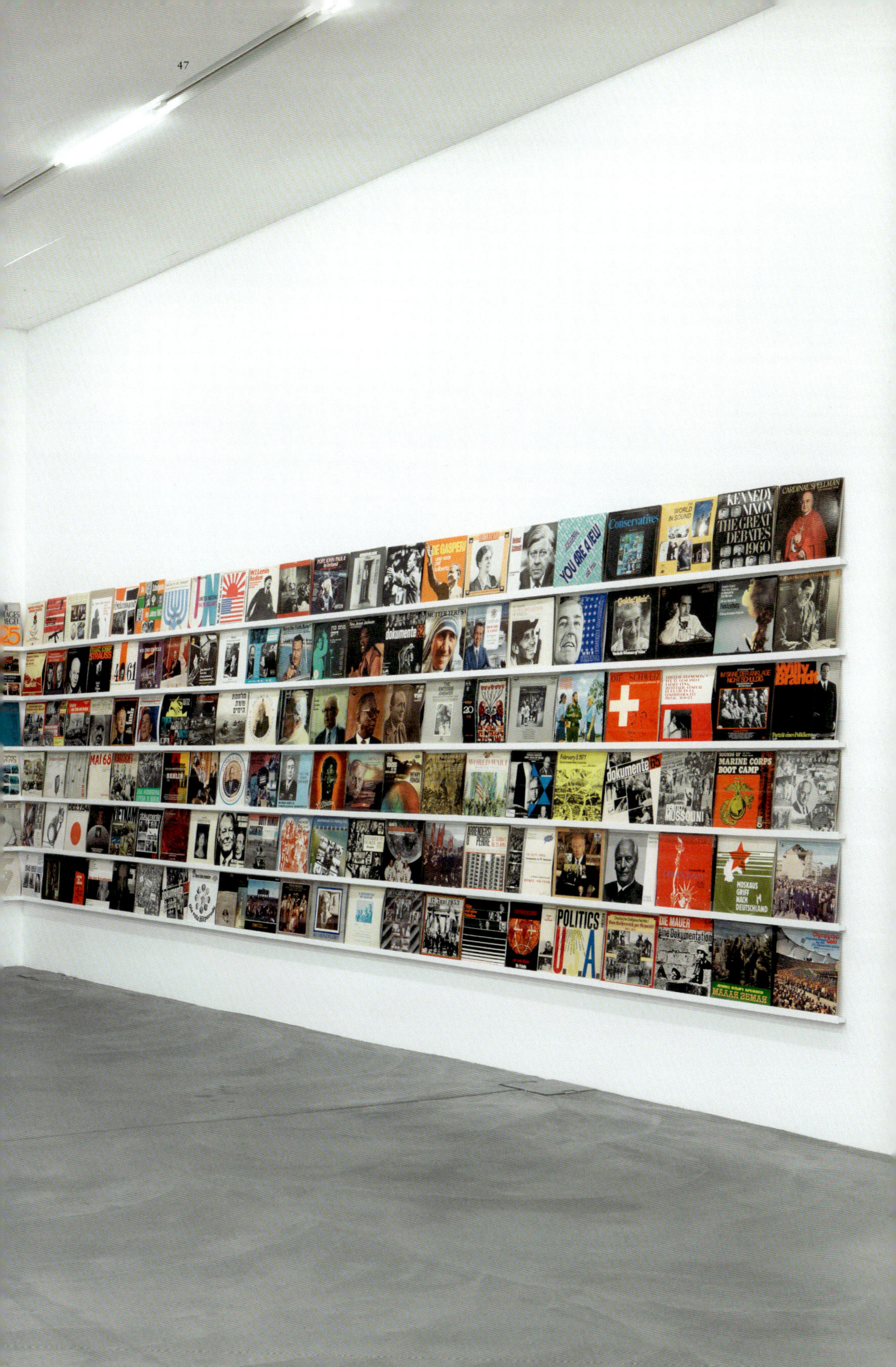

Now

When the Present Begins
Sophia Prinz

To define the mission of a museum of contemporary art, we should first clarify which present the term "contemporary" refers to and what distinguishes it from its historical predecessor, modernity. As it turns out, there is no clear-cut answer. The English philosopher Peter Osborne has argued that the question of when the present begins is first and foremost a matter of one's own standpoint.[1] An ambitious investment banker in placid Zurich will presumably see "his" present as circumscribed by a different temporal horizon than a Somali asylum seeker trying to build an entrepreneurial existence in Hong Kong by selling gold mining rights.[2] A conceptual artist in Chile who works on the depredation of natural resources faces different formal challenges than a landscape painter from southern Italy who adamantly refuses to let go of the paradigm of abstraction of the 1950s. Still, all these presents are loosely interconnected—be it by a notion of what successful entrepreneurship looks like, be it by the conviction that the "landscape" can become both a medium and an expression of profound historic shifts, or be it by the vague apprehension that one's own fate cannot be regarded and comprehended without a view to global constellations.

1   Peter Osborne, *Anywhere or Not at All: Philosophy of Contemporary Art* (London and New York: Verso, 2013), p. 25.
2   For the installation *A Season in Shell* that the duo Zheng Mahler (Daisy Bisenieks and Royce Ng) presented at the Johann Jacobs Museum, Zurich, in 2014, the two artists worked with the Somali asylum applicant "The Bull" to map the informal trade routes between China and Africa.

This awareness of global interdependency is where we part ways with
the spiritual founding fathers of modernity who thought of themselves as
standing at the center of history, but it must also be understood to be
an effect of the European process of modernization, a process that rested
in no small part on imperialist expansion and the colonial outsourcing
of exploitative practices. Yet modern Western thought has failed to develop
intellectual tools that would be even remotely adequate to the complexity
of such trans-cultural entanglements. A full four decades ago, this observation led Jean-François Lyotard to proclaim the "end of the grand narratives." And what is true of the histories of the progress of reason or capital
applies by extension to the universal categories of nineteenth-century
museology as well: neither straightforward chronology nor the rigid division
of the world into geographical zones (such as Africa, South America, or
Asia) nor the arbitrary distinction between autonomous and applied art
can help us understand how our present became what it is.

If all these conventional conceptual frameworks fall short, that is
primarily due to the fact that global modernity, though asymmetrical,
has not been a unilateral process. The things, practices, social forms, and
ego-ideals that Europe exported to the entire world have not remained
what they were; they were remodeled as they arrived overseas, adapted to
the prevailing local ways of living and working. One early modern example
would be the Portuguese woodcrafts of the Baroque period, which found
their circuitous way, via the Brazilian plantation economy, to the façades
of mosques on the African west coast. These manifold and historically
overdetermined translation processes retroactively affect the original, which
is beginning to be considered afresh in an altered perspective. Indeed,
Western modernity is compelled to change to the extent that it is confronted
with its global costs—especially since its creations have long led lives of
their own.[3]

But that seems to be the crux: we sorely lack a cogent social vision
that would do justice to the non-Western versions of modernity or, more
precisely, to their contributions to a global modernity. In the realm of
academic study, such a vision would have to be accompanied by a revised
theoretical vocabulary and a critical interrogation of the methodological

---

3   A related thought may be found in Homi K. Bhabha. In reflections informed by, though not uncritical of, Frantz Fanon's *Peau noire, masques blancs* (1952), Bhabha notes that the authority of colonial models of subjectivity and discourse is undermined by something so basic as their confrontation with the colonized population's failed attempts at mimicry; see Homi K. Bhabha, *The Location of Culture* (London and New York: Routledge, 1994), p. 88. However appealing this construal may be, we have reason to doubt that the will to assimilation as such inevitably breeds subversion. My assumption in the following will instead be that reinterpretations—even when they are not explicitly intended—always entail an active work on what is given.

approach. In the realm of art, the dilemma looms behind the label "contemporary art."

Following Boris Groys, we can read the ascent of the concept of "contemporary art" as a central cultural category over the past several decades as a symptom of a sustained crisis. Compared to the sense of time as rapidly elapsing bound up with modernity's emphasis on the "new" and the future, to reflect on the contemporary moment seems to be a kind of hesitation. To pause may allow us to assure ourselves of our historic standpoint: What was modernity, where has it swept us off to, and what of it may we still find useful in the future?[4]

In art, this genealogical question presents itself primarily as a formal problem: How can a work afford its audience an experience of the contemporary moment with its historical origins without reducing the immanent complexity and contradictoriness of today's reality to a single concept or image? Juliane Rebentisch has argued that the installation is the artistic form that is singularly capable of this balancing act between analytical rigor and speculative openness. Embodying a "distributive unity"[5] that sets different "bits of reality" (objets trouvés, fragments of writings, and objects that have undergone creative alteration) in relation to each other without ever forming a self-contained and self-consistent overarching whole, the form of installation art not only disputes the common formats of truth-making; it also urgently obliges viewers to accept the role of co-producer of possible meanings. We are prompted to trace its diverse formal as well as textual associations, pick up and enlarge upon them, and connect them to our own recollections and ideas. In this respect, installation art builds on central insights of conceptual art—the limitless possibilities of artistic media,[6] the genuine interpretive openness of aesthetic form, and the performative quality of orders of knowledge and perceptual regimes—

---

4   Boris Groys, "Comrades of Time," in Julieta Aranda, Brian Kuan Wood, and Anton Vidokle, eds., *What is Contemporary Art?* (Berlin: Sternberg, 2010), pp. 22–39. Juliane Rebentisch has proposed a definition of contemporary art that gestures in a similar direction, arguing that it must be seen as a critical engagement with and even rejection of certain aspects of modernity. See Juliane Rebentisch, *Theorien der Gegenwartskunst: Eine Einführung* (Hamburg: Junius, 2015), pp. 12–13.

5   Drawing on Kant's epistemological concept of "distributive unity" (Immanuel Kant, *Critique of Pure Reason* [Cambridge, UK: Cambridge University Press, 1997], p. A644/B672), Peter Osborne has proposed that the form of the (post-)conceptual work of art can no longer be conceived of as a closed and self-sufficient entity that remains identical to itself anywhere and at all times—on the contrary, it can take on different guises depending on the context; see Osborne, *Anywhere or Not at All* (see note 1), p. 49. While Osborne is primarily thinking of the photographic image, which materializes in infinitely many variants—as print on paper, as digital image, as poster—I would argue that his conception of "distributive unity" can be extended to include the work of installation art. The elements of the latter constitute a unified whole only insofar as they are formally and conceptually interrelated (and related to their respective environment) within a concrete spatial setting. The unity of the installation, that is to say, is distributive not only because it is variable across time and media but also because each of its embodiments is engendered in a performative act.

6   As Peter Osborne has argued, rigorously analytical anti-modernist conceptual art demonstrated not only that art is not defined by its aesthetic form alone, but also, paradoxically, that it cannot do without a medium; see Peter Osborne, "Art beyond Aesthetics: Philosophical Criticism, Art History and Contemporary Art," *Art History* 27, no. 4 (2004), pp. 663–665.

while rendering these insights useful for the analysis of concrete conditions of social existence.

Important precursors of an installation art that is "post-conceptual" (Osborne) in this sense can be found in the Latin American conceptual art of the 1960s, a movement that has also been described as "ideological conceptualism."[7] Unlike in the predominantly self-reflective conceptual art in the United States, which was locked in its struggle against Greenbergian modernism, in Latin America, the (re-)discovery of the reflective aspect of art was intertwined from the outset with a critique of precarious social conditions. The latter endeavor also entailed a critical engagement with the artists' own marginalization by kingmakers of the canon with their Western bias such as New York's Museum of Modern Art.

Gonzalo Díaz, who was born in Santiago de Chile in 1947, is one exponent of the first generation of Latin American conceptualists. Many of his works scrutinize the representational capacity of writing as well as its visual qualities; in this regard his art is comparable to the output of the group Art & Language. But where the latter are satisfied with playing epistemological games, Díaz uses the artistic analysis of visual and textual systems as a means to probe the limits of the representation of quite concrete historical and political themes. In his installation *Terras do Sem Fim* (2016), the artist literally disassembles a canonical work of Latin American literature, the Brazilian writer Jorge Amado's novel *Terras do Sem Fim* (1943).[8] Written when Amado, a young Communist, was living in exile in Uruguay, the novel paints the ruthless machinations of northeastern Brazil's cocoa barons in baroque scenes. Díaz breaks up the narrative by detaching the book's pages, framing them individually, and arraying them on the wall. Yet in so doing, he also lends the book a different form of coherency: the closely spaced frames mark a continuous line that runs around the exhibition space at eye level. The sculptural display impairs the legibility of Amado's story—who reads an entire novel during a visit to an exhibition?—but it transforms the book itself into a memorable figure: it appears as a horizon line. That figure reveals something that is implicit but at most hinted at in Amado's text: the colonial imagination that sniffed immeasurable profits on the horizon. Even when employed to emancipatory ends, Díaz's installation compellingly suggests, the literary means of

FIG. 1/2

---

7   See e.g. Mari Carmen Ramírez, "Blueprint Circuits: Conceptual Art and Politics in Latin America," in Waldo Rasmussen, Fatima Bercht, and Elizabeth Ferrer, eds., *Latin American Artists of the Twentieth Century* (New York: Museum of Modern Art, 1993), pp. 156–167.

8   An English translation was published under the title *The Violent Land* in 1945.

Western modernism are impotent or certainly insufficient when faced with the task of grasping the historical truth of the post-colonial world. The latter would seem to demand an artistic form that actively defies entrenched habits of perception and reading. Díaz underlines this challenge to engage in epistemic "disobedience"[9] by using the Portuguese original for his installation—a book in a language that, though it is spoken in numerous former colonies, is not part of the Western world's official artspeak. A museum visitor in Zurich who does not read Portuguese, that is to say, will have to make do with the figure of the horizon line. Yet if she knows her art history while also being alive to the contemporary moment, she might be reminded of Netherlandish seascapes of the seventeenth century. For the Dutch of the "Golden Age," after all, the horizon line was not an abstraction.

The decidedly analytical orientation we encounter in advanced forms of installation art demands not only a different receptive engagement but also a different kind of education. Presenting constellations of set pieces from the lifeworld of daily life, installation art appeals less to a canonical knowledge than to the implicit practical and perceptual knowledge of its various audiences.[10] Yet far from simply affirming this implicit knowledge, it puts it to the test with regard to its functionality and structural limitations. In other words, installation art impels a process of reception we may describe, with Kant, as an "aesthetic judgment of reflection," though the subject that enters into these feedback loops of reflection is not a universal subject but a socially situated one. Its "cognitive faculties" are of a historically specific kind, as Foucault would say, as is its capacity for aesthetic experience.[11] Hence Rebentisch's conclusion that "aesthetic experience is in an important sense individual—the experiencing subject is compelled to reflect on itself precisely to the degree to which it cannot simply situate itself vis-à-vis the object in terms of identification or counter-identification [...] In such experience, we do not simply receive political messages, rather in the face of specific works, we are confronted in a particular way with our own silent social and cultural assumptions."[12]

---

9 See Walter D. Mignolo, "Epistemic Disobedience, Independent Thought and Decolonial Freedom," *Theory, Culture & Society* 26, no. 7–8 (2009), pp. 159–181.

10 In the perspective of practice theory, most of the subject's activities are performed entirely automatically: driving a car, reading a novel, or visiting an exhibition—in all these situations the subject recalls a practical knowledge rehearsed in earlier similar situations that is only implicitly present, which is to say, that is not subject to conscious reflection. It stands to reason that how and what we perceive is not innate but formed in the practical engagement with the sensible order of the world.

11 Like the compass of what can be said or thought, which Foucault traces back to historic discursive strata, the conditions of the possibility of (aesthetic) perception must be described in their historical mutability. For example, the kinds of objects and visual forms the subject deals with in daily life presumably have a retroactive effect on its implicit perceptual knowledge. See also Sophia Prinz, *Die Praxis des Sehens: Über das Zusammenspiel von Körpern, Artefakten und visueller Ordnung* (Bielefeld: Transcript, 2014).

12 Juliane Rebentisch, *Aesthetics of Installation Art*, trans. Daniel Hendrickson (Berlin: Sternberg, 2012), p. 271.

What are the consequences these considerations have for the museum as an institution and the exhibition as an aesthetic form? What is required for a museum to develop a genuine relation to the present moment that would be more than a bald assertion of contemporariness? As I have mentioned above, the concepts that may be regarded as the as yet un-demystified inheritance of the type "museum of modern art"—historical linearity or the distinction between art and non-art—are inadequate to the multitemporal as well as polyphonic qualities of the contemporary. *Anything* is potentially contemporary, even a seventeenth-century Persian bowl decorated (for good reasons) with imitation Chinese ideographs.[13] This is not to say that the category of time becomes inoperative. On the contrary, as we might contend with Groys, the contemporary is distinguished precisely by its analytical posture vis-à-vis modernity: something appears as contemporary, one, because it inquires into the conditions of existence and historical origins of our present, and two, because it chooses a form for this inquiry that subverts modernity's Eurocentric truth regime. Post-conceptual installation art provides one such form. The technique of constellational montage makes it possible to draw associative connections without producing discursive or aesthetic closures. In so doing, it opens up a space of possibility accommodating different experiences that can vary widely depending on the beholders' schemes of perception, thought, and action.

With regard to the aspect of constellational montage, there is no essential difference between the work of installation art and the medium of the exhibition: any museum hall and any gallery is a scene of interrelations between exhibits engendered by their relative spatial positions. The classic white cube, however, pretends that the space shared by the individual works of art does not exist; each piece is supposed to remain itself without interfering with the others or shading their effect. This mode of presentation preserves the objects' art-historical identities, but it also deprives them of an opportunity to become or remain contemporary in the sense sketched above. A museum of contemporary art, by contrast, should—that would be my proposal—accept the epistemological and aesthetic challenge of post-conceptual art: instead of sticking to business as usual and exhibiting the oeuvre of this or that artist or surveying one or another tendency, the museum's work should take the form of a performative analysis that

---

7   The Museum für Kunst und Gewerbe Hamburg has one such bowl. On display in an exhibition that explores the genuine trans-cultural character of (contemporary) realms of things, it unexpectedly speaks directly to the present moment.

remains open to a speculative approach. When we can no longer draw a formal boundary between installation art and museum exhibition-making, though, the question of institutional responsibility becomes pressing. Although the interpretative authority of museological categories is beginning to crumble, the museum as an institution cannot forgo making its selection: What are the themes, the forms and models of knowledge that help us understand the global present? To address this question, the museum is dependent on cooperation with advanced forms of artistic and trans-disciplinary research. This is not the place to discuss in any detail the complex problems such an approach inevitably entails, but I should at least note that this sort of research often strikes out in the direction sketched above: toward a reappraisal of modernity's tainted legacy. Researching artists, however, often do not receive the support they need and lack the financial and scholarly resources to make a thorough study of the issues they choose to address. This is where the museum of contemporary art can live up to its educational mission: as a partner, think tank, and networking hub for different long-term research endeavors and formally open-ended projects. Only when a museum contributes to this work of bringing the present moment into being can it rightfully call itself contemporary.

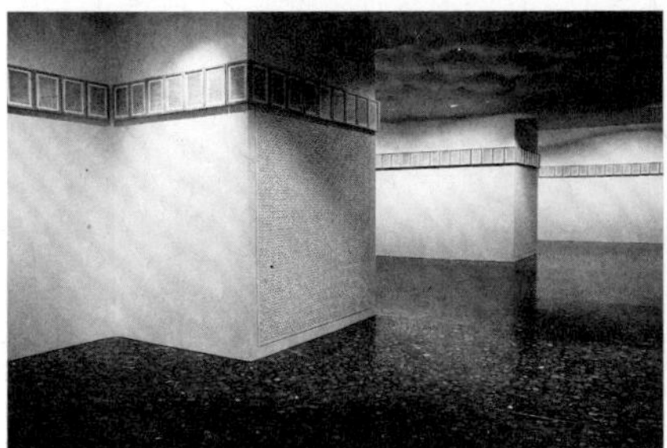
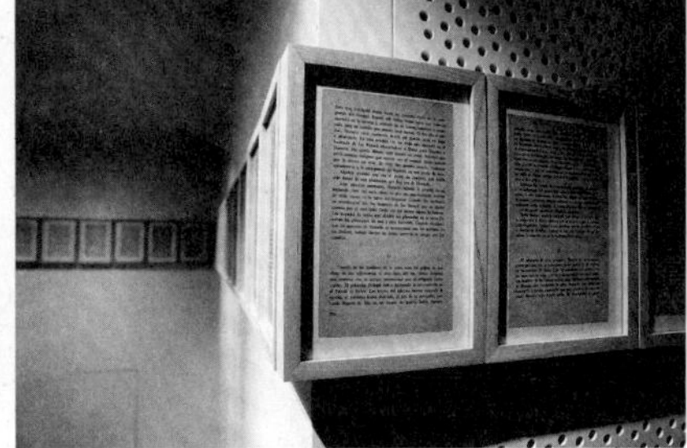

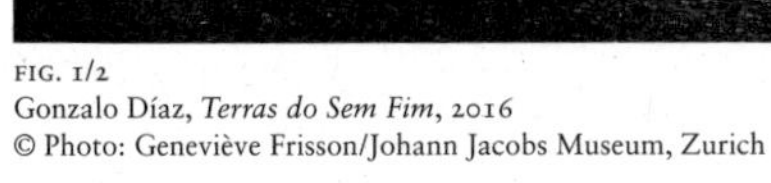

FIG. 1/2
Gonzalo Díaz, *Terras do Sem Fim*, 2016
© Photo: Geneviève Frisson/Johann Jacobs Museum, Zurich

The Time of Things in Space: Exhibition-Making as Memorial Theater

Beat Wyss

The Curatorial Act: Pro-ducing Truth

Two decades ago, the early modern term "Wunderkammer," usually translated as "cabinet of curiosities," was returned to currency by the Bonn and Copenhagen exhibition *Wunderkammer des Abendlandes*.[1] The term, which typically references a collection of diverse artifacts and artworks, also happens to be the name of a gallery in Berlin's Scheunenviertel, opened in 2010 by Thomas Olbricht, heir to the Wella hair product fortune. Olbricht, a trained chemist and professor of endocrinology, has built a collection that underlines the old alliance between art and knowledge. In one showcase, a coral crowns the assemblage: Doctor Olbricht has chosen the colorful *Cnidaria* skeleton, used since antiquity as an amulet against disease, for his personal coat of arms. Healing powers are attributed to the animal, which lives in tropical marine environments. If we spontaneously find that claim plausible, it is because of the way the coral is exhibited together with other things: a skull, hourglasses, a miniature globe, a portable crucifix, and found objects from natural and laboratory

FIG. I

---

1   *Wunderkammer des Abendlandes: Museum und Sammlung im Spiegel der Zeit*, ed. Annesofie Becker, Willie Flindt, and Arno Victor Nielsen, exh. cat. Bundeskunsthalle (Bonn, 1994). On the history and meaning of the cabinet of curiosities, see Horst Bredekamp, *Antikensehnsucht und Maschinenglauben: Die Geschichte der Kunstkammer und die Zukunft der Kunstgeschichte* (Berlin: Wagenbach, 1993); Frances A. Yates, *The Art of Memory* (Chicago: University of Chicago Press, 1966).

settings—what they are and which purpose they serve remains, at first sight, a mystery. All these things seem to form a murmuring chorus that is trying to tell us something. Or are we merely imagining that?

To answer this question, we must first get a better understanding of what a *thing* is. Martin Heidegger has proposed the pertinent definition. The word would seem to encompass everything that is, whatever it may be: from the "stupid thing" to the "Last Things," from the banality of everyday life to the intractable questions of philosophy. To get hold of the *thingness of the thing*, we must deliver it from its existence as *Zeug*, implement or mere stuff.[2] It is through the work of art that the thing inside the *Zeug* reveals itself.[3]

Domenico Remps's picture of a cabinet of curiosities illustrates this alchemical process. Translated into the medium of painting, all that stuff piled up in the cabinet and pinned to its walls recovers its thingness, enabling us to think of each individual thing—beyond what it might be good for as an implement or as a zoological specimen. Even the turned ivory spheres now appear before us not merely as examples of expert craftsmanship; in their painted guise, they join the chorus of murmuring things.

Iconology is the study of murmuring things. It is on to the words that seem to inhabit them. The historical-canonical building block of iconology is the *emblem*. The art of emblematics interleaves image-words in a sort of unbalance, with *icon* and *logos* forming a flywheel that, as a hermeneutic *perpetuum mobile*, continually revolves around its own axis.

Emblematics is also the cradle of what we call *curating* today. Exhibition-making, too, is a hermeneutic act that affords things an echo chamber so that their choral murmur can become more distinct. The question "What is that supposed to mean?" is thus not merely a formula of methodical doubt but a basic stance of philosophical curiosity, as Socrates taught Plato: θαυμάζειν, bafflement or marvel, marks the inception of reflective thought. The cabinet of curiosities retains the origin of philosophy in its name. The curious assembly of things is meant to make us marvel at how our thinking evinces a spontaneous propensity for depth. The relationship between words and things is not one of simple denotation; they take on a connotative dimension whose revolving openness is more

---

2   Martin Heidegger, *Being and Time*, trans. John Macquarrie and Edward Robinson (New York: Harper, 1962), pp. 97–98. The word *Zeug* is difficult to translate, and Macquarrie and Robinson chose the term "equipment," no doubt with a view to compounds such as *Werkzeug*, "tool." By itself, *Zeug* does not indicate utility or purposefulness.

3   Martin Heidegger, "The Origin of the Work of Art," in *Off the Beaten Track*, trans. Julian Young and Kenneth Haynes (Cambridge, UK: Cambridge University Press, 2002), pp. 4–19.

easily rendered in space than in the linear and explanatory medium
of writing.

Marvel is prompted by the dislocation of words and things out of
their wonted context, which initially seemed to be the only appropriate
one. The emblem and the cabinet of curiosities displace all sorts of stuff to
present them in a new light that, in the best of cases, translates the murmur
of things into an interminable polysemy. The essence of truth, ἀλήθεια or
unconcealedness, "is ruled throughout by a denial," as Heidegger says.[4] It's
just another way to describe the abstract murmur of things. Art and truth
come to pass in the "in-stalling."[5] So it is not the producer of the work who
engenders the message of this "in-stallation" as its author. On the contrary,
"the artist remains something inconsequential in comparison with the
work—almost like a passageway which, in the creative process, destroys
itself for the sake of the coming forth of the work."[6] Yet the work, too,
must be urged beyond its mere objecthood. The "happening of truth," that
is to say, comes to pass with the setting-to-work of the work.[7]

This figure of thought is visualized by a telling image from Andrea
Alciato's collection of emblems: it illustrates the "membra mentis," eye
and hand, the limbs the mind avails itself of to pro-duce truth.[8] Art and
knowledge reveal themselves in the course of an *exposition* in which words
and things appear in an order arranged by a discerning hand. In the act
of setting-to-work, truth comes to pass as the unconcealed.

Once we have understood this, the moment has come to summon
Michel Foucault. The two philosophers' approaches converge insofar
as both see truth as called forth by an ordering pro-duction. *Les mots et
les choses* is the title Foucault gives to his 1966 study into the history
of knowledge, published in English translation as *The Order of Things*.[9]
In Foucault, too, the term *la chose* refers to an otherwise indeterminate
thing. Things are the disposable material of the history of knowledge.
As *chose*, from the Latin *causa*, the thing in its semantic indeterminacy is
the *motive* for the business of construal. This is where the sublime fog
of fundamental ontology, exuded by Heidegger's peculiar diction, ought to
dissipate. Foucault's *Order of Things* enables us to uncover the historic
forms of thought involved in the "happening of truth." In what is no doubt
an ironic jibe at Immanuel Kant's terminology, Foucault introduces the

---

4   Ibid., p. 31.
5   Ibid., p. 23.
6   Ibid., p. 19.
7   Ibid., p. 37

8   Andrea Alciato, *Emblematum liber* (Augsburg: Heinrich
    Steyner, 1531), emblem no. 16: "Membra mentis," hand
    and eye.
9   Michel Foucault, *The Order of Things: An Archaeology
    of the Human Sciences* (London: Tavistock, 1970).

FIG. 3

historical a priori. Distinguishing various models of epistemic order from the sixteenth through the early twentieth centuries, he outlines three periods of knowledge: the Mannerist age of resemblances, the Baroque age of representation, and the Enlightened age of human history. The three exemplary disciplines that figure in his comparative analysis are the knowledge of language, economics, and the study of nature. In the following, I will seek to translate the three taxonomical models he unfolds into the history of exhibition-making.

The first to perform such a transfer into curatorial practice was Marcel Broodthaers, the congenial student of René Magritte and Marcel Duchamp. Inspired by reading *Les mots et les choses*, Broodthaers, starting in the mid-1960s, cultivated exhibition-making as an ephemeral art form. The Belgian poet of free association recognized an elective affinity in the forms of knowledge of the Renaissance, characterized by Foucault as the age of *ressemblance* and *similitude*. This affinity allowed him to embed Surrealist montage and strategies of conceptual art in the tradition of emblematics. *Musée d'Art Moderne, Département des Aigles*, a touring exhibition he staged afresh at each of several venues between 1968 and 1972, has become legendary. It featured a seemingly random congeries of things united by the motif of the eagle: banknotes, beer cans, champagne corks, even a few scattered pictures of the raptor from jumble sales that portrayed the king of the air in his habitat. Nothing survives of the exhibition but installation photographs and snapshots. After its final closing, the objects were returned to their owners or discarded as junk.

Three Historic Forms of Order for Things

As Foucault's leftist critics have objected, his analysis eschews sociological attributions. The history of curatorial strategies, then, would not be complete without the dimension of cultural sociology. Krzysztof Pomian, the doyen of the history of collecting, has highlighted its roots in bourgeois culture. Collectors' intellectual habitus was modeled on Roman literary sources: Cicero is said to have adorned his library with herms of Plato, the Muses, and the Olympian gods. According to this topos, Petrarch furnished his study with antiques.[10]

---

10   Krzysztof Pomian, "Sammlungen—eine historische Typologie," in Andreas Grote, ed., *Macrocosmos in Microcosmo: Die Welt in der Stube. Zur Geschichte des Sammelns 1450 bis 1800* (Opladen: Leske + Budrich, 1994), pp. 107–126. See also Krzysztof Pomian, *Collectors and Curiosities: Paris and Venice 1500–1800*, trans. Elizabeth Wiles-Porter (Cambridge, UK: Polity, 1990).

The first public collection north of the Alps was Basel's Amerbach Cabinet; its treasures form the nucleus of the holdings of the Historical Museum and the Kunstmuseum in the capital of the Swiss-French-German tristate area. The collection was nurtured by a dynasty of book printers, jurists, university professors, and merchants. The legal scholar Basilius Amerbach, Jr. (1533–1591), the third in this line of eminent men, initiated the earliest archaeological excavation north of the Alps, unearthing the Roman theater at Kaiseraugst in 1588–1590. The objects the Amerbachs compiled speak to the typical interests of men of learning: ancient coins, gems, small sculptures, copperplate and woodblock prints as well as the works of local painters.[11]

The humanist cabinet of curiosities may have been modest in size, but the erudition and research that underlay it were expansive. Its compass and function changed, however, when absolutist rulers appropriated the idea. In the late sixteenth century, the possession of a cabinet of curiosities became a princely hobbyhorse. By owning a collection, the monarch demonstrated his humanist education. In many instances, a bourgeois cabinet served as a cornerstone of subsequent aristocratic dilettantism; the Danish king, for example, acquired the objects assembled by Ole Worm, a physician in Copenhagen.

FIG. 4

Ownership of a collection sealed the *belle alliance* of sovereignty and wisdom at a time when Francis Bacon's pronouncement that knowledge is power became proverbial. Besides Bacon's *Novum Organon*, a Greek work was central to the education of Western Europe's princes: the Platonic dialogue about *The Republic*, translated by Marsilio Ficino into Latin in 1484 by the order of Cosimo de' Medici. Modern absolutism assimilated the idea of the ideal state, humanistically certified by the Athenian philosopher. A widely quoted passage praises the union of knowledge and power in one and the same person. Socrates proffers it in conversation with Plato's older brother Glaucon: the ideal state will not come into the world until ἢ οἱ φιλόσοφοι βασιλεύσωσιν ἐν ταῖς πόλησιν ἢ οἱ βασιλεῖς τε [...] φιλοσοφήσωσι, "either philosophers become kings in our states or [...] kings [...] take to the pursuit of philosophy."[12] One telling document of Plato's reception, translated into the courtly decorum of the early seventeenth century, is Anton Mozart's painting showing the presentation of the Pomeranian Art Cabinet. It captures the moment the art dealer and diplomat Philipp

FIG. 5

---

11   Elisabeth Landolt and Felix Ackermann, *Sammeln in der Renaissance: Das Amerbach-Kabinett* (Basel: Historisches Museum, 1991).

12   Plato, *Republic*, trans. Paul Shorey, vol. 5 (Cambridge, MA: Harvard University Press, 1969), 473c,d.

Hainhofer delivers a drawer filled with collected objects to his patron, Duke Philip II of Pomerania.

The staging of the figures in the pictorial space reflects the three estates of the Platonic corporative state: the ruling class at the center is surrounded by the court guard, representatives of the guardian class Plato portrays with such devotion. The third estate, the productive class, consists of the ordinary citizens of Pomerania, including the craftsmen who manufactured this famous masterpiece of an art cabinet. These commoners may draw some satisfaction from the fact that they rank above the monkeys, which can do no more than ape humans, and the patient dog suffering a boy to ride on its back.

Stored in the art cabinet, that analog *computator*, and ready to be recalled by opening its various drawers, are found natural objects, mechanical instruments, and works of art. The painting symbolizes the relationship between power and knowledge as the two poles between which the ruler must maintain an appropriate balance: governing, that is to say, is an intellectual challenge. Duke Philip II and his cabinet of curiosity are engaged in a *sacra conversazione*, assisted by the people as the eyewitnesses to this rational mystery. The Platonic figure of the philosopher king is born—or, more precisely, reborn in the spirit of occidental absolutism.

This rebirth, we should note, involves a twofold appropriation. The ruler takes possession of the craftsmanship of artists and artisans while also assimilating the humanist collector's habitus of expository erudition. With a view to Heidegger's argument about the setting-to-work of the work, it is not the art cabinet as such but only its ceremonial staging in which the truth of its mission unfolds. The cabinet of curiosities was meant to be a microcosmic replica of the macrocosmic world. Its pioneers were humanist scholars who thought of their collections as quasi-alchemical laboratories of operative knowledge.

Its successor, the encyclopedic art cabinet of the mid-sixteenth century, effaces that magical sense of real symbolism. The cabinet of curiosities' pandemonic order is disbanded; the new order of knowledge introduces new classifications and establishes a division of things in accordance with the methods of the disciplines practiced at the academies: into botanical and zoological preserved specimens, mineralogical finds, the physical cabinet, and the showroom for mechanical automata. Works of art are moved to the separate picture gallery. The collections, often on display in rooms specifically built for them, are owned by princes secular and spiritual. Whereas the cabinet of curiosities as an allegory of encompassing knowledge attested to the inquisitive mind of the scholar who personally accumulated all these things, the aristocratic art cabinet serves the representational purpose of lending aesthetic legitimacy to the ruler-collector's political power. The library, where the content of the collection, the book, coincides with the formative power of language, is the ideal type of this epistemic order. The regulative role of the alphabet culminates in the encyclopedia of the eighteenth century.

The representation of knowledge is structured by academic discourse, by a formal taxonomy of identity and difference defined by logical deduction. The exhibited thing is the exemplar representing a definition, a class, a genus. Display cases, herbariums, and catalogues alphabetize the rich diversity of species in fauna and flora.

The third epistemic form of collection-building to emerge is the bourgeois museum. The Enlightenment discovered life and history as the categorial structures of all its knowledge and bequeathed them to the Idealist generation of the nineteenth century. One German thinker of time, life, and history, the philosopher Georg Wilhelm Hegel, sat on the committee overseeing the planning for the museum in Berlin. Schinkel's four-wing complex adjacent to the Lustgarten park unfolds the historical evolution of art in step with the progression of the World Spirit from Orient to Occident, from the Persians and Egyptians to the Greeks and Romans and onward to us citizens of the West.[13] The nineteenth-century museum completes the transfer of the aristocratic collection into the domain of public education. The new institution is closely associated with the genesis of the modern state. The museum as the nation's treasure house illustrates its historical and cultural origins. The things on display in it perform a genealogical parade that binds the nation to the glorious canon of occidental culture.

On the Episteme of the Present

This epistemic mode of collecting, too, is now history. The postwar art system is marked by the decline of the museum, which comes to be seen as an old-fashioned monument to the educated bourgeoisie, and the rise of contemporary art as the focus of broad-based public attention and interest. One architectonic attempt to chart a way forward in this crisis is the

---

13   See Beat Wyss, *Hegel's Art History and the Critique of Modernity* (Cambridge, UK: Cambridge University Press, 1999). Originally published as *Trauer der Vollendung* (Munich: Matthes & Seitz, 1985).

Centre Pompidou, for whose designs Renzo Piano and Richard Rogers took inspiration from the neo-Futurist programs of the London-based group Archigram. Inaugurated in 1977, at the tail end of a decade of student revolt in Paris, the complex, in keeping with its statutes, offered free admission to everyone. Yet far from heralding a renaissance of the bourgeois museum, the "Beaubourg" is the brilliant final act of its reign. There is no contradiction in noting that the crisis of the museum in the 1980s coincides with a building boom. Postmodern museum architecture reflects the increasingly desperate struggle to lure the consumerist and leisure-minded members of a deregulated society into the old temples of the Muses.

The second symptom of the museum's crisis is the emergence of the self-employed internationally active exhibition organizer and artist-curator in the mold of Marcel Broodthaers. The latter was born in 1924; so was Pontus Hultén, founding director of the Centre Pompidou. Hultén's friend Harald Szeemann, who studied with Broodthaers, rounds out the triumvirate of charismatic curators. The three regarded the exhibition gallery as a laboratory, a scene of artistic research, reviving, in a sense, the tradition of the early modern humanists with their emblematic-alchemical conception of the cabinet of curiosities. Broodthaers, Hultén, and Szeemann chiefly worked in public institutions, as members of the permanent team or collaborators on specific projects. But this division of responsibilities is not the end of it. A takeover in the business of displaying art has occurred with respect to ownership and collectionism, and it has likewise wrought changes in exhibition-making and curatorial policy.

We can sketch a historical sequence:

One: Humanist scholars start collecting and exhibiting art and knowledge.

Two: In the age of absolutism, rulers buy up the cabinets of curiosities. Possession of a cabinet of natural curiosities and works of art allows the monarch to pose as an erudite humanist.

Three: This sequence repeats in contemporary collectionism.

And so the long history of collecting presents itself as a chain of more or less friendly takeovers: from the humanist scholar to the ruler and on to private collectors and corporations who amass art. The museum was a brief interregnum emerging with the bourgeois state's legal succession to the monarchies that have made, step by step, their exit from the political stage. Where the resulting hybrid absolutism implied a kind of monopoly on major collections, the encroachment of capitalist structures has now deregulated the art market. Prices have skyrocketed to heights that are beyond the means of public institutions. That is why contemporary forms of collecting and curating merit the term *post-museum*.

Art collecting has become a mode of distinction among wealthy individuals. They are the new protagonists whose spending power affords them discretion over exhibitions and the architecture in which they are presented. Just as the absolutist ruler of the early modern era appropriated the habitus of the inquisitive humanist scholar, the post-museum collector appropriates the habitus of the artist-curator. Like the modern ruler, the post-museum collector transmutes the intellectual's modest cabinet of curiosities into a lavish spectacle.

The private art collector is postmodernity's heir in two ways: in his artist-curator's habitus and in the architectonic staging of his endeavor. The private "museum" visualizes the "the collector's choice" in its sovereign arbitrariness and provides an aesthetic stage for the owner's profiling. It is a post-museum scenario in the sense that it no longer serves the museum's classic functions; neither the cultural history of a region nor the public educational mission plays a part in shaping the post-museum collection.

The curators of traditional museums have become aware that their previous core business—the work of collecting and preserving—runs directly counter to the contemporary art world. Their publicly funded institutions have little to offer to the interests of a current episteme categorically structured in accordance with the capitalist logic of surplus value and commodity circulation. As a consequence, public collection-building efforts are monopolized by the select few institutions that act as "global players." The "Bilbao effect" is the last vestige of the museum's erstwhile pedagogical aspirations, with an imperial tinge. The New York-based private collection of the Solomon R. Guggenheim Foundation is open about its ambition to disseminate its idea of collecting across the world in a supermarket chain–style franchise operation. While the strategy has worked out fairly well in Venice, Bilbao, and Berlin, though at the expense of the municipal leaseholders, Rio de Janeiro was sensitive enough to reject the Western-culture theme park it was offered as a neocolonial imposition. The Louvre–Abu Dhabi joint venture functions along similar lines. A public institution dreams of a return to the age of colonial France, which, ever since Napoleon, had a patriarchal *flair* for the Arab world. The Musée du Louvre, the mother of all museums, renders an institution placeless whose ideational purpose was once to locate culture as a *lieu de mémoire* by architectural means.

The contemporary global art world is mobile: being on the move is everything. The Guggenheim principle rests on the economic practice of generating surplus value through circulation. Marx's capital formula has prevailed in the art system. The art trade is no longer about the simple transaction of exchanging works of art for money, the ultimate purpose of such transactions being a collection. The inverse is true: the work of art is regarded as the vehicle of an exchange value to be increased through iterative transactions. The ultimate purpose of the operation is asset appreciation in the merry-go-round of circulating commodities. Collections send their holdings to international art fairs and temporary blockbuster exhibitions that cater to mass tourism's need for spectacles. The museum is expected to adapt to this dynamic by serving, like the art fair, as a temporary storage facility and showroom for circulating art assets and continuous-flow heater stoking their surplus value.

In this light, what would be the model of epistemic order of our time: after the cabinet of curiosities, the encyclopedic library, and the bourgeois museum? Our peripatetic tour across the scenography of knowledge opened with the cabinet of curiosities. But the discursive line has led us to the conclusion that the contemporary renaissance of the *Wunderkammer* is a nostalgic response to the phantom pain caused by the demise of the museum. In the perspective of the history of knowledge, collecting is in a crisis because, like all domains of life, it is being remolded by the advance of economic liberalism. The patient work of building and preserving a collection is no longer the focus of interest. Spectacular auction sales and temporary exhibitions—the characteristic manifestations of an art world in which the work is in permanent circulation—draw far more public attention. Art is expected to keep moving, from biennials to art fairs. Its travels parallel the global cash flows. The epistemological meta-emblems of today are the auction house, the shipping crate, and the trolley case.

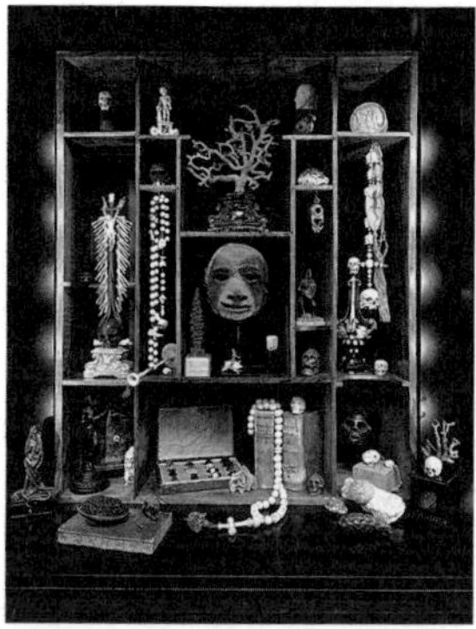

FIG. 1
Wunderkammer Olbricht
© me Collectors Room Berlin
Photo: Bernd Borchardt

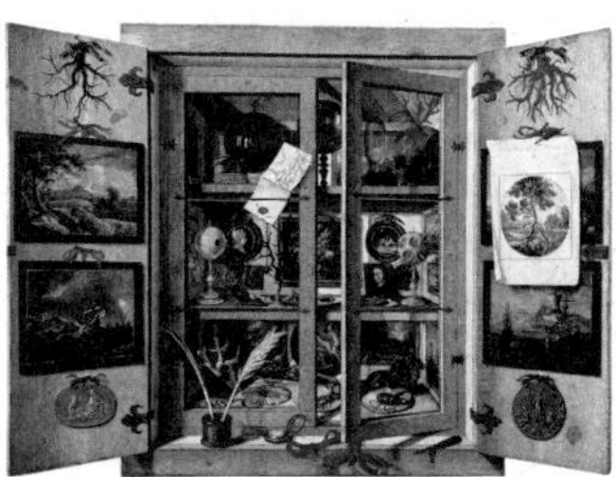

FIG. 2
Andrea Domenico Remps, *Cabinet of Curiosities*, ca. 1690,
Opificio delle Pietre Dure, Florence, Italy.
Wikimedia Commons

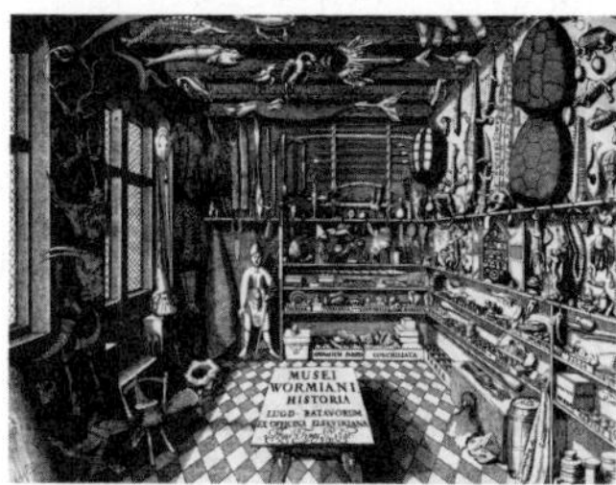

FIG. 4
The Cabinet of Curiosities of Olaus Wormius (1588–1654).
Frontispiece in: *Musei Wormiani Historia* (Copenhagen, 1655)

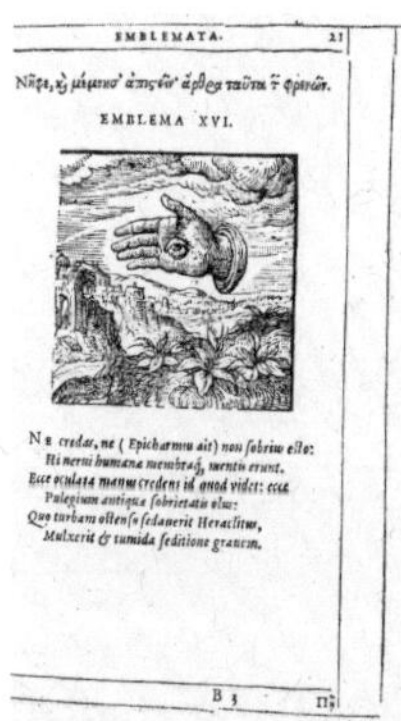

FIG. 3
Emblema XVI: Νήφε καὶ μέμνησο ἀπιστείν
(Epicharmos: Keep sober and remember to be mistrustful),
in: *Emblematum liber* (Augsburg, 1531)

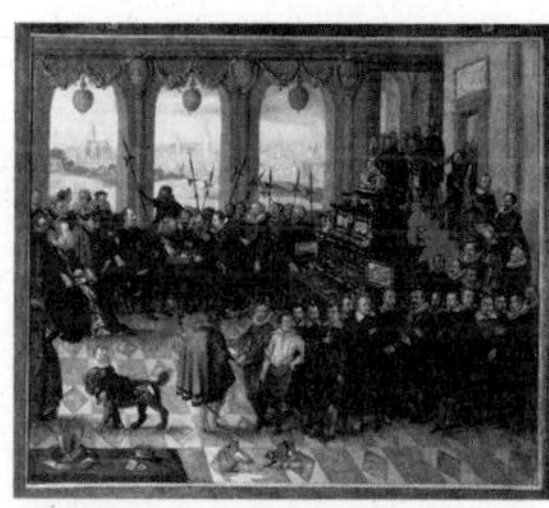

FIG. 5
Anton Mozart, *The Presentation of the Pomeranian
'Kunstschrank' to Duke Philip II of Pomerania*, ca. 1615–1616,
Kunstgewerbemuseum, Staatliche Museen Berlin.
Wikimedia Commons

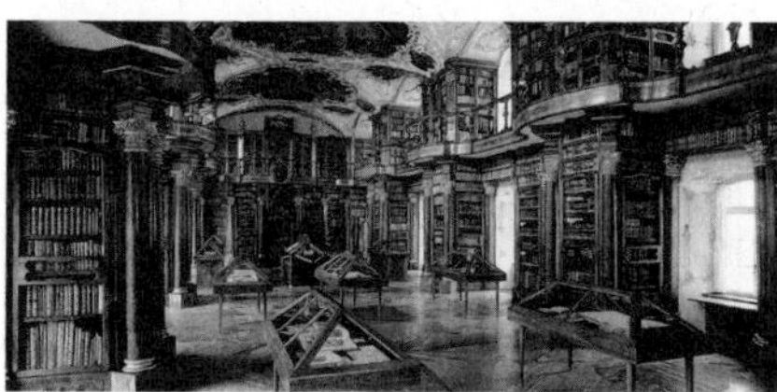

FIG. 6
Peter Thumb, Monastic library, Sankt Gallen, 1768.
Wikimedia Commons

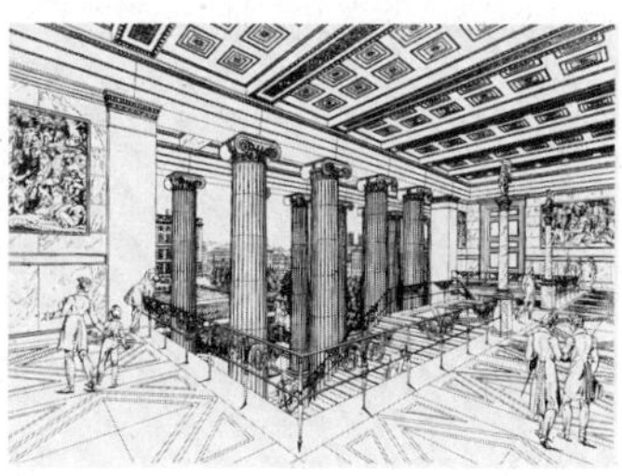

FIG. 7
Carl Friedrich Schinkel, Altes Museum, Berlin, view toward
the staircase, 1823.
Wikimedia Commons

Placing the Present in Relation to the Present
Bettina Funcke

April 2015: a friend accompanies me on a first visit to the Whitney
Museum's new location downtown. Afterwards we take in Untitled—the
museum's restaurant, not an artwork. We're trying to figure out, after
our stroll through the debut collection show, why it's the architecture that
dominates our first impression. How masterfully it highlights the urban
setting of the museum. The galleries seem to widen on each side, directing
visitors away from the art and toward wall-sized windows that give onto
stunning terraces and views beyond: to the east, the Meatpacking District
and Greenwich Village; to the west, the Hudson River and the setting sun.
At Danny Meyer's ground-floor restaurant every table is occupied, there's
chatter all around, the menu is delicious and completely 2015 (small plates,
heavy on locally sourced vegetables). To our right, Glenn Lowry sits with
Adam Weinberg; I try to imagine the thoughts the directors must be sharing
on the new roles, audiences, and architectures of their museums. Behind
me, a man and woman are busy taking and posting pictures of their food.
The woman is ready to upload but pauses to contemplate the proper
hashtag, asking, "Where are we again?"

 Her question captures some of the conundrums museums face today.
The Whitney has built a successful new brand, a new building, and a new
restaurant, all of which are things museums need. Museums have always
been part of tourism, as have adventurous dining and architecture, but each

has increasingly skewed younger and broader in search of greater attendance numbers. Name-brand architecture plus a destination restaurant is the basic recipe for a place where people will want to gather, consume, and socialize. But the museum obviously doesn't want patrons to be unaware of where, exactly, they happen to be. Now that museums are fashionable destinations, what will they do with all the visitors they've summoned, particularly the ones who don't know where they are? One could even say that the disoriented diner's question implies other, larger questions: Where are we with museums in general, and how did we arrive at this new sort of institution?

For centuries, a museum's collection was central to its role and identity. Museums placed the present in dialogue with the past by preserving and presenting objects from different periods. In the ancient world the *museion*, or "seat of the Muses," was invented in Alexandria, an institution for contemplation, teaching, and discussion centering on books and later also objects. The Renaissance revived the term to describe the renowned collection of Lorenzo de' Medici, the word now denoting not a building but the fact of the collection's comprehensiveness. In seventeenth-century Europe the term was used to describe collections of curiosities. After the French Revolution, in keeping with a general movement toward the public, museums made formerly private collections accessible to all. In the early stages of modern capitalist society, with its newly created public sphere and bourgeoisie, museums became places to emphasize national consciousness by giving nascent identities a historical context of objects and documents.

The present era, however, is marked by an intense preoccupation with the contemporary combined with a lack of understanding of its relation to the past, a combination that creates a false sense of existing outside historical time. History and its objects have mostly moved into the background or are used to punctuate the present for effect. Our dominant new museological model, the museum of contemporary art, is often founded without a collection and with little consideration of a dialogic relation to history. In fact, in light of the history of the word *museum*, the phrase "museum of contemporary art" has come to seem practically oxymoronic. So what is it that has replaced the collection in these museums of contemporary art?

While leading a tour of his recent Marcel Broodthaers exhibition at the Museum of Modern Art in New York, curator Christophe Cherix said that "museums are just a platform to try to find out what art is." It's an intriguing statement, implying that museums now are about the flux

of current art and the present moment.[1] The goal it expresses is entirely
contemporary and can be opposed to the traditional museological goals of
illuminating beauty, faith, truth, history, or nation. We might say that while
the traditional museum placed the present in relation to the past, the
museum of contemporary art now places the present in relation to the
present. The museum becomes a designated space for this self-reflexive
activation. As far as funding is concerned, museums almost literally cannot
afford to focus primarily on the past, so activation of the audience has
replaced activation of the historical because that's what attracts the largest,
most diverse crowd. Museums have traditionally expanded our sense of
time by examining periods: the Renaissance focused on the past, and
modernity was about imagining the future. Today, however, audiences want
to imagine the present.

The public still wants to experience objects, of course, but contemporary objects, including paintings and sculptures, are hard to make sense
of without a frame and a context. The museum must be this frame, offering
an experience of the present that is distinct from everyday life and commodity culture. How, then, to make the contemporary perceptible? One
answer is performance, which has always played out, in real time, the
audience's encounter with itself and its own moment. For this the museum
needs the right form, which means not traditional viewing galleries but art
shells, art bays, white cubes, black boxes—the kinds of apparently neutral,
flexible spaces that are necessary to stage performance in the broadest
sense: dance, theater, concerts, screenings, lectures, readings, tours, discussions, meals, therapy sessions, haircuts. These activities are typically
documented, uploaded, and live-streamed, and this makes today's activated
museum of contemporary art eminently compatible with the Internet.[2]

It makes sense to try to open up to a larger discussion around art,
to emphasize the relationship to one's own time, to embrace a younger and
more diverse public. The dead objects of the mausoleum are brought to life
and made to appear more welcoming. As Thomas Hoving, former director
of the Metropolitan Museum of Art, put it in the title of his memoir, the
job is about "making the mummies dance." On the other hand, the friendly
openness that museums seek might compromise art's tensions, its edge,
by helping to gloss over provocations and unresolved conundrums. Art is
not always necessarily welcoming or friendly. Of course there is a part of

---

1   Broodthaers himself already understood this impending
change half a century ago, when he made himself the
director of his fictitious Musée d'art moderne.

2   See Boris Groys, "Entering the Flow," in Groys, *In the Flow*
(New York: Verso, 2016), pp. 3–22.

art that wants to communicate and share, but art also wants to hide something; an artwork is also there to challenge. If a viewer no longer senses this challenge, what remains is a visual surface barely distinct from any other in a highly aestheticized world.

The powerful interests that have recently attached themselves to contemporary art—urban renewal, tourism, financial speculation—distract from the difficult, reclusive, and uncompromising core of art. This resistant nature arises, in part, from an attempt to withstand the flow of time, from a longing to leave traces beyond the lifetime of the artist. In response, the museum traditionally offered a material eternity, secured politically and economically if not ontologically. Are modern museums of contemporary art—perhaps even modern societies—avoiding a consideration of the eternal and metaphysical? The turbulence of the early twenty-first century has certainly undermined any sense of material or political perpetuity. Today's sense of transience, and the absence of any claim on eternal essence, may be signs of the lateness of our era. Despite this, or perhaps because of it, museums have only become more relevant and more visited. This raises a question: Who is the intended consumer of art? Or, to put it differently: What constitutes the economic basis of radical contemporary art? Historically it has been the ruling class, be that the church, the aristocracy, or the modern state. Capitalism's elite have now taken on the role, and ideological interests have always been attached to such support. Might it be that the framing of museums for a mass audience is related to an elite's need to stay in power? Are museums a tool? We know that power needs to propose a (false) promise of equality in order to perpetuate itself, and that it uses an aesthetic of equality (e.g. "art for all") to do so. One could say, then, that to retain political power, the ruling class pretends to erase distinctions of taste, creating an illusion of aesthetic solidarity.[3]

Consider the 2016 redesign of the Metropolitan Museum's logo. Part of an institutional rebranding effort, the new logo is intended to signal a more welcoming, accessible, and current Met. The older logo, in use since 1971, featured a capital *M* set against a circle and square, with a smaller circle nestled in each serif, recalling Leonardo da Vinci's famous *Vitruvian Man* (ca. 1490), in which proportional geometries formed an image of relation and harmony. The *M* itself originated in an illustration from the 1509 book *De divina proportione* by Fra Luca Pacioli, da Vinci's math teacher and collaborator; in his illustration the letter was already a logo,

---

3   See Groys, "Clement Greenberg: Engineer of Art," in Groys,
      In the Flow (see note 2), pp. 101–114.

as it stood for the word *mathematica*. The older Met design was thus grounded in knowledge, history, and a visualization of their relations. In the new design, the words *THE MET* are stacked, one over the other, in bright red letters whose conjoined shapes are meant to evoke both modernity and classicism while also embodying a theme of connection. In explaining the desire to rebrand, the institution used the words "friendlier," "simpler," and "contemporary." "It's the right direction," said the museum's chairman, Daniel Brodsky. "It's a changing institution; the world is changing around us, and I think it's time for the Met to move forward."[4]

From divine proportion to the friendliness of contemporary branding: this is the new direction that the contemporary museum and its audience have to contend with. The question remains: What will these more fashionable institutions do with the new audiences they attract? In "Avant-Garde and Kitsch," Clement Greenberg suggested that the mark of kitsch is the way it imitates the effects of art.[5] In their efforts to activate spaces, stage encounters, and entertain the public, museums of contemporary art are increasingly engaging in such mimicry. Does that make them kitsch? The Whitney's new restaurant borrows from art gestures in calling itself Untitled; In Situ, the restaurant at the San Francisco Museum of Modern Art, goes even further: at what may be the first conceptual restaurant, star chef Corey Lee offers no recipes of his own, instead curating the menu as a "group show" composed entirely of recipes by other well-known chefs. Where are we again?

Art's power is to make visible the rules governing social behavior. By offering a dialogue with historical objects, museums traditionally played a decisive role in demonstrating the transitory character of the current order, helping audiences imagine a beyond, offering the possibility of transcendence. If you erase a dialogue with history, or if that dialogue only considers the last fifty years or so, it makes it very hard to imagine the future or anything beyond the material world we live in, producing frustration and confusion. Museums may draw larger, broader, younger publics, but people still expect to understand, to be moved, to have a moment of clarity or a connection to eternal values. As much as they want to imagine the present, they also still desire all that the museum once represented.

---

4   Robin Pogrebin, "The Met, Courting Criticism, in Caps,"
New York Times, February 20, 2016, New York edition, C1.

5   Clement Greenberg, "Avant-Garde and Kitsch," *Partisan
Review* 6, no. 5 (Fall 1939), pp. 34–49.

Radical Museology, or, What's "Contemporary" in Museums of Contemporary Art?

Claire Bishop

I. Going Inside

Rosalind Krauss's 1990 essay "The Cultural Logic of the Late Capitalist Museum" was arguably the last polemical text to be written on museums of contemporary art by an art historian. Her essay is indebted to Fredric Jameson's critique of late capitalist culture not just in its title but also in its relentless pessimism. Drawing from her experience of two contemporary art museums—the Musée d'Art Moderne de la Ville de Paris and the projected site of Mass MoCA in North Adams, Massachusetts—Krauss argued that a profound encounter with the work of art had become subordinated to a new register of experience: the unanchored hyperreality of its architectural container, which produced effects of disembodiment that, in her view, correlated to the dematerialized flows of global capital. Rather than a highly individualized artistic epiphany, visitors to these galleries encountered a euphoria of space first, and art second.[1] Krauss's essay was prescient in many ways: the decade to come saw an unprecedented proliferation of new museums dedicated to contemporary art, and increased scale and a proximity to big business have been two central

---

[1] Rosalind Krauss, "The Cultural Logic of the Late Capitalist Museum," *October* 54 (Fall 1990), p. 14. Krauss goes on to discuss an article in *Art in America* that reports museums deaccessioning their collections, noting the incursion of a managerial mindset and the pressure of the art market upon museum activities.

characteristics of the move from the nineteenth-century model of the museum as a patrician institution of elite culture to its current incarnation as a populist temple of leisure and entertainment.

Today, however, a more radical model of the museum is taking shape: more experimental, less architecturally determined, and offering a more politicized engagement with our historical moment. In the longer version of this paper, I discuss three museums in Europe that are doing more than any individual work of art to shift our perception of art institutions and their potential: the Van Abbemuseum in Eindhoven, the Museo Nacional Centro de Arte Reina Sofía in Madrid, and Muzej sodobne umetnosti Metelkova (MSUM) in Ljubljana.[2] All three present compelling alternatives to the dominant mantra of bigger is better, and better is richer. Rather than following the blue-chip mainstream, these museums draw upon the widest range of artifacts to situate art's relationship to particular histories with universal relevance.[3] They do not speak in the name of the one percent, but attempt to represent the interests and histories of those constituencies that are (or have been) marginalized, sidelined, and oppressed. This doesn't mean that they subordinate art to history in general, but that they mobilize the world of visual production to inspire the necessity of standing on the right side of history.

It is no coincidence that each of these museums has also engaged in the task of rethinking the category of "the contemporary." In this essay, I set two models of contemporaneity against each other. The first concerns presentism: the condition of taking our current moment as the horizon and destination of our thinking. This is the dominant usage of the term "contemporary" in art today; it is underpinned by an inability to grasp our moment in its global entirety, and an acceptance of this incomprehension as a constitutive condition of the present historical era. The second model, which I want to develop here, takes its lead from the practice of these three museums: here the contemporary is understood as a dialectical method and a politicized project with a more radical understanding of temporality. Time and value turn out to be crucial categories at stake in formulating a notion of what I will call a "dialectical contemporaneity," because it does

---

2   See Claire Bishop, *Radical Museology, or, What's Contemporary in Museums of Contemporary Art?* (London: Koenig Books, 2013).

3   Here I am referring to Susan Buck-Morss's arguments in *Hegel, Haiti and Universal History* (Pittsburgh: University of Pittsburgh Press, 2009). Buck-Morss argues that universal history involves the denationalization of events in order to reinscribe them as questions of universal concern. (The Holocaust, for example, does not belong to German history or to Jewish history, but is a calamity for all humankind.) In retrieving the universal as a category, Buck-Morss joins a number of recent thinkers, including Slavoj Žižek and Alain Badiou, who seek to recuperate the universal after its dismantling by poststructuralist assaults on metanarratives. Her aim is not to interpret universality as inclusivity (i.e., pulling everything into the same narrative), but rather to use it as a methodological intervention into history.

not designate a style or period of the works themselves so much as an *approach* to them. One of the consequences of approaching institutions through this category is a rethinking of the museum, the category of art that it enshrines, and the modalities of spectatorship it produces.

II. Museums of Contemporary Art

Although the last twenty years have seen a huge diversification of museums as a category, a dominant logic of privatization unites most of their iterations worldwide. In Europe, there has been an increasing dependence on donations and corporate sponsorship as governments gradually withdraw public funding from culture in the name of "austerity." In the United States, the situation has always been thus, but is now accelerating without any pretense to a separation of public and private interests: an art dealer, Jeffrey Deitch, was appointed head of the Museum of Contemporary Art, Los Angeles, in January 2010. Two months later, the New Museum controversially installed the collection of its multimillionaire trustee Dakis Joannou and employed the artist Jeff Koons—already in Joannou's collection—to guest curate the exhibition. Meanwhile, it is well-known that the Museum of Modern Art in New York regularly rehangs its permanent collection on the basis of its trustees' latest acquisitions. Indeed, it can sometimes seem as if contemporary museums have ceded historical research to commercial galleries: Gagosian, for example, has mounted a series of blockbuster shows of modern masters (Manzoni, Picasso, Fontana) as carefully curated by famous art historians as those in a traditional museum.

In Latin America, although publicly funded institutions of contemporary art have existed since the 1960s—for example in São Paulo and Lima, where two museums form part of university campuses (MAC-USP and LiMAC)—the highest-profile contemporary art spaces are all private: Jumex in Mexico City (established in 1999), MALBA in Buenos Aires (2001), Inhotim near Belo Horizonte, Brazil (2006). In Asia, the biggest collection-based contemporary art museums have been established under the aegis of wealthy individuals (such as the Mori Art Museum, Tokyo, 2003, or the Dragon Museum in Shanghai, 2012) or corporations (such as the Samsung Museum of Art, Seoul, 2004). It is only recently that the Chinese government has opened its first state-run contemporary art museum, the Power Station of Art, based in a former Shanghai industrial plant (October 2012), to be followed by the M+ museum in Hong Kong, slated to be the world's largest contemporary art museum, which will open in 2019. However, many Asian museums could just as well be described as "Kunsthallen" that show temporary exhibitions, as their commitment to a collection policy is negligible: think of the Beijing Today Art Museum (2002), Shanghai's Minsheng Art Museum (2008) and Rockbund Art Museum (2010), or the Guangdong Times Museum, Guangzhou (2010).

As critics have observed, the visual expression of this privatization has been the triumph of "starchitecture": the museum's external wrapper has become more important than its contents, just as Krauss foresaw in 1990, leaving art with the option of looking ever more lost inside gigantic post-industrial hangars, or supersizing to compete with its envelope. Although museums have always endorsed signature architecture, the extreme iconicity of new museum buildings is comparatively recent: I. M. Pei's Pyramids for the Louvre in 1989 are an early benchmark, while the most recent avatars in Europe are the Centre Pompidou-Metz by Shigeru Ban and Zaha Hadid's MAXXI, Rome, both of which opened in 2010. The future shadow of Abu Dhabi adds further, intercultural tension to this list: a franchised Louvre and a Guggenheim will form part of a slew of eye-popping over-scaled buildings destined to house art and performance. Looking at this global panorama of contemporary art museums, what binds them all together is less a concern for a collection, a history, a position, or a mission than a sense that contemporaneity is being staged on the level of *image*: the new, the cool, the photogenic, the well-designed, the economically successful.[4]

When did contemporary art become so desirable a category? Back in 1940, an artists' manifesto, designed by Ad Reinhardt, queried MoMA's ability to show the present rather than merely exhibit the past, asking "How Modern is the Museum of Modern Art?" Artists picketed the museum and demanded more exhibitions of contemporary US art, rather than endless shows of early twentieth-century European painters and sculptors.[5] It is telling that for MoMA's then director, Alfred H. Barr, Jr., modern denoted aesthetic quality (the progressive, original, and challenging) compared to the safe, academic, and "supine neutrality" of the contemporary, which simply meant work by living artists.[6] In the postwar period,

---

4   As artist Hito Steyerl notes, "Contemporary art is a brand name without a brand, ready to be slapped onto almost anything for a quick face-lift touting the new creative imperative for places in need of an extreme makeover [...] If contemporary art is the answer, the question is: How can capitalism be made more beautiful?" Steyerl, "Politics of Art: Contemporary Art and the Transition to Post-Democracy," *e-flux journal* 21 (December 2010), available online at: http://www.e-flux.com/journal/politics-of-art-contemporary-art-and-the-transition-to-post-democracy/.

5   In fact, as Richard Meyer has shown, MoMA's program during the 1930s had been remarkably varied, including exhibitions of prehistoric rock painting, Persian frescoes, and reproductions of Cézanne paintings. US artists had been shown at the museum, but Reinhardt and the organization American Abstract Artists objected to the fact that these artists were too old, too conventional, or too popular to qualify as authentically modern. See Richard Meyer, *What Was Contemporary Art?* (Cambridge, MA: MIT Press, 2013), chapter 4.

institutions tended to favor the term "contemporary art" as a substitute
for "modern": the Institute of Contemporary Arts in London was founded
in 1947, opting to show temporary exhibitions rather than building up
a permanent collection, as did many similarly titled venues.[7] In these
examples, once again, the "contemporary" refers less to style or period than
to an assertion of the present. By contrast, the Institute of Modern Art in
Boston was renamed the Institute of Contemporary Art in 1948 as a way to
distance itself from MoMA's vanguard internationalism; it turned to the
more capacious category of the "contemporary" to legitimate a regionalist,
commercial, and conservative agenda.[8]

The New Museum in New York is an important transitional case
in the story of museums becoming presentist. Established in 1977 as an
alternative to MoMA and the Whitney Museum of American Art, the
New Museum initially built up a "semi-permanent collection" under the
aegis of its first director, Marcia Tucker. Begun in 1978, the collection was
devoted to the kind of work that then had no place in the traditional
museum: dematerialized, conceptual, performance, and process-based art.
These works represented marginalized subject positions and staked out a
position against Reagan-era politics. The museum's idea was to destabilize
the idea of collecting by keeping its sights on the present: work would be
selected from shows in the building, as a form of documentation, but after
a decade these works would be deaccessioned to create room for more
recent pieces.[9] On the one hand, the semi-permanent collection functioned
as an "anti-collection," allowing works to flow in and out, refusing a
correct or authoritative story of contemporary art. On the other hand, this
perpetual motion rendered the museum "compliant with notions of
obsolescence and the march of fashion."[10] Tucker later recognized that the

6   Alfred H. Barr, Jr., letter to Paul Sachs, October 5, 1929, cited in: ibid., p. 366.

7   The outlier here is the City Gallery of Contemporary Art in Zagreb, founded in 1954. It changed its name to the Museum of Contemporary Art in 1998.

8   "The Institute's intermingling of curating and commerce would, for better or worse, increasingly come to mirror the logic of contemporary art in America." Meyer, *What Was Contemporary Art?*, p. 251. In 1950, MoMA, the Whitney Museum, and the ICA Boston issued a joint manifesto declaring the modern tradition alive and well—a public reversal of Boston's previous assertion that modernism had died in 1939. See J. Pedro Lorente, *Cathedrals of Urban Modernity* (Aldershot: Ashgate Publishing, 1998), p. 250.

9   This model of collecting was not new: it was more or less the same as that implemented in 1818, when the Musée du Luxembourg in Paris became the "musée des artistes vivants"—a designation chosen to position the institution in direct contrast to the Louvre, which was reserved for artists who were "historical" (i.e., dead). This model was also followed by Barr at MoMA as of 1931: works would either be deaccessioned after fifty years, or passed on to the Metropolitan Museum of Art for posterity—a practice that continued until 1953. What makes the New Museum's "semi-permanent collection" distinctive is that it formed a bridge between alternative art practices of the 1970s (informed by institutional critique and systems art) and the market logic of the 1980s (exemplified by the continual turnover of Charles Saatchi's collection). Saatchi's acquisition strategy has controversially involved buying young artists' work wholesale and then reselling the entire set once the market value has increased. See, for example, Arifa Akbar, "Charles Saatchi: A Blessing or a Curse for Young Artists?" *The Independent*, June 13, 2008: "Saatchi's most outspoken protegé-turned-critic was the Italian neo-expressionist painter Sandro Chia, whose work was bought and then disposed of in the 1980s. There was speculation that Saatchi's sale of his entire holdings of Chia's work effectively destroyed the Italian's reputation."

10   See Brian Goldfarb et al., "Fleeting Possessions," in *Temporarily Possessed: The Semi-Permanent Collection* (New York: The New Museum of Contemporary Art, 1995), pp. 9ff.

collection's semi-permanence refused access to the past in favor of the present, rather than setting the two in dialogue. Today, there is no mention of the New Museum's collection of circa 670 works on the institution's website, which states that it is a "non-collecting institution."[11] The emphasis is instead on high-profile solo shows by living (or recently deceased) artists, group exhibitions, and a triennial, and there is very little to differentiate its activities from those of the Guggenheim, Whitney, MoMA, or even the Metropolitan, all of which now show contemporary art. The only discernible difference is branding: the New Museum's demographic is younger and hipper.

III. Theorizing the Contemporary

In tandem with this proliferation of contemporary art museums, the study of contemporary art has become the fastest-growing subject area in the academy since the turn of the millennium. Here, the definition of "contemporary" has become a moving target par excellence: until the late 1990s, it seemed synonymous with "postwar," denoting art after 1945; about ten years ago, it was relocated to start somewhere in the 1960s; now the 1960s and 1970s generally tend to be viewed as high modernist, and the argument has been put forward that we should consider 1989 as the beginning of a new era, synonymous with the fall of communism and the emergence of global markets.[12] While each of these periodizations has its pros and cons, the central drawback is that they operate from a Western purview. In China, contemporary art tends to be dated from the late 1970s (the official end of the Cultural Revolution and the beginning of the democracy movement); in India, from the 1990s onwards; in Latin America, there is no real division of the modern and the contemporary, because this would mean conforming to hegemonic Western categories—indeed, a prevalent discussion there still revolves around whether or not modernity has actually been realized. In Africa, contemporary art dates variously from the end of colonialism (the late 1950s/1960s in Anglophone and Francophone countries; the 1970s in the case of former Portuguese colonies), or as late as the 1990s (the end of apartheid in South Africa, the first African

---

11 See http://www.newmuseum.org/files/nm_press_faq.pdf. Recent work to have been purchased for the museum by its trustees includes Ugo Rondinone's *Hell, Yes!* (2001), installed on the façade of the building 2007–2010. None of the collection has been included in any of the exhibitions at the New Museum since its move to the Bowery in 2007. Email from Gabriel Einsohn, press officer at the New Museum, March 29, 2013.

12 See, for example, Alex Alberro, response to "Questionnaire on 'The Contemporary,'" *October* 130 (Fall 2009), p. 55; *Global Contemporary: Art Worlds After 1989*, exhibition at ZKM | Karlsruhe, 2011; Alexander Dumbadze and Suzanne Hudson, eds., *Contemporary Art: 1989 to the Present* (Oxford: Wiley-Blackwell, 2013).

biennials, and the start of the publication *NKA: Journal of Contemporary African Art*).[13]

It almost goes without saying, then, that the attempt to periodize contemporary art is dysfunctional, unable to accommodate global diversity. Most recent theorists have therefore positioned it as a *discursive* category. For philosopher Peter Osborne, the contemporary is an "operative fiction": it is fundamentally a productive act of the imagination, because we attribute a sense of unity to the present, one that encompasses disjunctive global temporalities we can never grasp; as such it is a time of stasis.[14] For Boris Groys, modernism was characterized by a desire to surpass the present in the name of realizing a glorious future (be this avant-garde utopianism or the Stalinist five-year plan); contemporaneity, by contrast, is marked by "a prolonged, potentially infinite period of delay," prompted by the fall of communism.[15] For both Osborne and Groys, a future-oriented modernism has been replaced by a static, boring present ("we are stuck in the present as it reproduces itself without leading to any future").[16] Groys points to the secular ritual of repetition that is the video loop as contemporary art's instantiation of this new relationship to temporality, which creates, he argues, a "non-historical excess of time through art."

Other theorists have claimed the contemporary as a question of temporal disjunction. Giorgio Agamben, for example, posits it as a state of being founded on temporal rupture: "contemporariness," he writes, "is *that relationship with time that adheres to it through a disjunction and an anachronism*," and it is only by this untimeliness or "dys-chrony" that one can truly gaze at one's own era.[17] He evocatively describes contemporariness as being able "to fix your gaze on the darkness of the epoch" and "being on time for an appointment that one cannot but miss."[18] Anachronism also permeates the reading of Terry Smith, one of the few art historians to tackle this question. He has persuasively argued that the contemporary should be set equally against the discourses of modernism and postmodernism, because it is characterized by antinomies and asynchronies: the simultaneous and incompatible coexistence of different modernities and ongoing social inequities, differences that persist despite the global spread of

13   See also Okwui Enwezor and Chika Okeke-Agulu, *Contemporary Art in Africa Since 1980* (Bologna: Damiani, 2009), p. 12: "Contemporary African art comes both at the end of traditional arts (seemingly precolonial) and at the end of colonialism; that is to say, its condition of existence in the present is postcolonial."

14   Peter Osborne, "The Fiction of the Contemporary," in *Anywhere or Not At All: Philosophy of Contemporary Art* (London and New York: Verso, 2013), pp. 15–35.

15   Boris Groys, "Comrades of Time," in *Going Public* (Berlin: Sternberg Press, 2010), pp. 84–101.

16   Ibid., p. 90, and the following quote, p. 94.

17   Giorgio Agamben, "What Is the Contemporary?" in *What is an Apparatus? and Other Essays* (Stanford: Stanford University Press, 2009), p. 41. Italics in the original.

18   Ibid., p. 46.

telecommunications systems and the purported universality of market logic.[19]

These discursive approaches seem to fall into one of two camps: either contemporaneity denotes stasis (i.e., it is a continuation of postmodernism's post-historical deadlock) or it reflects a break with postmodernism by asserting a plural and disjunctive relationship to temporality. The latter is of course more generative, as it allows us to move away from both the historicity of modernism, characterized by an abandonment of tradition and a forward propulsion towards the new, and the historicity of postmodernism, equated with a "schizophrenic" collapse of past and future into an expanded present.[20] Certainly, an assertion of multiple, overlapping temporalities can be seen in many works of art since the mid-1990s by artists from countries struggling to deal with a context of recent war and political upheaval, especially in Eastern Europe and the Middle East.[21] Art historian Christine Ross has argued that contemporary artists look backwards in order to "presentify" the modernist regime of historicity and thereby to critique its futurity; artists are less interested in Walter Benjamin's approach to history as radical discontinuity, she writes, than in "potential[izing] remains as forms of resistance to and redeployment of modern life."[22] However, other critics have questioned whether these artistic efforts are ultimately more nostalgic and retrospective than prospective: Dieter Roelstraete has lambasted contemporary art's turn towards history-telling and historicizing for its "inability to grasp or even look at the present, much less to *excavate the future*."[23]

A less contested approach to disjunctive temporalities can be found in the revival of interest in anachronism among art historians. Its central advocate, Georges Didi-Huberman, has argued that anachronism is so pervasive an operation in art throughout history that we should see its

---

19   This world came into being in the late 1980s, he argues, but exists decisively in common consciousness after 9/11. Terry Smith, *What Is Contemporary Art?* (Chicago: Chicago University Press, 2009).

20   The term "historicity" is used by the French historian François Hartog to describe the dominant order of time in a given era: how society conceptualizes and treats its past. See Hartog, *Régimes d'historicité* (Paris: Editions du Seuil, 2003). "Schizophrenic" is the term deployed by Fredric Jameson to characterize postmodernism's preference for heightened but disconnected experiences of the present. See Jameson, "Postmodernism and Consumer Society," in *The Anti-Aesthetic: Essays on Postmodern Culture*, ed. Hal Foster (New York: The New Press, 2002), pp. 13–29.

21   In Eastern Europe, the disavowal of the Communist past in official discourse has given rise to numerous video works exploring the psychological impact of the transition, therapeutically incorporating old film stock or technology (such as Anri Sala's *Intervista* and Deimantas Narkevicius's *His-Story*, both 1998); in the Middle East, a powerful body of work has addressed the Lebanese Civil War and episodes from the history of the Israel/Palestine conflict (consider the extensive archival work of the Atlas Group/Walid Raad or Emily Jacir). In Western Europe and North America, by contrast, artists have seized upon overlooked moments in the history of psychotherapy, colonialism, feminism, and civil rights—at their best, interested less in the past for its own sake than in the possibilities it contains for opening up alternatives for the future (Stan Douglas, Sharon Hayes, Harun Farocki).

22   Christine Ross, *The Past is the Present; It's the Future Too: The Temporal Turn in Contemporary Art* (London: Continuum, 2013), p. 41.

23   Dieter Roelstraete, "The Way of the Shovel: On the Archaeological Imaginary in Art," *e-flux journal* 4 (March 2009), available online at: http://www.e-flux.com/journal/the-way-of-the-shovel-on-the-archeological-imaginary-in-art/. Italics in the original.

presence in *all* works: "in each historical object, all times encounter one another, collide, or base themselves plastically on one another, bifurcate, or even become entangled with each other."[24] Building on the work of Aby Warburg (1866–1929), Didi-Huberman puts forth the idea that works of art are temporal knots, a mixture of past and present; they reveal what persists or "survives" (*Nachleben*) from earlier periods, in the form of a symptom in the current era. To gain access to these stratified temporalities, he writes, requires a "shock, a tearing of the veil, an irruption or appearance of time, what Proust and Benjamin have described so eloquently under the category of 'involuntary memory.'"[25] Taking their lead from Didi-Huberman, Alexander Nagel and Christopher Wood demonstrate in *Anachronic Renaissance* (2010) the co-existence of two temporalities in works of art circa 1500, as culture shifted from religious medieval to secular Renaissance. Arguing against the historicist idea that each object or event belongs in a specific time and place (the idea upon which anachronism is founded), they instead propose the term "anachronic" to describe the way in which works of art perform a recursive temporality.[26]

Nagel and Wood's investigation, while compelling, is mono-directional: by their own admission, they "reverse engineer" from the work of art backwards (into its own past, its own chronotopology), rather than beginning with a diagnosis of the present that necessitates research into the early Renaissance as a means to mobilize a different understanding of today.[27] By contrast, what I call a dialectical contemporary seeks to navigate multiple temporalities within a more political horizon. Rather than simply claim that many or all times are present in each historical object, we need to ask *why* certain temporalities appear in particular works of art at *specific* historical moments. Furthermore, this analysis is motivated by a desire to understand our present condition and how to change it.[28] Lest this method be interpreted as yet another form of presentism, a preoccupation with the now masquerading as historical inquiry, it should be stressed that sightlines are always focused on the future: the ultimate aim is to disrupt the

---

24 Georges Didi-Huberman, "History and Image: Has the 'Epistemological Transformation' Taken Place?" in *The Art Historian: National Traditions and Institutional Practices*, ed. Michael Zimmermann (Williamstown, MA: Clark Studies in the Visual Arts, 2003), p. 131.

25 Georges Didi-Huberman, "Before the Image, Before Time: The Sovereignty of Anachronism," in *Compelling Visuality*, ed. Claire Farago and Robert Zwijnenberg (Minneapolis: University of Minnesota Press, 2003), p. 41. See also Didi-Huberman, "The Surviving Image: Aby Warburg and Tylorian Anthropology," *Oxford Art Journal* 25, no. 1 (2002), pp. 59–70.

26 Alexander Nagel and Christopher Wood, *Anachronic Renaissance* (New York: Zone Books, 2010), p. 14.

27 Ibid., p. 34.

28 My position also differs from that of Thomas Crow, for whom the work of visual art has a unique temporality compared to that of literature, music, or dance, because its objects are "the actual things fashioned and handled by the subjects of history themselves." (Thomas Crow, "The Practice of Art History in America," *Daedalus* 135, no. 2 [Spring 2006], p. 71.) The use of reproductive technologies in contemporary art has weakened the viability of this claim; see the discussion of documentation at the Reina Sofía, in: Claire Bishop, *Radical Museology, or, What's Contemporary in Museums of Contemporary Art?* (London: Koenig Books, 2013).

relativist pluralism of the current moment, in which all styles and beliefs are considered equally valid, and to move towards a more sharply politicized understanding of where we can and should be heading. If, as Osborne claims, the global contemporary is a shared fiction, then this doesn't denote its "impossibility," but rather provides the basis for a new political imaginary. The idea that artists might help us glimpse the contours of a project for rethinking our world is surely one of the reasons why contemporary art, despite its near total imbrication in the market, continues to rouse such passionate interest and concern.

Where do museums fit into this? My argument is that museums with a historical collection have become the most fruitful testing ground for a non-presentist, multitemporal contemporaneity. This is in direct contrast to the commonplace assumption that the privileged site of contemporary art is the globalized biennial; the operational logic of the latter remains locked within an affirmation of the zeitgeist, and any navigation of the past tends to serve only as a foil for younger artists. Of course, for many curators, the historical weight of a permanent collection is an albatross that inhibits the novelty so essential to drawing in new audiences, since the incessant turnover of temporary exhibitions is deemed more exciting (and profitable) than finding yet another way to show the canon. Yet today, when so many museums are being forced to turn back to their collections because funds for loan-based temporary exhibitions have been slashed due to austerity measures, the permanent collection can be a museum's greatest weapon in breaking the stasis of presentism. This is because it requires us to think in several tenses simultaneously: the *past perfect* and the *future anterior*. It is a time capsule of what was once considered culturally significant at previous historical periods, while more recent acquisitions anticipate the judgment of history to come (in the future, this *will have been* deemed important). Without a permanent collection, it is hard for a museum to stake any meaningful claim to an engagement with the past—but also, I would wager, with the future.[29]

This text originally appeared in Radical Museology, or, What's Contemporary in Museums of Contemporary Art? (London: Koenig Books, 2013) *and has been edited by the author.*

---

29 At the New Museum, for example, history appears only in the register of fashionability, like a well-chosen retro interest. Even group exhibitions whose themes provide a perfect opportunity for historical research are presented without argumentation. For example, *Ostalgia* (2011), a survey of Russian and Eastern European art since the 1960s, juxtaposed works on the basis of sensibility, without any acknowledgment of the ideological transition that took place 1989–1991. The show replaced the frame of political history with that of good taste, effectively permitting the market to hold sway (appropriately, the show was funded by a Russian gas oligarch, Leonid Mikhelson, whose art foundation is called VICTORIA—the Art of being Contemporary [*sic*]). Moreover, the exhibition title grouped all work under the rubric of "ostalgia," despite the fact that the majority of exhibits dated from the pre-1989 period.

Production
This image series features works on a grand scale that were produced
in collaboration with the Migros Museum für Gegenwartskunst.

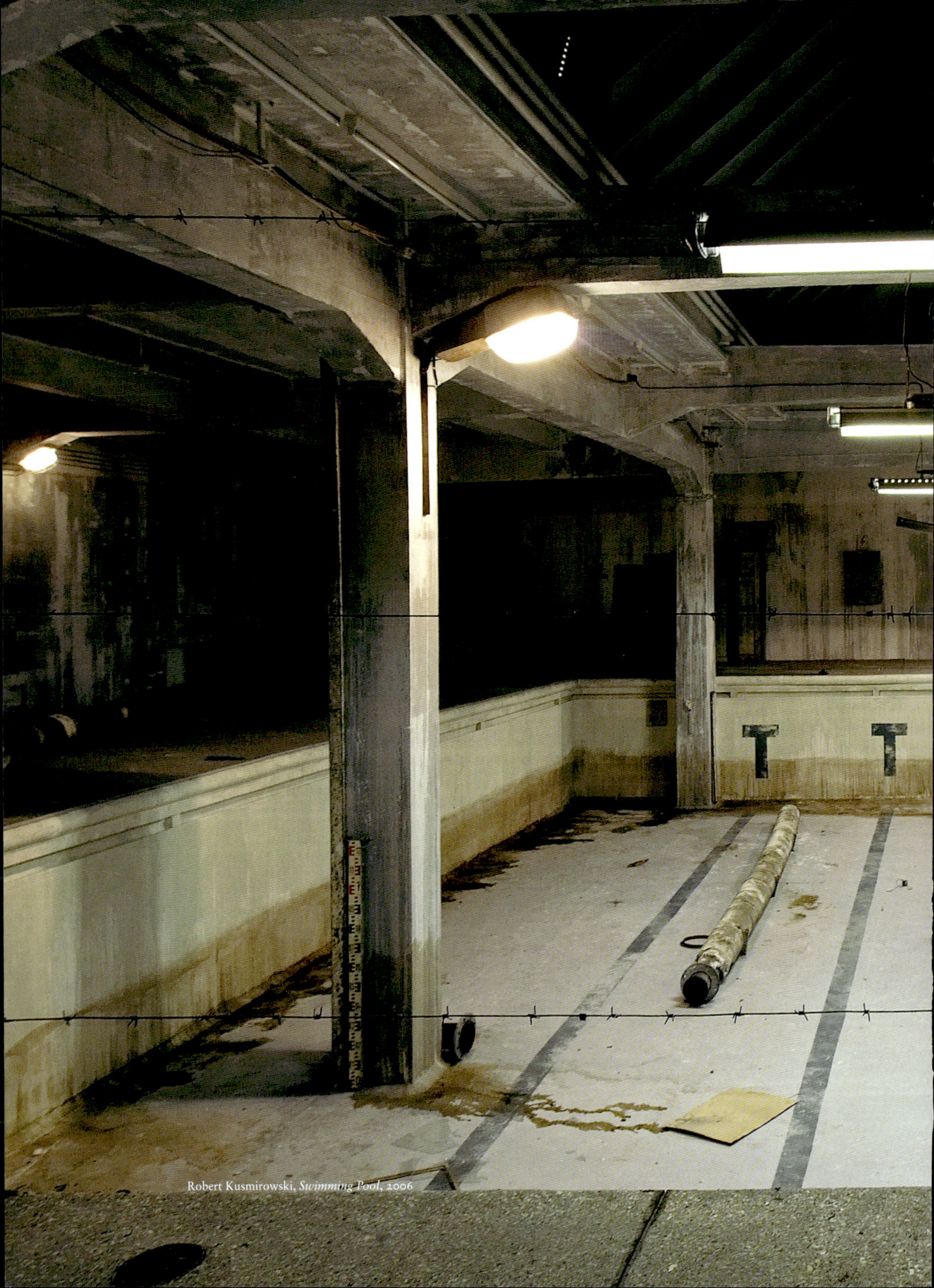

Robert Kusmirowski, *Swimming Pool*, 2006

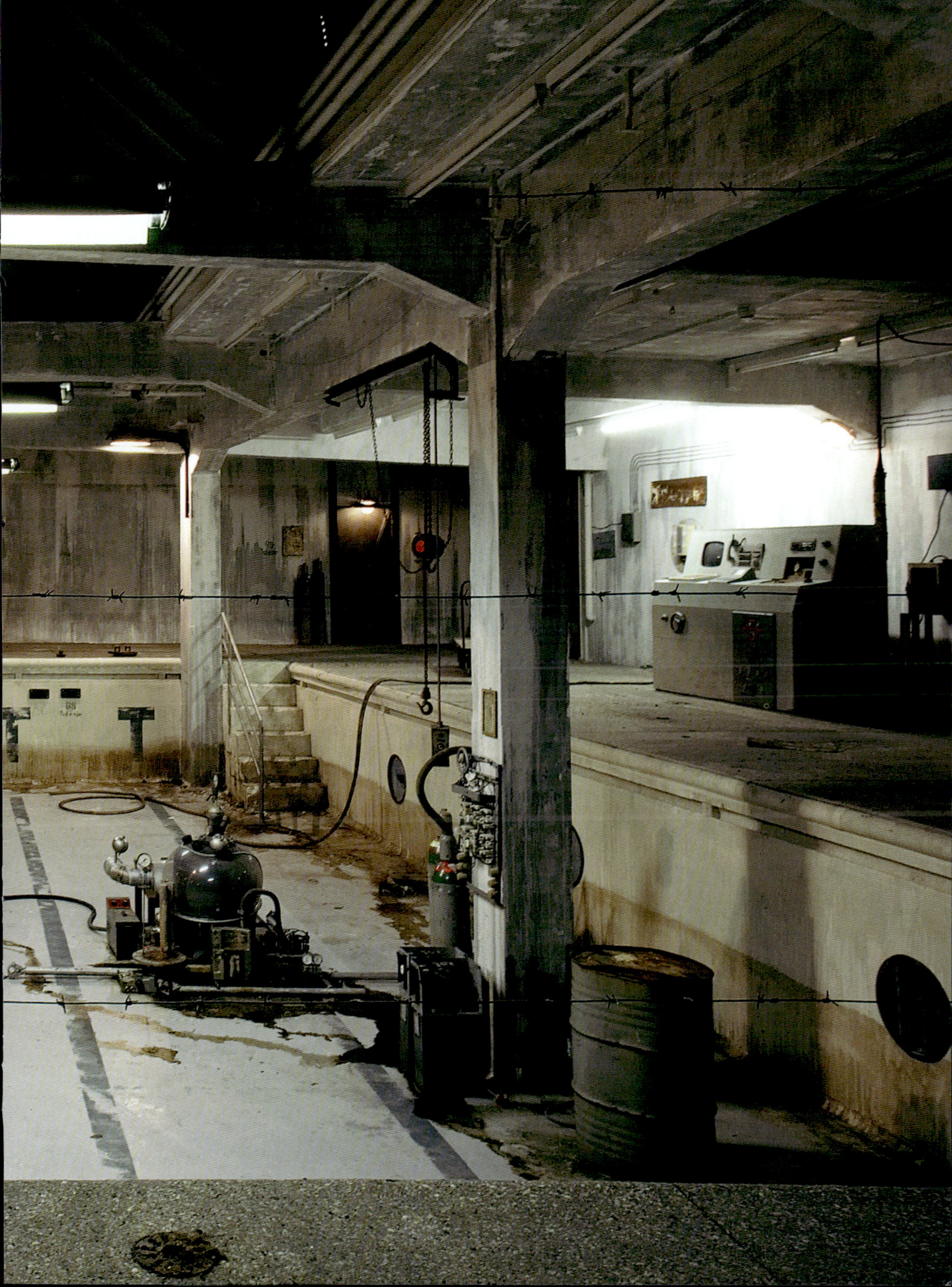

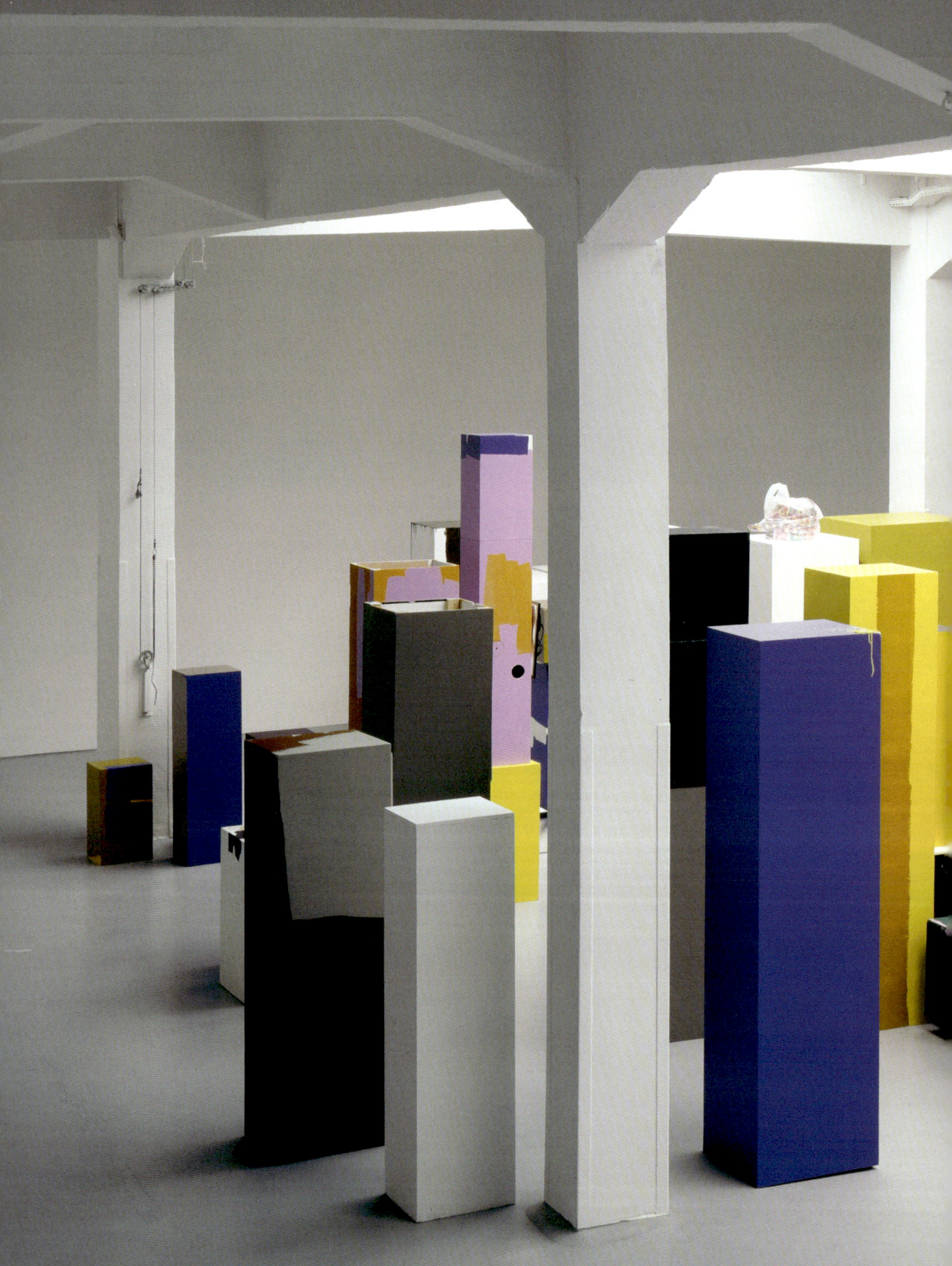

Rachel Harrison, *Trees for the Forest*, 2007

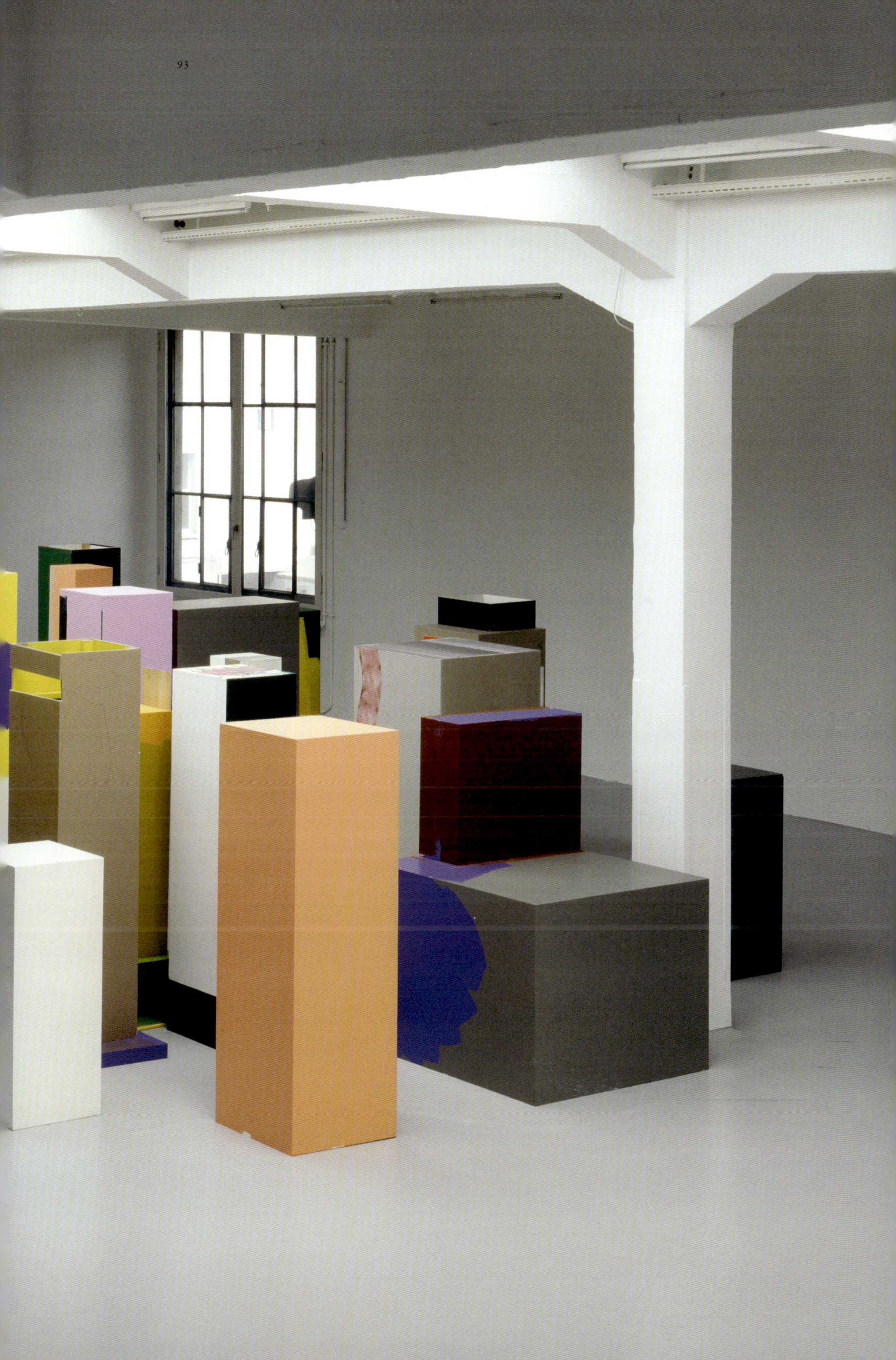

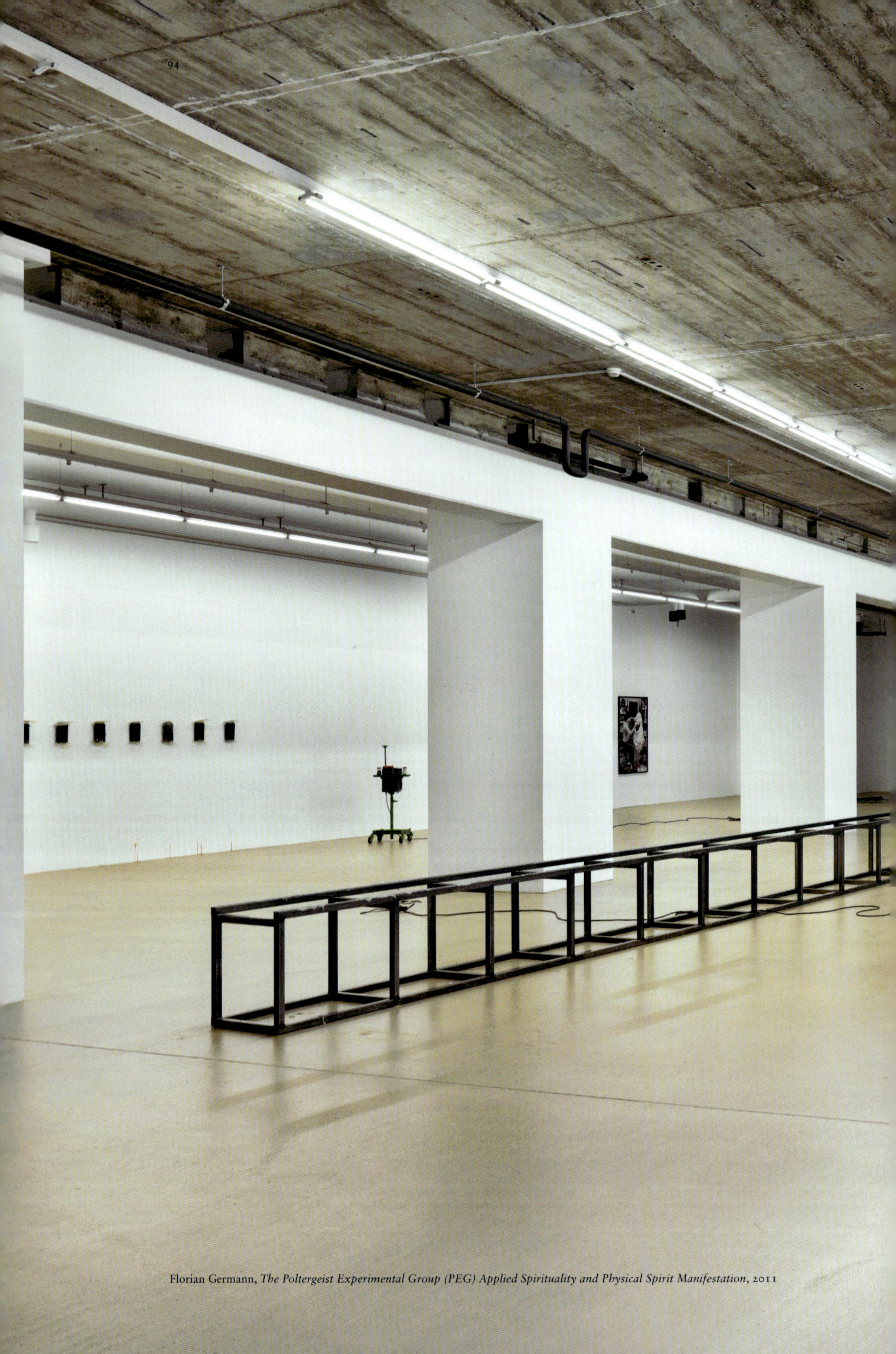

Florian Germann, *The Poltergeist Experimental Group (PEG) Applied Spirituality and Physical Spirit Manifestation*, 2011

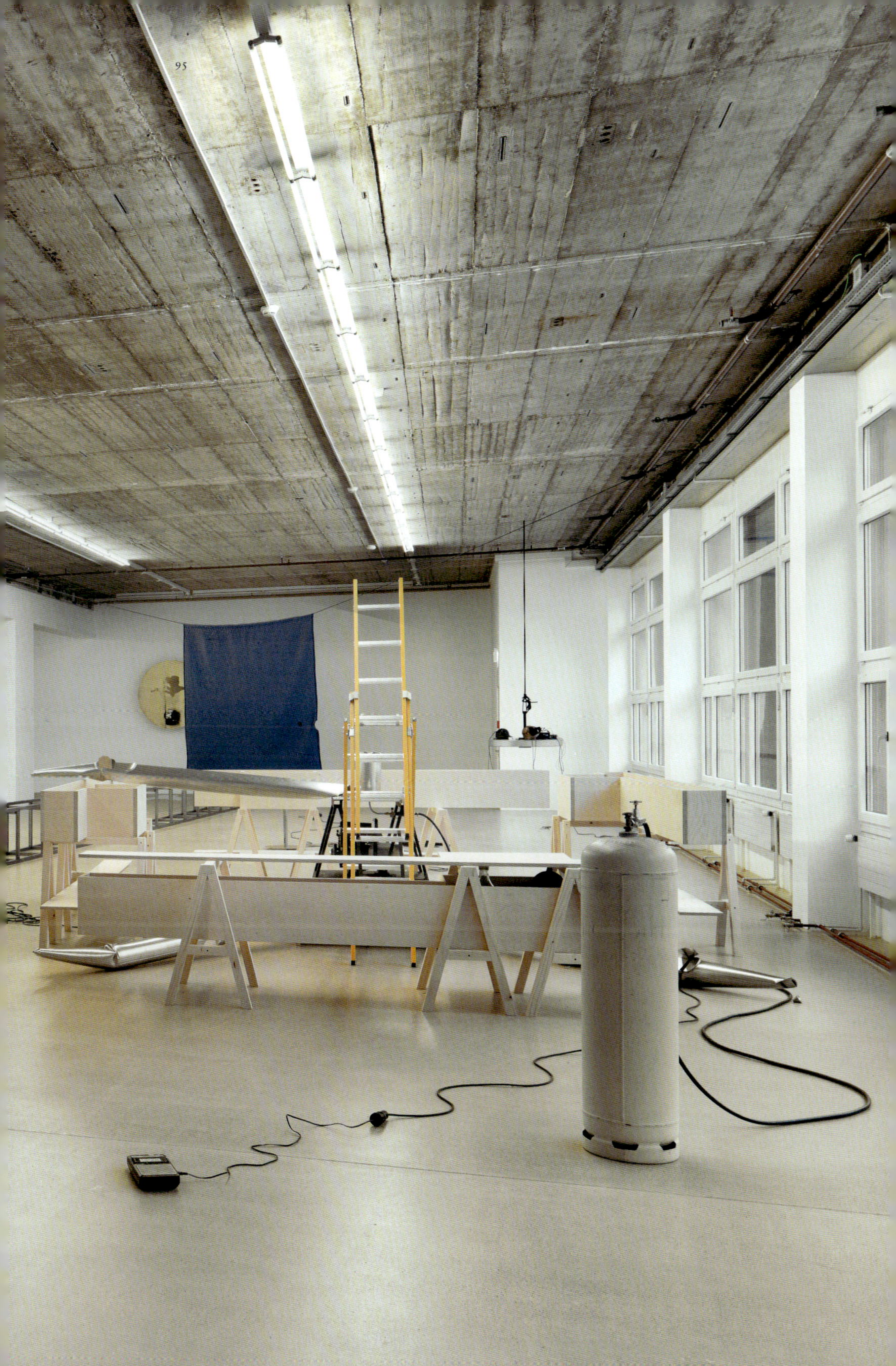
95

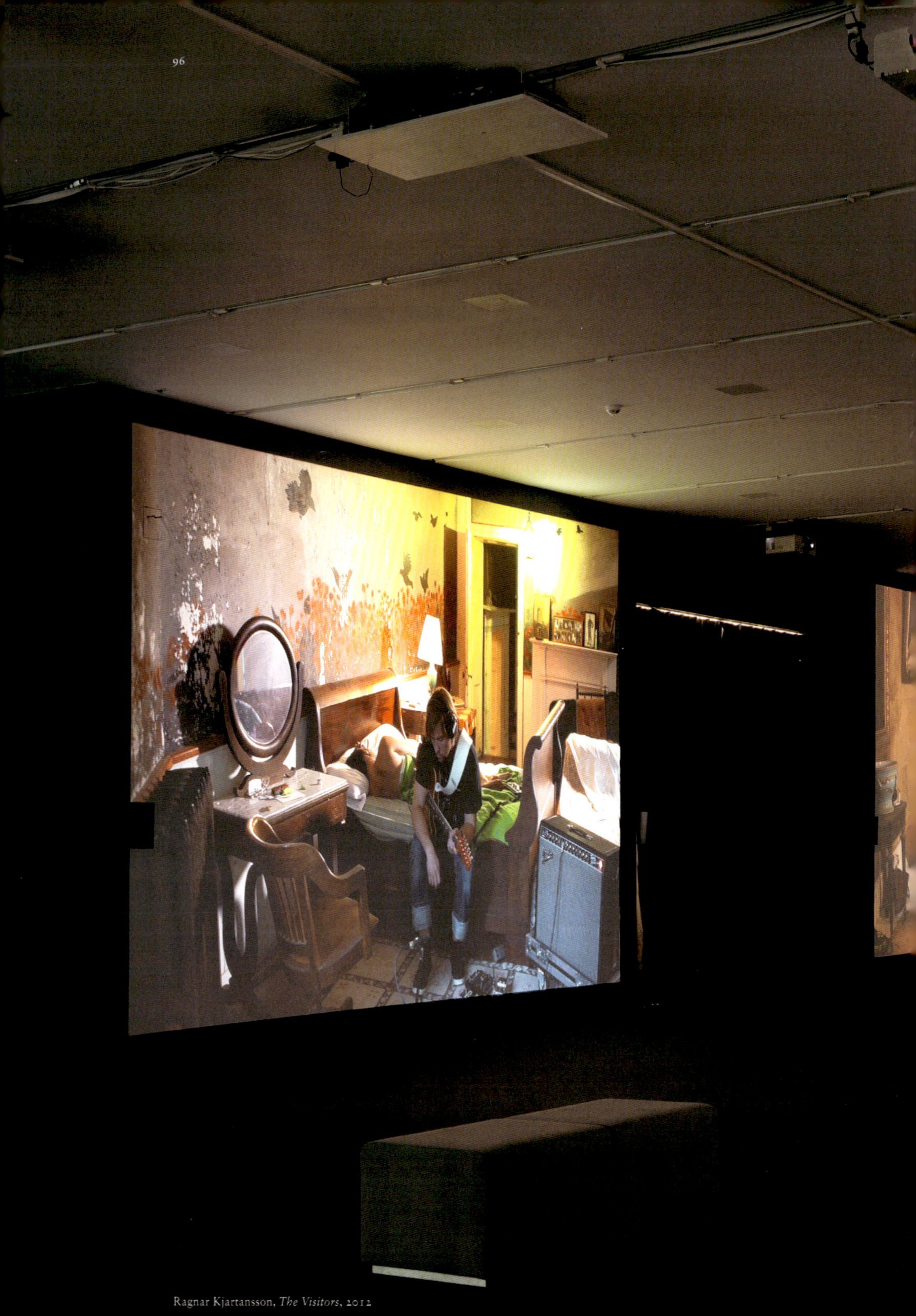

Ragnar Kjartansson, *The Visitors*, 2012

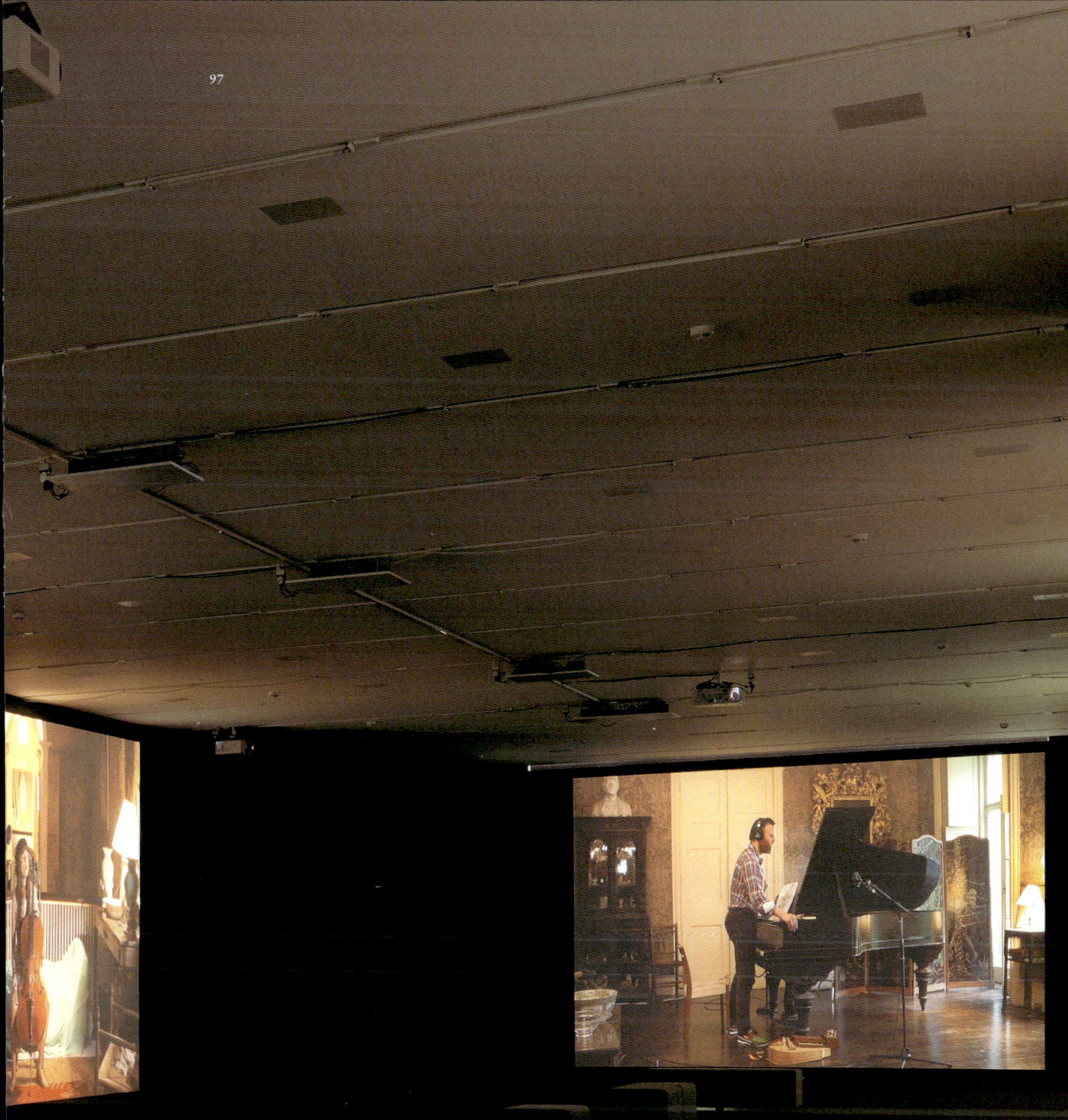

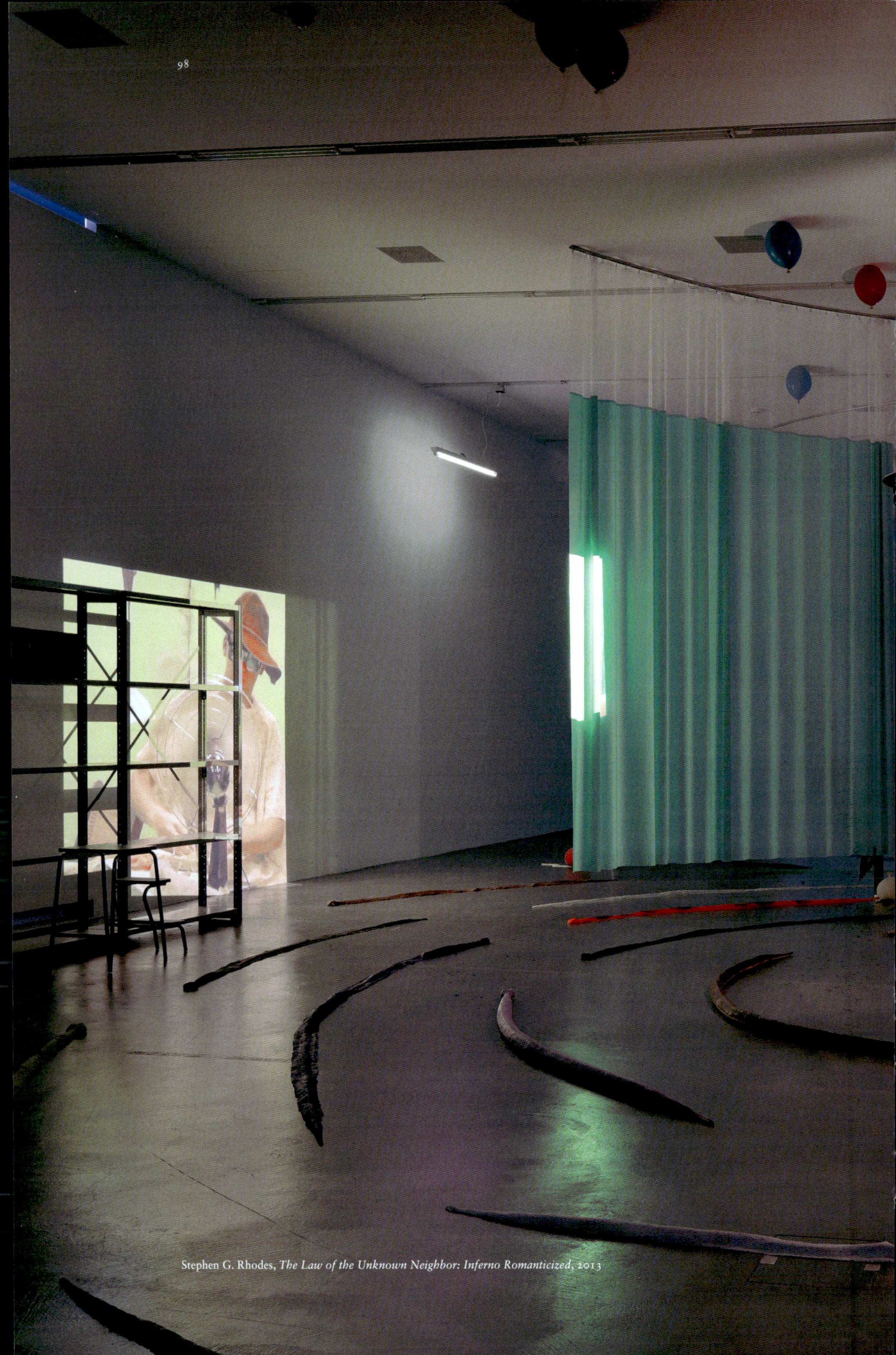

Stephen G. Rhodes, *The Law of the Unknown Neighbor: Inferno Romanticized*, 2013

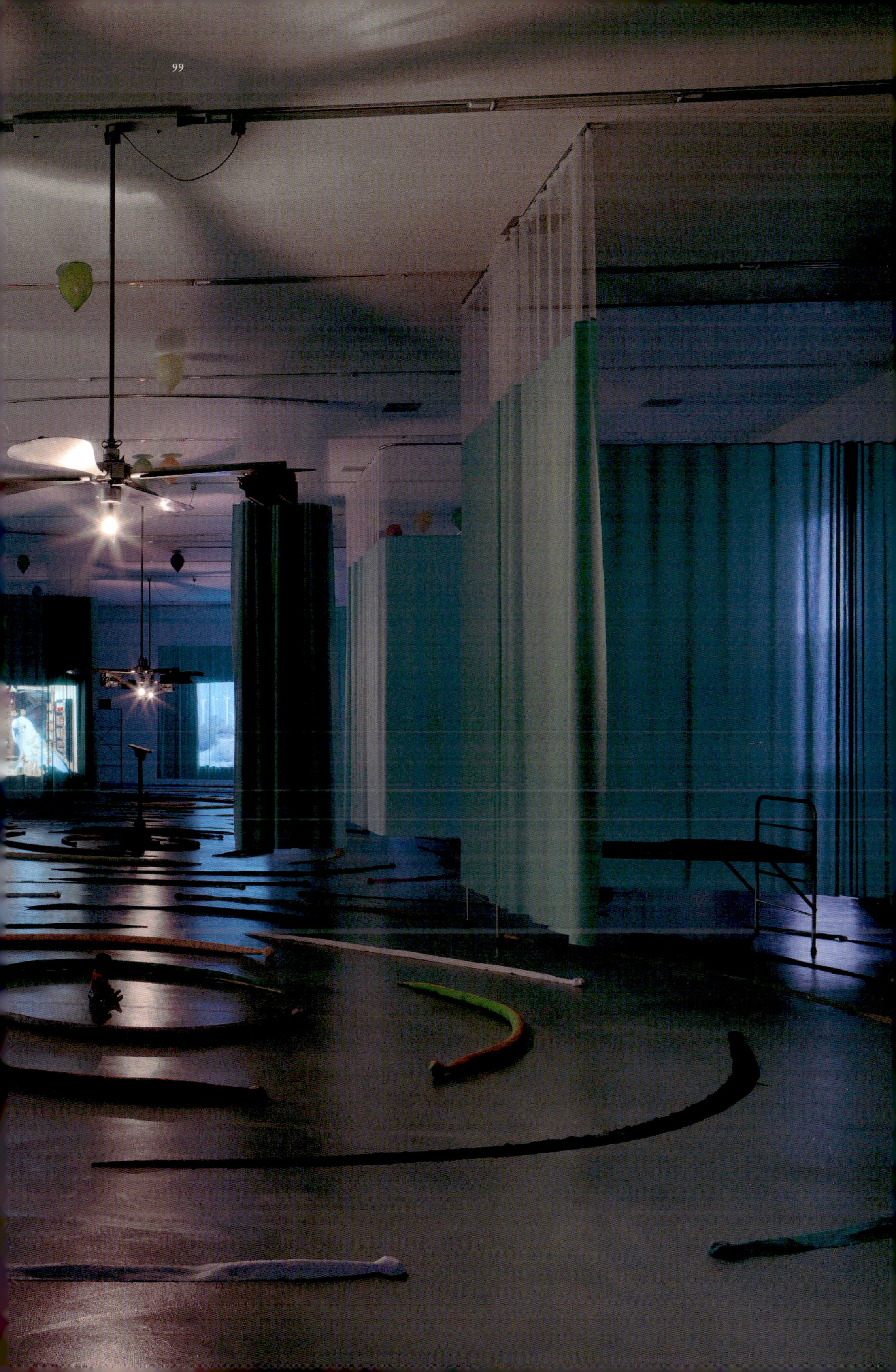

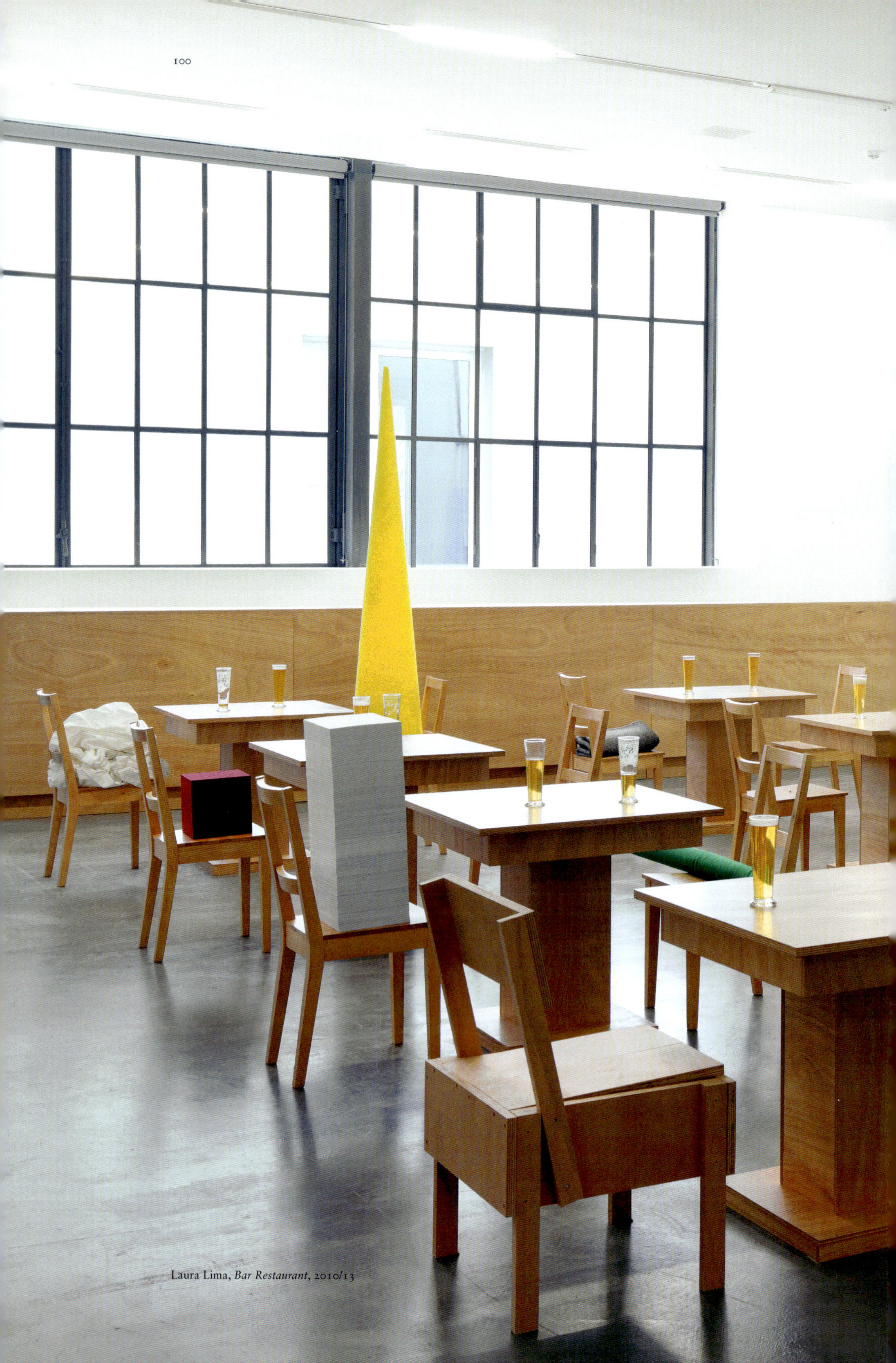

Laura Lima, *Bar Restaurant*, 2010/13

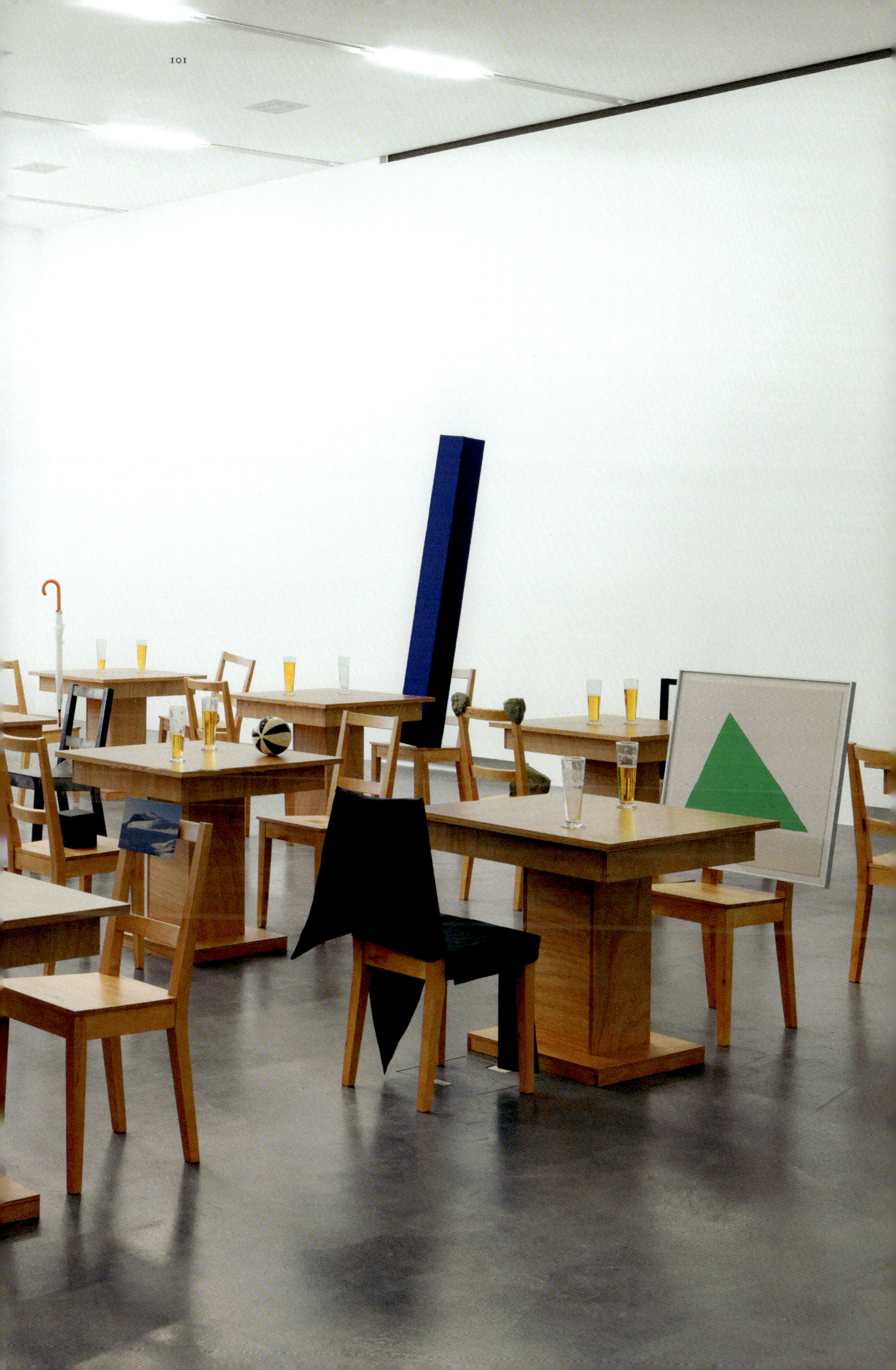

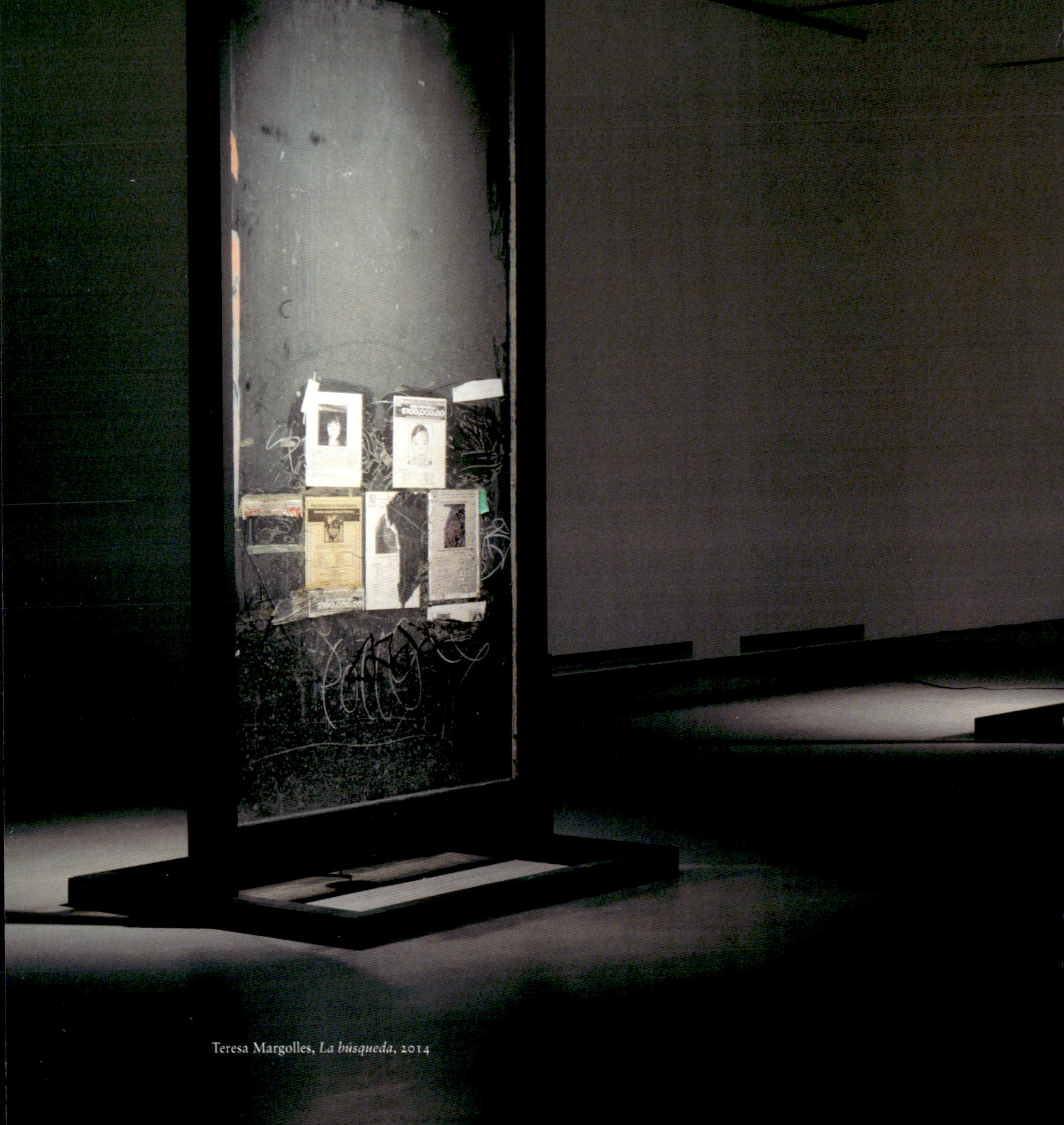

Teresa Margolles, *La búsqueda*, 2014

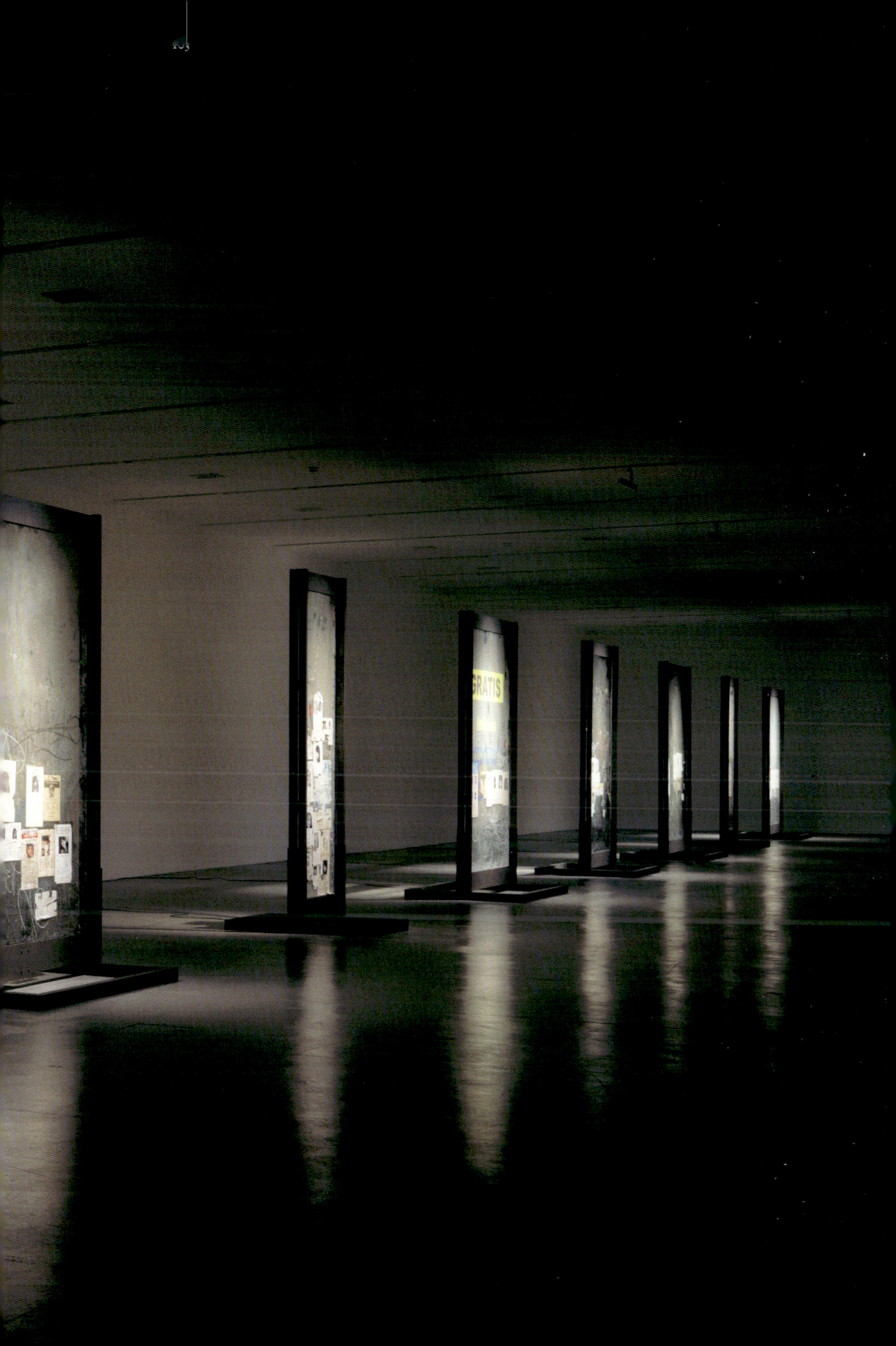

Tomorrow

The Museum as Producer
Martha Buskirk

When the artist's vision for an installation involves such elements as an entire movie theater, a two-story house, various types of vehicles, and many tons of other material in a gallery the size of an athletic field, what could possibly go wrong? As Christoph Büchel's *Training Ground for Democracy*, his ultimately unfinished project for Mass MoCA that was originally slated to open in December 2006, demonstrates, a great deal. Büchel envisioned an environment similar to ones constructed for military training exercises, but reconceived as a setting where the audience could play out roles and conflicts associated with democratic society. Tensions between artist and institution over the procurement of specific elements, funding, and an array of related issues, however, resulted in delays and eventually a complete breakdown in relations, relegating the unfinished installation to a state of limbo that lasted until it was finally disassembled in September 2007.

The conflict between Büchel and Mass MoCA is well known for both the initial problems and the legal challenge mounted by Büchel to prevent the museum from showing the incomplete arrangement. Issues revealed by the lawsuit included the museum's continued work on the project after the artist and his assistants had left the site and questions about the status of the unresolved configuration. One striking feature was the absence of a contract between artist and institution clearly spelling out division of responsibility, timeline, and budget issues. However, the most interesting aspect of the legal back and forth (decided in Büchel's favor on appeal, long after the material had been removed) concerned whether Büchel could prevent its display on moral rights grounds if it was unfinished and therefore had never actually become a work of art in the first place.[1]

Once upon a time, things were simple: the artist made the work, and in a few cases, if judged important by enough people, it might wind up in a museum. But not really—since survey collections are filled with a wide range of objects made well before the wave of museum formation in the eighteenth and nineteenth centuries. The idea of the museum as primarily a repository for past art was also relatively short lived, having been upended over the course of the twentieth century by an increasing focus on contemporary practices. In the process, the gap between conception and embrace has not just narrowed, but can enter into negative territory when museums commission the art that they exhibit rather than showing work understood as complete and self-sufficient before leaving the studio.

Transformations in the status of the artist and the relationship to the collecting institution are bound up with dramatic shifts in materials and procedures over the last half century. The idea that an author should continue to be able to control aspects of his or her work even after it changes ownership is the basis for moral rights protections incorporated into certain international conventions by the late nineteenth century. But site-specificity and associated strategies of institutional critique have to be understood in relation to the activism that led, among other things, to the foundation of the Art Workers Coalition in New York in 1969. Key AWC demands were incorporated in the 1971 "Artists' Reserved Rights Transfer and Sale Agreement," drafted by Robert Projansky and Seth Siegelaub—which gained notoriety for its resale royalty clause but was also striking for the power it envisioned the artist retaining, including control over where works would be exhibited and reproduced.[2]

In a somewhat ironic twist, the proliferation of institutional critique paved the way for a new tradition of collaboration between artists and museums, with the work emerging from a process of negotiation that blurs distinctions among artist, curator, conservator, historian, and even museum

---

1   See Virginia Rutledge, "Institutional Critique: On Christoph Büchel and Mass MoCA," *Artforum* 46, no. 7 (2008), pp. 151, 382, and K. E. Gover, "Artistic Freedom and Moral Rights in Contemporary Art: The Mass MoCA Controversy," *Journal of Aesthetics and Art Criticism* 69, no. 4 (2011), pp. 355–365. In the United States, the 1990 Visual Artists Rights Act, or VARA, provides limited integrity rights protections at the federal level.

2   On the Projansky-Siegelaub contract, see Maria Eichhorn, *The Artist's Contract: Interviews with Carl Andre, Daniel Buren, Paula Cooper, Hans Haacke, Jenny Holzer, Adrian Piper, Robert Projansky, Robert Ryman, Seth Siegelaub, John Weber, Lawrence Weiner, Jackie Winsor,* ed. Gerti Fietzek (Cologne: Verlag der Buchhandlung Walther König, 2009). Hans Haacke appears to be the only artist who has used a version of the Projansky-Siegelaub contract on a long-term basis.

lawyer. Although widespread resistance to ongoing artistic control articulated in the Projansky-Siegelaub contract resulted in its limited adoption, the increasingly contingent nature of recent practices has meant that many artists are unavoidably involved in the life of their work over time. Despite the fact that much contemporary work entails collaborative and delegated production, however, it largely continues to be presented to the museum public according to an organizing principle that prioritizes individual artistic achievement.

Illusory Autonomy

As part of his insistent refutation of autonomy claims in his 1934 essay "The Author as Producer," Walter Benjamin sketched a breakdown of genre divisions as well as distinctions between author and public. But the realignment Benjamin was envisioning, via his attention to production, was between author and worker. The transformation of production under discussion here emphasizes a rather different model, related to a phenomenon provocatively characterized by Caroline Jones as the rise of the executive artist.[3] Boris Groys also invoked and quickly refuted the figure of the autonomous creator to outline associated shifts in the relationship between artist and curator: rather than the curator selecting from work fully formed in the studio and serving as mediator between artist and public, the roles are no longer clearly defined.[4] Groys accentuates the readymade as a crucial shift, with the act of selection constituting a form of creation and, as a corollary, exhibition becoming the crucial moment in a work's definition as art. Taken in this light, one can read the Büchel lawsuit as an attempt by the artist to use his legal rights over works of art displayed under his name to prevent the museum from officially exhibiting material already assembled in a gallery space, even if designated as unfinished.

One aspect of this blurring of roles is evident in the various ways that curators have relied on artists to interrupt the pseudo-neutrality of collection arrangements based on a chronological unfolding of regional periods and styles—thus helping to push back against an important distinguishing characteristic of public museums, as opposed to both the royal collections from which some were formed and the eccentric associations private collectors are free to establish. A well-established counter

---

3 Caroline A. Jones, *Machine in the Studio: Constructing the Postwar American Artist* (Chicago: University of Chicago Press, 1996).

4 Boris Groys, "Multiple Authorship," in Groys, *Art Power* (Cambridge, MA: MIT Press, 2008), pp. 93–100.

tradition of inviting such disruptions includes MoMA's "Artist's Choice" exhibition series, inaugurated in 1989 with Scott Burton's presentation of the bases from Constantin Brancusi's sculptures; Fred Wilson's well-known fusing of artist and curator roles; or the popular strategy of inviting artists to present their own work in dialogue with historical displays.[5]

The idea that simply arranging the objects already in the collection could constitute a work of art is an interesting extrapolation from the readymade turn. But if a surprising assembly can, under certain circumstances, be understood as a creative act in itself, this raises issues for curators who want to take similar liberties. Visitors to Boston's historically staid Museum of Fine Arts in summer 2016 who ascended the stairs by the Fenway entrance encountered, in quick succession, two somewhat different contemporary insertions into the survey-collection fabric: for his *Alchemy*, part of the museum's "Megacities Asia" exhibition, Choi Jeong Hwa chose to present a series of colorful plastic forms strung together vertically between the classical columns of the second-floor landing; and just off the staircase area, Josiah McElheny's 2007 *Endlessly Repeating Twentieth Century Modernism*, his mise-en-abyme sculpture incorporating blown glass and mirrors, was set into a gallery displaying historic European porcelain. Given that the McElheny work was both owned by the museum and unencumbered by documentation indicating specific placement requirements, there was no obligation per se that the artist should be consulted. But the play with context was sufficiently novel that Jen Mergel, the MFA's senior contemporary curator, took it upon herself to okay the unexpected setting with McElheny.[6]

The increasing shift from inviting artists rather than curating extant works has meant not only that museums are frequently involved in every stage of producing the art on display, but that they also often wind up choosing to acquire work that they have helped to bring into existence. At the Migros Museum für Gegenwartskunst, two interesting examples of this tendency are evident in Ragnar Kjartansson's 2012 *The Visitors* and Teresa Margolles's 2014 *La búsqueda*. After both were created for initial exhibition at the Migros Museum für Gegenwartskunst, the museum acquired part of each for the permanent collection: from the Kjartansson,

SEE P. 96

SEE P. 102

---

5   For a survey of artists' projects created in response to museum collections and conventions, see James Putnam, *Art and Artifact: The Museum as Medium*, rev. ed. (London: Thames & Hudson, 2009). See as well, Martha Buskirk, ch. 4, "Context as Subject," in Buskirk, *The Contingent Object of Contemporary Art* (Cambridge, MA: MIT Press, 2003), pp. 161–208, and chs. 1 and 2, "Now and Then" and "The Collection," in Buskirk, *Creative Enterprise: Contemporary Art between Museum and Marketplace* (New York: Continuum, 2012), pp. 25–114.

6   Conversation with Jen Mergel, July 11, 2016; at issue was not just the juxtaposition with historic decorative arts, but the decision to rotate the work forty-five degrees in relation to the axis of the gallery space.

which was issued in an edition, the entire work in the form of one of the multiples; and from the Margolles, two of the glass panels that were components of the installation.

To create *The Visitors*, Kjartansson recorded eight musicians in separate rooms of a large house in upstate New York, all in a single take, simultaneously and repetitively performing a composition based on a poem by Ásdís Sif Gunnarsdóttir. The genesis of the nine-channel video (with each individual performer projected on a separate screen, plus one showing a space where various people congregate) was a concept proposed by the artist to the museum—which supported the realization of the work but was not directly engaged in its production. The Migros Museum für Gegenwartskunst was more closely involved in the technical realization of the *La búsqueda* installation by Margolles, which featured glass shop windows from long-closed stores in Ciudad Juárez, Mexico, that still had missing person posters dating from twenty to twenty-five years earlier affixed to their surfaces. The glass itself, with its potent reminder of the city's infamous femicides, was transported to Switzerland, but another element of the work—the incorporation of sound and vibrations associated with a train that runs through the center of Ciudad Juárez—was produced by the museum's team working in collaboration with a Zurich sound technician.[7]

The Migros Museum für Gegenwartskunst is quick to stress that anytime a work enters the collection after being shown, it is acquired as a purchase (with production expenses subtracted), a transaction that is separate from the honorarium paid to artists to create temporary exhibitions. Complexities that arise from these types of collaborative arrangements include how museums should be compensated in cases where they help to produce objects that cycle back into the commercial gallery system, along with the rate of payment to artists for their involvement in the realization of more ephemeral manifestations. This dialogue is also inseparable from the increasing significance of performance art in museum programming as well as permanent collections—with its integration suggested, among other things, by MoMA's decision to add the position of "performance producer" to their curatorial roster.[8] While the AWC demand that museums should pay a rental fee to artists when they exhibit their

7   Email from Barbara Biedermann, Migros Museum für Gegenwartskunst, July 7, 2016. And see also René Ammann, "Teresa Margolles," *Kunst Bulletin*, issue 7–8 (July 2014), pp. 38–45, available at http://www. kunstbulletin.ch/router.cfm?a=140630113420KQ2-1 (accessed July 14, 2016).

8   In a June 22, 2016, conversation with the author, Lizzie Gorfaine, MoMA's performance producer, discussed museum initiatives focused on different types of performance, including durational work and evening events, as well as the importance of establishing documentation protocols and cross-departmental coordination that encompasses not just different curatorial areas, but also human resources, digital media, security, education, legal, etc.

object-based works never gained traction, changes to the nature of work collected and displayed have opened the door to renewed attention to alternative models, including Andrea Fraser's emphasis on the artist as service provider and recent activism around minimum fee standards by the W.A.G.E. group.[9]

Remaking the Collection

Conservation has long been an important aspect of the museum enterprise. Yet many forms of contemporary art require not just preservation in the traditional sense, but far more extensive forms of remaking—often via initiatives undertaken in collaboration with the artist or artist's studio. The intersection between conservation's object-oriented approach and potentially ephemeral or contingent practices associated with conceptual, performance, and installation art has given what would previously have been understood as secondary documentation an increasingly central role in the life of the work.

Deriving inspiration from the idea of the performative articulated in J. L. Austin's *How to Do Things with Words*, Philip Auslander has probed how the audience for performance art (including many scholars) often depends on documents for their after-the-fact understanding. Rather than simply conveying information, the document is itself performative—producing the event as a performance—and for this reason, he argues, Austin's division between performative and constative or descriptive does not hold.[10] For a wide range of contemporary practices, it is equally important to consider the far less evident performative function of documents that may include installation records, loan agreements, sales contracts, and research interviews as the basis of ongoing decisions about how to update or even remake a whole range of malleable or ephemeral works. It is also striking how little access most viewers (including critics and art historians) have to behind-the-scenes negotiations that can dramatically shape art's public presentation.

---

9   Andrea Fraser, "How to Provide an Artistic Service: An Introduction," in Fraser, *Museum Highlights: The Writings of Andrea Fraser*, ed. Alexander Alberro (Cambridge, MA: MIT Press, 2005). The agenda of the W.A.G.E. initiative can be found at http://www.wageforwork.com/. Regarding demands for rental payment in the AWC context, see in particular Sol LeWitt's statement during the AWC Open Hearing, April 10, 1969, archived on Siegelaub's "Primary Information" site, http://primaryinformation.org/files/FDoc.pdf (accessed June 25, 2016).

10   Philip Auslander, "The Performativity of Performance Documentation," *PAJ A Journal of Performance and Art* 84 (September 2006), pp. 1–10. Austin's examples of performatives include the "I do" of a wedding ceremony or the "I bequeath" of a will. See as well Amelia Jones, "'Presence' in Absentia: Experiencing Performance as Documentation," *Art Journal* 56, no. 4 (1997), pp. 11–18, and Kathy O'Dell, "Displacing the Haptic: Performance Art, the Photographic Document, and the 1970s," *Performance Research* 2, no. 1 (1997), pp. 73–81.

Gwynne Ryan, sculpture conservator at the Hirshhorn in Washington, DC, has emphasized how frequently contemporary art acquired by the museum requires some degree of refabrication or replacement as part of the preservation process. For work that is potentially ephemeral due to variable installation possibilities, unstable materials, obsolescent technologies, or the incorporation of performance, its initial exhibition may constitute only the first moment in a long process of definition. Ryan, among others, uses anthropomorphic language to discuss the lifespan of art, describing certain works acquired in their "infancy" as an opportunity to discover, alongside the artist, the full identity of the work.[11]

Many of these dialogues take place behind closed doors; but one long-term project that Ryan has discussed extensively is her collaboration with Janine Antoni to explore replacement parameters for the soap component of the Hirshhorn's example of two busts from Antoni's 1993–1994 *Lick and Lather*, made from paired life-sized self-portraits, cast in soap and chocolate, and then altered by the artist's act of lathering herself with the soap and licking the chocolate. Given the inherent issues, it is not surprising that Antoni already had a long history of being asked to reengage with early works she made using cholate, soap, and lard—in other words, the opposite of the AWC idea of the artist being compensated with a rental payment when object-based work is exhibited by a museum, since she has to invest fresh time and energy into long-ago sold work. In relation to *Lick and Lather*, such requests have included establishing a new way of attaching the bust to its base or securing the base to the museum floor. Surprisingly, given that the cylindrical support is an integral part of the sculpture, one proposal was to add a visible metal clip (a traditional display technique for classical marbles) to secure the connection between the bust and the base.[12]

Antoni's collaboration with Ryan addressed the full replacement of the soap component—both short term and long term—including extensive research into different soap-making techniques and recipes as well as a discussion about the feasibility of using a mold taken from the post-lathered shape to cast subsequent replacements. In giving her permission for the

11   Gwynne Ryan, presentation, "Conversations with Contemporary Artists," VoCA Artist Interview Workshop, Musem of Fine Arts, Boston, April 14–15, 2016, and conversation with the author, June 21, 2016. Ryan's work with Antoni was profiled in Anika Gupta, "The Art of Chocolate (and Soap)," *smithsonian.com* (website), February 10, 2015, available at http://www.smithsonian-mag.com/smithsonian-institution/art-chocolate-and-soap-180954180 (accessed June 25, 2016).

12   Janine Antoni, conversation with the author, July 11, 2016. According to Antoni, both the Metropolitan Museum of Art, in relation to the example from *Lick and Lather* borrowed for their 2016 *Unfinished* exhibition, and the National Gallery, vis-à-vis their acquisition of the original group of fourteen, were in dialogue with Antoni regarding requests to incorporate new elements for securing the bust to the columnar base and the base to the gallery floor.

latter, Antoni concluded that the importance of her experience of washing as part of the work's initial production did not translate into requiring her literal touch in the future.[13] And this research was in turn shared with the National Gallery after their acquisition of the original set of fourteen paired busts.

While all museums that collect contemporary art have to face questions about how to ensure the longevity of work riddled with issues that fall under the general conservation category of "inherent vice," the Whitney Museum is perhaps unique in establishing a "replication committee," founded in 2008, that includes conservators, curators, archivists, a lawyer, and a registrar. In a *New Yorker* profile focused on the committee's brief, Ben Lerner described witnessing a detailed interview between committee members and artist Josh Kline as "watching conservation shade into collaboration"—a suggestion resisted by Carol Mancusi-Ungaro, the Whitney's chief conservator.[14]

Kate Lewis, media conservator at MoMA, has also highlighted the importance of installing a work in order fully to understand it.[15] In one telling example, Nalini Malani's 2003 *Gamepieces* (first shown at the 8th Annual Istanbul Biennial and acquired by MoMA in 2007) gained a slash date of 2003/2009 once it was installed at the museum for the first time— reflecting a relatively substantial, but not necessarily unusual degree of reconceptualization at that point. The basic elements of the work were six cylinders, made from a clear polycarbonate painted with figures from Hindu mythology, suspended and slowly spinning in the center of the room, and a four-channel video incorporating animation and documentary footage of nuclear destruction projected through the cylinders onto the surrounding walls. When first shown, the cylinders were arranged in a single row; MoMA's high ceilings, however, allowed them to be divided into upper and lower registers. Museum staff worked closely with Malani's husband (her main installation manager) on the exhibition and used it as an occasion to document the assembly process for future reference. MoMA registrar Sydney Briggs, who served as the museum's point person for this project, has also described a standard debriefing procedure after an installation is complete, when everyone involved can bring up potential issues or challenges posed by the work.[16]

13 Antoni, conversation with the author, July 11, 2016.

14 Ben Lerner, "The Custodians: How the Whitney Is Transforming the Art of Museum Conservation," *The New Yorker*, January 11, 2016, available at http://www. newyorker.com/magazine/2016/01/11/the-custodians-onward-and-upward-with-the-arts-ben-lerner (accessed August 15, 2016).

15 Kate Lewis, presentation, "Case Study: Conservator's Perspective," VoCA Artist Interview Workshop, Museum of Fine Arts, Boston, April 14–15, 2016.

In the context of earlier aristocratic collections, it was not uncommon for art to be altered, including being cut down or added to, based on decorative requirements. By contrast, the field of conservation associated with the museum era has, at least until facing the challenges posed by contemporary art's multitude of forms, emphasized minimal and reversible interventions. The idea that a work would acquire different interpretations over time, as it moves through history and is experienced by changing audiences, is hardly new. But the contemporary era's dramatically expanded field of materials and procedures has opened up the possibility that preservation can include extensive and even wholesale remaking; and it has radically reshaped the ongoing relationship between artist and institution.

There is a somewhat ironic convergence between activism around artists' rights and a fracturing of artistic authorship based on delegated production. For any large-scale installation, museum staff—including curators, conservators, exhibition designers, art handlers, registrars, carpenters, audiovisual technicians, access experts, museum educators, and lawyers—are all potentially involved in the dialogue about a work's initial form as well as its ongoing life. So, too, are the artist's studio assistants and outside fabricators, representatives of the artist's gallery, and many others. But unlike a Hollywood film, art is generally presented without a credit roll, meaning that there is little obvious evidence of the many separate contributions shaping the work that the audience encounters.

Given their increasing expertise in making the art on display themselves, as well as the significance of exhibition for art's definition, will museums continue to need artists? The fact that the answer appears to be a resounding "yes" is certainly a function of the long-standing emphasis on authorship bound up in museum history—even if its traditional counterpart, the study of the object known as connoisseurship, is no longer relevant to many forms of contemporary art. It remains to be seen whether the sometimes extensive involvement by museums in both initial realization and later reconfiguration of the art they exhibit and collect will precipitate a revised understanding of the authorship principles upon which the institution was founded.

16   Sydney Briggs, conversation with the author, June 21, 2016. These debriefing meetings, according to Briggs, generally include the curator, conservator, registrar, exhibition designer, art handler, and, as relevant, AV techs, carpenters, framers, or others involved in specific issues. One important decision made by sculpture conservation concerned whether to disassemble the cylinders again, and store the material flat, or to crate them as cylinders—with the latter ultimately decided. See also Briggs, "Gamepieces: An Installation Deconstructed," *Inside/Out* (MoMA/MoMA PS1 blog), March 13, 2015, http://www.moma.org/explore/inside_out/2015/03/13/nalini-malani-gamepieces-an-installation-deconstructed (accessed August 15, 2016), where she describes how, in the initial installation, "Images of war and violence were concentrated toward the center of the room while the blue skies were pushed to the extremities," but at MoMA, the double-height space allowed the imagery to be split, "into an upper and lower domain—blues skies above, earthly images below."

The Museum after Art
Beatriz Colomina

"Art is everywhere in the street, which is the museum of the present and the past."—Le Corbusier, 1923

In her 1990 essay "The Cultural Logic of the Late Capitalist Museum," Rosalind Krauss identified the signature of the contemporary museum as one in which the experience of the space of the museum takes precedence over the experience of the artworks. In other words, the space between the works is more important than the experience of the works themselves. She described the experience of seeing the Panza Collection in the Musée d'Art Moderne de la Ville de Paris, guided by then director Suzanne Pagé, as a kind of walk in a landscape—even if Krauss doesn't say as much—an itinerary in which she encountered works of art (in her words, "old friends" of the 1960s) the way one might encounter a big rock, tree, or pavilion in a park, but where the overall experience of the space dominates; what is about to happen becomes more relevant than what you are seeing right now. She recalled how her guide viewed the highlight of the exhibition as its spaces rather than the individual works on display, stopping at one point to draw attention to the way the space was lit by the glow of another space coming from a Dan Flavin piece. In a much earlier essay, "Sculpture in the Expanded Field" (1978), Krauss had defined sculpture, following the structuralist logic of the double negative, as that which is "not-architecture" and "not-landscape." In the face of the contemporary museum experience, it is not just sculpture that assumes this negative position but art, as exhibited, in general. And Krauss didn't seem very happy about it.

Tate Modern, which opened in 2000, a decade after Krauss's article, magnified this new logic of the museum and made millions of people happy just to spend time in a museum, make out in a museum, lie down on the floor in some kind of ecstatic contemplation, spiral down a chute, eat, drink, dance, listen to music, go to lectures, shop, meet friends, etc. The spaces between the art have become the main event. Vast circulation spaces dominate the experience with more traditional galleries in the background. And circulation is no longer between works of art. Art can be found in circulation and circulation itself can be turned into art. A quiet white room with a few static works of art becomes almost startling, as if what is on display is not just the art but also an older way of engaging with it. The line between these two worlds has been thinned down architecturally to just a doorway where tickets are checked. The world of spectacle is free, the world of contemplation has a price. And visitors are deep in the museum by the time they cross this line, if they cross it at all. It is not simply that the outside world has come all the way in, with the circulation spaces continuing the streets outside. In fact, these spaces are in some ways more active, more social, and more densely populated than the streets of the city. It is a kind of utopian ideal of the street, stripped of cars, potential violence, cacophonous sounds, smells, street vendors, the weather, the homeless. The museum today is a hyper-controlled, theatrical space, a contemporary image of "public space" where people perform for each other, and broadcast that performance through social media.

Curiously, both of Krauss's essays privileged minimalism to the exclusion of artists such as Gordon Matta-Clark, Dan Graham, and many others who, from the mid-1970s, were experimenting more directly with the medium of architecture, trying to break away from the art gallery and the museum by engaging with buildings. It was precisely during the late 1970s and early 1980s that architecture entered the museum and gallery system. In 1978 Max Protetch, who had been exhibiting minimalist and conceptual artists, but also the work of Andy Warhol, early performances by Dan Graham, Vito Acconci, and others, moved his gallery from Washington, DC, to New York and started to specialize in architectural drawings. In 1980 Leo Castelli put on the exhibition "Houses for Sale" for which eight international architects were invited to put their visions of the modern house up for "sale." Castelli felt the need to clarify that "drawings

may be purchased separately from the commission of the project."
Storefront for Art and Architecture, a non-profit gallery, opened in SoHo,
New York, in 1982 as a catalyst for new work and new energy. It promptly
exhibited architects and artists such as Diller+Scofidio, Morphosis,
James Wines, Lebbeus Woods, Steven Holl, Dan Graham, Dennis Adams,
Jenny Holzer, Krzysztof Wodiczko, Wolf Prix, Tadashi Kawamata, Mike
Webb, Enric Miralles and Carme Pinós, Mel Chin, Camilo José Vergara,
Antoni Muntadas, Matthew Ritchie, and Julia Scher—many of them at
a very young age and all of them working at the intersection of art and
architecture. The first Venice Architecture Biennale did not take place until
1980, with the postmodern manifesto of the "Strada Novissima" of Paolo
Portoghesi (preceded by a small number of exhibitions of architecture
within the Art Biennale, starting in the mid-seventies under Vittorio
Gregotti). The first museums and archives of architecture are also a postmodern phenomenon and are even housed in postmodern buildings—
for example, the Canadian Centre for Architecture in Montreal (1979)
and the Deutsche Architektur Museum in Frankfurt (1984).

It is not by chance that at the same time architecture started to get
its own territory in museums, galleries, and biennials, artists started
to take over the architect's territory. In the 1976 Biennale "Ambiente/Arte,"
organized by Germano Celant, Dan Graham built his *Two Audiences:
Public Space,* a rectangular room with the proportions of the golden
section, divided into two square chambers by a pane of acoustic glass.
One of the far walls of the room was a mirror, and the other far wall was
white. Graham likened the Venice Biennale and other art fairs to world
fairs, in which countries have their own pavilions and art is the commodity.
In Venice, he attempted to upset the system by making the audience into
the exhibit. Visitors to the pavilion would see themselves seeing themselves.
They have become the artwork, the commodity. Graham's pavilion complicated the art scene by turning the viewing subject into the object.

Dan Graham's work is closely linked to modern architecture and to
the historical figure of Mies van der Rohe through the idea of the glass
pavilion. When commissioned to build the German Pavilion for the International Exhibition in Barcelona in 1929, Mies asked the Ministry of Foreign
Affairs what was to be exhibited. It is a normal question for an architect:
What is this building for? An artist never needs to ask that. The answer
was: "Nothing will be exhibited. The pavilion itself will be the exhibit."[1]

---

1   Quoted in Julius Posener, "Los primeros años: de Schinkel a
     De Stijl," *A&V: Monografías de Arquitectura y Vivienda 6,*
     no. 33 (1986), author's translation.

Interestingly, Mies was being treated as an artist. His pavilion doesn't even have plumbing. If for Gordon Matta-Clark the difference between architecture and sculpture was that one has plumbing and the other not, then the Barcelona pavilion was art. It was precisely in the absence of a traditional program that the pavilion became an exhibit about exhibiting. All it exhibited was a new way of looking. The act of viewing was itself on display, rather than objects to be seen.

Despite its prominent position in the layout of the 1929 International Exhibition in Barcelona, the Barcelona Pavilion went largely unnoticed. Even critics from professional journals passed over it entirely, unable to detect its significance. Some local journalists with no particular training in architecture provided the only testimony to its existence. They commented on the "mysterious effect" of the pavilion, "because a person standing in front of one of these glass walls sees himself reflected as if by a mirror, but if he moves behind them he then sees the exterior perfectly."[2] From the inside, visitors would see people on the outside looking at themselves, in the position they had themselves just vacated. The pavilion is a place of encounter with oneself and others, an encounter with an encounter.

The Barcelona Pavilion is a kind of house, complete with front and rear entrances, a stone garden, and pools, but it is a house with no interior. The inside is constructed of reflections of the outside, multiplied by the shiny surfaces of the marble, chrome, and glass. The play of reflections one normally encounters in the streets of the modern city, catching one's reflected image in a shop window suspended alongside the commodities on display, is multiplied and treated as a building material. The pavilion turns the street into a domestic interior where you see both yourself and others seeing. This internalization, even domestication, of the street could be the very project of modern architecture, and is inseparable from the project of the modern museum.

Modern architecture, it can be argued, was incubated in a series of domestic projects that were explicitly set up to exhibit modern art and ultimately absorbed and transformed the logic of exhibition. Indeed, the modern museum and the modern house follow the same logic.

2   Local journalist from Barcelona reviewing the pavilion, quoted in José Quetglas, "Fear of Glass: The Barcelona Pavilion," in Beatriz Colomina, ed., *Architectureproduction* [*Revisions* 2] (New York: Princeton Architectural Press, 1988), p. 130.

3   Today Maison La Roche-Jeanneret is the headquarters of the Fondation Le Corbusier, a foundation and museum displaying Le Corbusier's paintings, furniture, drawings, photographs, and all the documentation of his projects, as well as his correspondence, telephone bills, electricity bills, laundry bills, bank statements, postcards, suitcases and trunks, travel snapshots, family pictures, court proceedings (he was often involved in lawsuits), pottery, rugs, sea shells, pipes, books, magazines, newspaper clippings, mail order catalogues, drafts for lectures, doodles, scribbles, notebooks, sketchbooks, diaries; in short, a museum of everything.

Le Corbusier's idea of the museum started with a house, the Maison
La Roche-Jeanneret, in Paris, of 1922–1923.[3] The client, Raoul La Roche,
a young Swiss banker and director of the Crédit Commercial de France,
was one of the major sponsors of the magazine *L'Esprit nouveau*; he
commissioned its editors, painter Amédée Ozenfant and Le Corbusier, to
purchase a collection of Cubist paintings for him. At Le Corbusier's
prodding, La Roche ended up also buying Purist paintings by both himself
and Ozenfant.[4] Once the collection was assembled, Le Corbusier talked
La Roche into making a house for the paintings, writing: "La Roche, when
you have a fine collection like yours, you should also have a house built
worthy of it."[5] Modern domestic architecture was developed as a frame for
Cubist and Purist paintings.[6]

FIG. 2

La Roche used to open the house to the public on Tuesdays and
Fridays, turning it into a private museum with public visiting hours. Soon
the issue of whether what was on show was the paintings or the building
became blurred, a source of conflict between Le Corbusier and both La
Roche and Ozenfant. Le Corbusier wanted some of the walls to be kept free
of paintings. He wrote to Ozenfant: "The La Roche house should not take
on the look of a house of a (postage-stamp) collector. I insist absolutely that
certain parts of the architecture should be entirely free of paintings, so as to
create a double effect of pure architecture on the one hand and pure painting
on the other."[7] La Roche responded to Le Corbusier's desire to exhibit
the house itself: "I commissioned from you a 'frame for my collection.' You
provided me with a 'poem of walls.' Which of us two is most to blame?"[8]
Here we already have exactly the same concern that Rosalind Krauss
voiced in the face of the postmodern museum, but almost seventy years
earlier. The intrusion of architecture into the space for the contemplation of
art is not a postmodern phenomenon but a quintessentially modern one.

The paintings in the La Roche house were hung in a specific
sequence along the spiraling promenade of the house, and it is important

---

4 Le Corbusier and Ozenfant acted as La Roche's bidders
for the confiscated paintings by Picasso, Braque, Léger, and
Gris from the Kahnweiler Collection at four art auctions
held in June and November 1921, July 1922, and May
1923. See Russell Walden, "New Light on Le Corbusier's
Early Years in Paris: The La Roche-Jeanneret Houses,"
in idem, ed., *The Open Hand: Essays on Le Corbusier*
(Cambridge, MA: MIT Press, 1977), p. 135.

5 Letter from La Roche to Le Corbusier, May 24, 1926,
Fondation Le Corbusier.

6 Beatriz Colomina, "Where Are We?" in Eve Blau and Nancy
J. Troy, eds., *Architecture and Cubism* (Cambridge, MA:
MIT Press, 1997).

7 Letter from Le Corbusier to Ozenfant, April 16, 1925,
Fondation Le Corbusier; dossier La Roche. Quoted in

Tim Benton, *The Villas of Le Corbusier: 1920–1930*
(New Haven: Yale University Press, 1987), p. 67.

8 "Do you recall the origin of my undertaking? 'La Roche,
when you have a fine collection like yours, you should also
have a house built worthy of it.' And my response: 'Fine
Jeanneret, make this house for me.' Now, what happened?
The house, once built, was so beautiful that on seeing it
I cried: 'It's almost a pity to put paintings into it!' Neverthe-
less I did so. How could I have done otherwise? Do I not
have certain obligations with regard to my painters, of
whom you yourself are one? I commissioned from you
a 'frame for my collection.' You provided me with a 'poem
of walls.' Which of us two is most to blame?" Letter
from La Roche to Le Corbusier, May 24, 1926, Fondation
Le Corbusier. Quoted in ibid., p. 70.

to remember that it was precisely here, in this house, that Le Corbusier invented the *promenade architecturale*—the idea of an architecture experienced in choreographed movement along a predetermined path. The itinerary in the La Roche house was meant to guide the public past the paintings in a way that—conveniently for Le Corbusier—demonstrated the triumph of Purism over Cubism. This logic of exhibition through internalized promenade became most polemical in the Villa Savoye in Poissy (1928–1931) where the visitor literally drives into the house and the movement continues up the spiral ramp that organizes the whole experience of the house. There is no longer an art collection here, but the promenade continually opens up framed views to the inside and the outside of the house. The house is all street, neither interior nor exterior space. As Le Corbusier put it: "In this house [Villa Savoye] it is a question of a real architectural promenade, offering constantly changing views, unexpected, sometimes astonishing."[9] The inhabitants have become visitors in their own house, constantly on the move and watching others move.

Indeed, Le Corbusier went so far as to speak about the inhabitants of the modern house as "visitors." Writing specifically about Villa Savoye, he said: "The visitors [...] turn round and round in the interior, asking themselves what is happening, understanding with difficulties the reasons for what they see and feel; they do not find anything of what is called a 'house.' They feel themselves in something entirely new. And [...] I do not think they are bored!"[10] The occupants of Le Corbusier's house are displaced. First, because they are disoriented. They do not know how to place themselves in relation to this building—it does not look like a "house." But also because the occupant is only a "visitor." Le Corbusier's subject is detached from the house with the distance of a visitor, a viewer, a photographer, a tourist… a museum-goer even. And crucially, visitors are not "bored." Against the nineteenth-century boredom of the interior, modern architecture is a form of entertainment.

Le Corbusier's and Mies van der Rohe's idea of the museum emerged literally out of the house.[11] Domesticity is the real source of modernity in

---

9   "L'architecture arabe nous donne un enseignement précieux. Elle s'apprécie *à la marche*, avec le pied; c'est en marchant, en se déplaçant que l'on voit se développer les ordonnances de l'architecture. C'est un principe contraire à l'architecture baroque qui est conçue sur le papier, autour d'un point fixe théorique. Je préfère l'enseignement de l'architecture arabe. Dans cette maison-ci, il s'agit d'une véritable promenade architecturale, offrant des aspects constamment variés, inattendus, parfois étonnants." Le Corbusier and Pierre Jeanneret, *Œuvre Complète*, vol. 2, 1929–1934 (Zurich: Les Éditions d'Architecture, 1964), p. 24.

10 Le Corbusier, *Précisions sur un état présent de l'architecture et de l'urbanisme* (Paris: Éditions Crès, 1930), p. 136.

11 Mies van der Rohe's houses likewise act as the basis of a radical proposal for a new kind of museum, as with the Museum for a Small City in 1942, a project that stands with Le Corbusier's Museum of Unlimited Growth as the two most significant proposals for museums of the modern movement. See Beatriz Colomina, "The Endless Museum: Le Corbusier and Mies van der Rohe," in *When Things Cast No Shadow*, exh. cat. 5th Berlin Biennial for Contemporary Art (Zurich, 2008).

museums. The spiraling ramps that define Le Corbusier's domestic architecture are simply exaggerated and celebrated in a kind of hyper-ramp in his museum projects. The carefully choreographed views of nature through the windows in the houses are simply replaced with the view through the frame of each painting. In each of the multiple versions of his spiral museum, Le Corbusier emphasized the surprising lateral views within the labyrinthine spaces. Viewing is what is on view.

The internalized street of the domestic projects became the museum as internalized street with Le Corbusier's project for the Mundaneum in 1929, to be built in Geneva, Switzerland. The client, Paul Otlet, a Belgian industrialist, wanted to establish an international organization of intellectuals based on a large campus which included an airport, a university, a stadium, botanical and mineral gardens, exhibition spaces, a world library, and a museum: "Our desire is that in one place on the globe the total image and significance of the world should be visible and understood; that this place should become a holy place [...] a contribution from science to universal organization."[12] The central element of the Mundaneum was the "world museum": a pyramid made out of a square spiral, a continuous gallery that would show the various stages of civilization in evolution. Visitors would take an elevator to the top of the pyramid (the beginning of civilization) and walk down the spiral ramp until they reached the ground: the present day.

Le Corbusier flattened out the spiral when he proposed a "Museum of Contemporary Art" in Paris in 1931. The museum is now made out of a single continuous wall folded into a square spiral. This system provided a linear exhibition space that could be extended as the collection grew. Le Corbusier's radical idea was that the museum could even be started with a collection of just one painting, with the donor also donating a length of wall. With each new painting, more wall would be added. When describing the project he insisted:

> The museum has no facade; the visitor will never see a facade; he will only see the interior of the museum. One enters the heart of the museum by means of an underground passage and the wall opening for the entrance door would, once the museum has reached its full

---

12 Paul Otlet, UAI (Union of International Associations), 1925, p. 4. Promotional booklet, quoted in *Le Corbusier: Architect of the Century*, ed. Michael Raeburn and Victoria Wilson, exh. cat. Hayward Gallery, London (London, 1987), p. 165.

magnificent size, comprise the 9000th meter of the total developed length of the museum.[13]

The space of the traditional museum has been transformed into a length, a wall continuously folding upon itself. Only a few cuts are made in the wall to allow the visitor to break the fixed trajectory and move through the building in different ways. The museum is entered through an underground passage and the collection is to be experienced in a singular guided promenade along a seven-meter-wide space—a spiral that keeps expanding as more wall is added. Le Corbusier even recommended that "a mason and a laborer [...] be permanently employed in building this museum in an interrupted and perennial operation."[14] The endless museum would be endlessly under construction.

In 1939, Le Corbusier called his latest version of the museum for Philippeville in Algiers the "Museum of Unlimited Growth." The museum is an ever-expanding interior without an exterior. It is a machine for swallowing the outside. The idea that museums will continuously expand becomes the very basis of the museum and the inevitable consequence of internalizing the street. Already in 1923, Le Corbusier had written in the pages of *L'Esprit nouveau*: "Art is everywhere in the street, which is the museum of the present and the past."[15]

The carnivorous spiral museum became part of the civic center of Le Corbusier's Saint-Dié town plan in 1945. In fact, Le Corbusier seemed to insert a museum of unlimited growth project wherever he went. The first version to be actually built was designed for Ahmedabad in India between 1952 and 1956. In anticipation of contemporary ideas, the director Prithwish Neogy declared that the aim of the museum was "to bring about the active participation of people [...] instead of encouraging mere irresponsible contemplation of rare luxury objects torn from their contexts [...] The objects will appear not in unique isolation but as a reality—against [...] the pattern of culture that produced the artifacts."[16] The program included a library, open-air theater, traveling exhibitions, audience participation, music, and cinema all housed in one collection of buildings:

13 "Le musée n'a pas de façade; le visiteur ne verra jamais de façade; il ne verra que l'interieur du musée. Car il entra au cœur du musée par un souterrain dont la porte d'entrée est ouvert dans un mur qui, si le musée arrivait a une étape de croissance magnifique, offrirait à ce moment le neuf millième mètre de cimaise." Letter from Le Corbusier to Christian Zervos, December 8, 1930, in *Cahiers d'art*, reprinted in Le Corbusier and Pierre Jeanneret, *Œuvre Complète*, vol. 2, (see note 9), p. 73. English trans. in Willy Boesiger and Hans Girsberger, eds., *Le Corbusier 1910–65* (Zurich: Les Éditions d'Architecture, 1967), p. 236.

14 Le Corbusier, *My Work*, trans. James Palmes (London: The Architectural Press, 1960), p. 101.

15 Le Corbusier, *L'Esprit nouveau* 19 (1923).

16 Prithwish Neogy, Director, Brochure for the Cultural Centre, Ahmedabad. Quoted in *Le Corbusier: Architect of the Century* (see note 12), p. 301.

"The whole world was to be there," in the words of the director.[17] The museum that swallows the outside is no longer quiet. It increasingly becomes a space of performance, interaction, and participation.

As the spiral project kept traveling, Le Corbusier successively added a pavilion to it for temporary exhibitions and a building for theatrical experiments that he called a "Box of Miracles" (as in the Tokyo National Museum of Western Art of 1957–1959), and then a "Spontaneous Theatre" (as in the 1963 project for an "International Art Centre" near Frankfurt).[18] From 1964 to 1968, the project returned to India when Le Corbusier brought yet another version of the museum to Chandigarh, and finally, in 1965, to Paris when Le Corbusier was commissioned by André Malraux, then minister of culture in France, to do a "Museum of the 20th Century" to be sited in Nanterre. Le Corbusier, however, kept insisting that it should be in the center of Paris, near the Grand Palais. He dreamed of a museum of the twentieth century set on ten-meter (or higher) *pilotis* above the streets and squares of Paris. The museum would float over the world it swallowed. Le Corbusier even thought of bridging the river Seine across the Quai d'Orsay. He was at work on a version of the museum project to be placed in Nanterre when he died in August 1965 and the project was never realized. Once again, he was arguing for a square box that could grow endlessly, absorbing and classifying the entire world outside.

"The true museum is the one that contains everything," Le Corbusier wrote alongside an image of a bidet in *L'Esprit nouveau* in 1924. With this definition, the world and the museum are conflated. Museum architecture, in the literal sense of a bounded space, an enclosure containing objects, becomes redundant. In 1951 Malraux would famously call for a "museum without walls," an imaginary museum that comes into being with the new means of communication that allows any object to be collected without the need for a physical space. Le Corbusier's project for an endless museum tested the limits of an equally radical concept of a museum that is only wall. A museum that can be anywhere, collect anything—an architecture independent of the ground and of culture, a nomadic architecture for a globally networked world. Such a museum made of a folded street has no interior. It brings the world in, domesticating the outside rather than

---

17   Ibid.
18   Le Corbusier and his atelier rue de Sèvres 35, *Œuvre Complète*, vol. 7, 1957–1965 (Zurich: Les Éditions d'Architecture, 1967), p. 163. Le Corbusier presents the project in a book entitled *Le Musée du XXe siècle*, showing how this project to represent the whole world is to be positioned on a key node in a transnational network. Ibid., pp. 164–177.

looking out at the world. Detached static contemplation becomes mobile social action and architecture becomes the event.

The idea of internalizing the street increasingly defined the twentieth-century museum, most obviously with the "inverted ziggurat," as Frank Lloyd Wright described the Guggenheim Museum in New York (1943–1959) to *Time Magazine* in a press conference in 1947—even speculating that such a ziggurat could be expanded infinitely, unlike a traditional one. The spiral ramp became the gallery itself and complaints from artists, curators, critics, and even the director of the museum that the architecture was intruding on the experience of art, upstaging the art, were voiced from the very beginning of the project to its completion. John Canaday, a critic for the *New York Times*, described it on the very day it opened as "a war between architecture and painting in which both come out badly maimed."[19] Wright kept insisting that architecture itself would be the frame for art: "The only 'framing' needed by the painting is this relationship to architectural environment."[20] He had even called the project "Archeseum" on all the drawings, specifications, and correspondence until told to stop doing so in 1956 by Harry Guggenheim. The hostility to the building continued for a long time. Some of the many legends surrounding the building include the hip problems that its guards supposedly develop, presumably from standing on the ramp with one leg lower than the other. Ironically enough, it is only in recent years that a new generation of artists has appreciated the challenge, the pushback the building presents, happily engaging with the architecture. And it is useful to remember that Wright's original vision for the museum was also of a profoundly social space. Drawings and sketches of the project show individual paintings and other works of art being looked at by groups of people assembled in the alcoves, but most visitors are looking across the void and at each other, or down to the crowded, loungy, almost festive ground floor where most of the action is.

The Centre Georges Pompidou of Renzo Piano and Richard Rogers in Paris (1971–1977)—yet another commission from André Malraux—made the next quantum leap in the concept of the museum as mass medium. It went one step further with the creation of a new public square in the city that was then "pulled" into the building to form a public library and bookshop, up the side of the building as circulation and information spaces, with the visitors on display passing each other on escalators in

FIG. 6

FIG. 7

19   "Wright Versus Painting: The Guggenheim Museum," *The New York Times*, October 21, 1959.

20   Frank Lloyd Wright, "The Solomon R. Guggenheim Museum" [June, 1958], in Bruce Brooks Pfeiffer, ed., *Frank Lloyd Wright Collected Writings*, vol. 5 (New York: Rizzoli, 1995), p. 248.

tubed-shaped vitrines, and across the roof as restaurant and terraces—with the galleries sandwiched in between. The project was a watered-down version of Cedric Price's Fun Palace, the polemical project for a building without any walls that he symptomatically called "a university of the streets." The Pompidou made the line between street and gallery even thinner and brought it even deeper into the museum, turning the very act of visiting the museum into a spectacle.

With Tate Modern, this entire scenario was digested and amplified: the public square became a huge internal volume extended by a massive vertical circulation system including public landings with books, objects, interfaces, performances, installations, cafes, education areas, restaurants, and terraces. Each of these present multiple occasions to congregate and meet other people and to look back at the city, as if inviting visitors to situate themselves and admire the city like any other work of art or installation in the collection. The most popular artwork in the permanent collection is the framed city of London itself—with the galleries as secondary, optional experiences.

The museum of the twentieth century has thus traveled from its origins in the domestic house to what is likely its endgame—the vast structure of Tate Modern. Institutions like MoMA and the Guggenheim began with domestic rooms that were successively expanded by bringing more and more of the street inside. They have often been accused of bringing the logic of shopping arcades and department stores into the museum, for example with the escalators introduced by Cesar Pelli in 1984 in the first expansion of MoMA's original 1939 building. The anxiety is not only about the ever more explicit treatment of art as a commodity, but also about the related possibility of bringing anything inside the museum, including an ever wider public, the world-absorbing ability of the arcades described so eloquently by Walter Benjamin. The very first page of his massive study of the arcades quotes a nineteenth-century illustrated guide of Paris on the emergence of a new internalized city, which he associates with the birth of consumerism: "These arcades, a recent invention of industrial luxury, are glass-roofed, marble-paneled corridors extending through whole blocks of buildings, whose owners have joined together for such enterprises. Lining both sides of these corridors, which get their light from above, are the most elegant shops, so that the *passage* is a city, a world in miniature." The Tate Modern inherited this interiorization of the city project, but what is consumed now is art, or, more precisely, the experience of art, or even the experience of the space of art.

With the first Tate Modern project, artists were extensively surveyed for their opinions and they all seem to have used the occasion to condemn museum architecture for interfering with art. In the meantime, the building itself has left this old view behind. With the latest project, it is notable that artists were not asked. Only the public was surveyed. It is the real users of the building that matter. The visitor is treated like an artist, a performer, engaged with the museum in unexpected ways. The museum learns from the visitor as much as the visitor learns from the museum. And this new kind of interactive partner is steadily getting younger. More than half of the five million annual visitors to Tate Modern are under thirty-five years old. The museum that invited them in to perform is obliged to perform in return.

Tate Modern may well be the apogee of this kind of massive museum. As the Tate continues to eat the streets, other museums seem to be heading in the reverse direction, getting out of their skins to occupy the streets in an ever more expansive gesture that ultimately threatens the big architectural statement. The proliferation of biennales, festivals, fairs, temporary pavilions, and the like is bringing the museum logic to cities all over the world in a kind of urban performance. Every such pop-up event produces a kind of hypothetical urbanism. They create a temporary city within a city. This is obvious in old biennales like Venice with its own streets lined with pavilions, but it is equally true when installations and events are dispersed throughout a city. With each of these exhibition-events, there is a special map to guide the visitors, the map through an alternative urbanism that is temporarily superimposed on the existing city. The usual urban circuits give way to new patterns, and the performance of temporary architecture, like that of an artist, provokes new movements, new interactions, and new thinking. This confusion, even dissolution, of the art object into a kind of landscape experience is equally a dissolution of the line between the inside and outside of the museum. As architecture enters the space of exhibition and systems of exhibition enter the street, new kinds of museums or post-museums become possible.

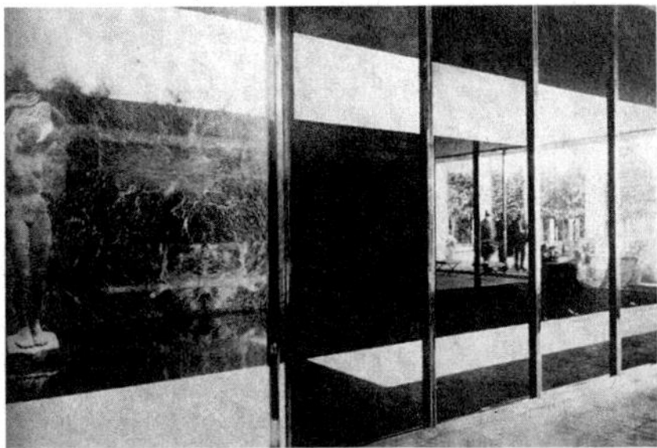

FIG. 1
Mies van der Rohe, Barcelona Pavilion, International Exhibition
in Barcelona, 1929. *Diario Oficial de la Exposición Internacional
de 1929–30.* Biblioteca Nacional de Madrid.
© 2016, Pro Litteris, Zurich

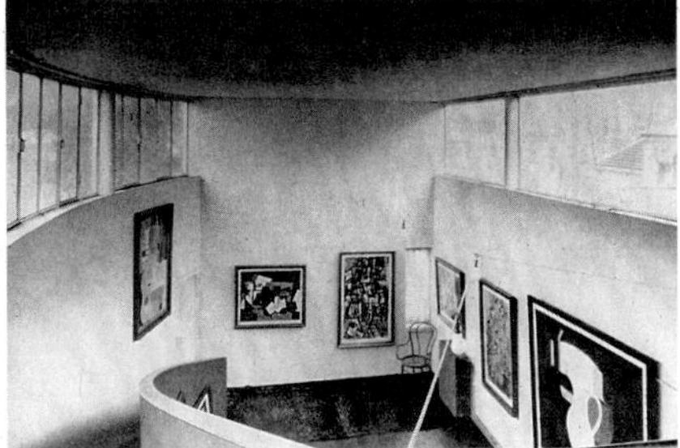

FIG. 2
Le Corbusier, Villa La Roche-Jeanneret, Paris-Auteuil, 1923.
Photo: Fred Boissonnas
© FLC/2016, Pro Litteris, Zurich

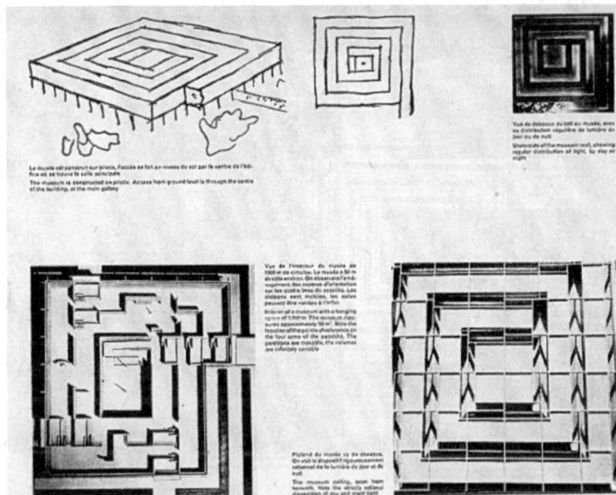

FIG. 3
Le Corbusier, page dedicated to the spiral museum, *Œuvre Complète*,
vol. 4, 1938–1946, p. 17.
© FLC/2016, Pro Litteris, Zurich

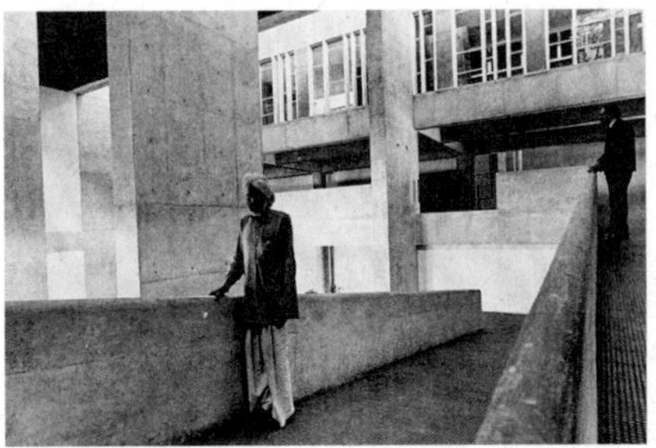

FIG. 4
Le Corbusier, Government Building and Art Gallery, Chandigarh, 1952,
Œuvre Complète, vol. 8, 1965–1969, p. 99.
Photo: Grasser, Zurich
© FLC/2016, Pro Litteris, Zurich

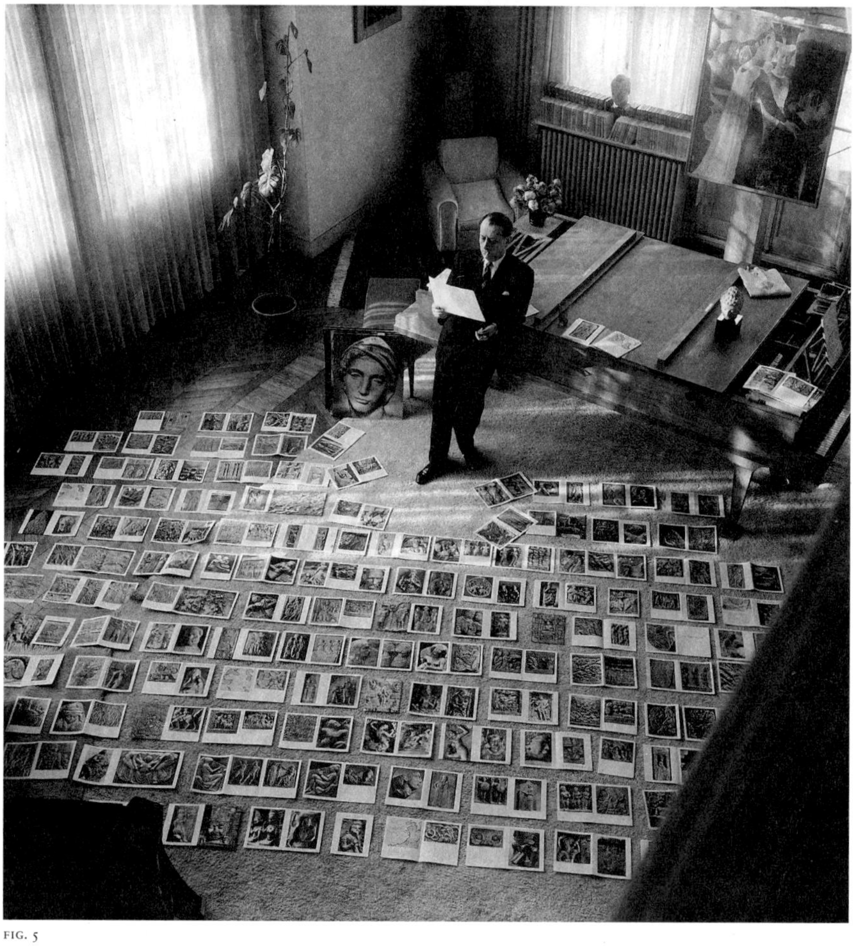

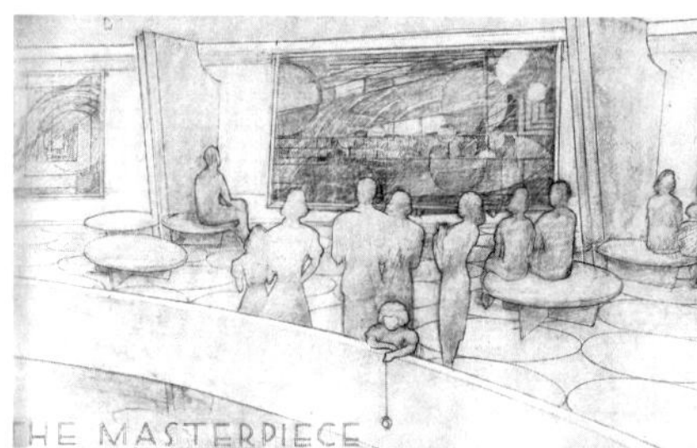

FIG. 5
Maurice Jarnoux, André Malraux surrounded by images for the Imaginary Museum, 1953.
© Paris Match Archive

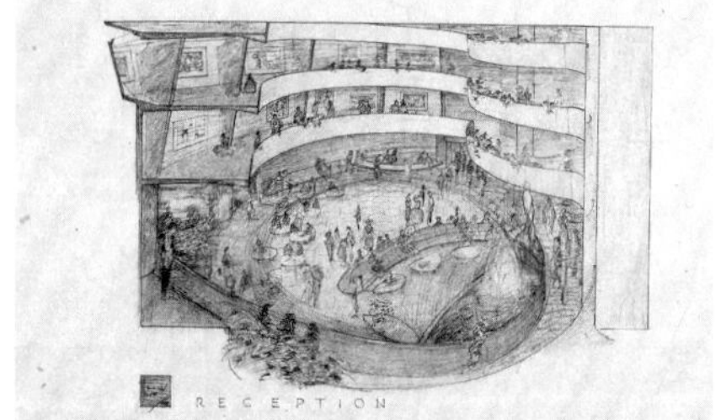

FIG. 6
Frank Lloyd Wright, *The Masterpiece*, ca. 1958.
The Frank Lloyd Wright Foundation Archives (The Museum of
Modern Art | Avery Architectural & Fine Arts Library, Columbia
University, New York).
© 2016, Pro Litteris, Zurich

FIG. 7
Frank Lloyd Wright, *The Reception*, ca. 1958.
The Frank Lloyd Wright Foundation Archives (The Museum of
Modern Art | Avery Architectural & Fine Arts Library, Columbia
University, New York).
© 2016, Pro Litteris, Zurich

Carving from Airy Nothing a Local Habitation and a Name
Donald Preziosi

What is this "airy" nothing such that it could be "carved"? Is this nothing a "zed"; a "zero"?[1]

Are "habitations" and "names" the products and artifacts of activities such as carving? Can a habitation exist without a name, or a name without a site; a *locus* being spoken from? An enunciation without a place of speaking? Carving as a mode not only of fabricating but of speaking?

And also: Who is allowed or authorized to "carve"? How exactly does one carve?
Carving as a residue of *craving*?

There are several parts to the following: a first regarding *habitation*, a second regarding *naming*, and a third about their conjunction, their juxtaposition, as palimpsests.

---

1   The number zero arrived in Europe ca. 1200 CE, most famously by the Italian mathematician Fibonacci ("Filius Bonacci," aka Leonardo of Pisa), who brought it, along with the rest of the Arabic numbers, from his travels in North Africa. It first appeared in Mesopotamia, in Babylon, ca. 400–300 BCE, but some argue that it originated much earlier in Sumer as a placeholder denoting an empty number column in cuneiform texts, written as a pair of angled wedges. It was later used in India in the fifth century CE as a placeholder—for example, to distinguish 1 from 10. Arguments have also been made for an independent origin in the Americas, among the Olmec peoples in Mexico, during the first millennium BCE. For a useful discussion of these issues, see the online article by John Matson, "The Origin of Zero," *Scientific American* (August 21, 2009), www.scientificamerican.com/article/history-of-zero/ (accessed September 22, 2016).

Prologue

1.   1939, Jorge Luis Borges:
*We [...] have dreamt the world. We have dreamt it as firm, mysterious,
visible, ubiquitous in space and durable in time; but in its architecture we
have allowed it tenuous and eternal crevices of unreason which tell us it
is false.*[2]

2.   1945, Maurice Merleau-Ponty:
*What protects the healthy man against delirium or hallucination is not
his reason [sa critique], but rather the structure of his space: objects remain
in front of him, they keep their distance and [...] they only touch him
with respect.*[3]

3.   2004, Andrea Nightingale:
*In the effort to conceptualize and legitimize theoretical philosophy, the
fourth-century [BCE] thinkers invoked a specific civic institution: that
which the ancients called "theoria." In the traditional practice of theoria,
an individual (called the* theoros*) made a journey or pilgrimage abroad for
the purpose of witnessing certain events and spectacles. In many cases, the
theoros was sent by his city as an official ambassador: this "civic" theoros
journeyed to an oracular center or festival, viewed the events and spectacles
there, and returned home with an official eyewitness report.*[4]

4.   1595–1596, William Shakespeare, *Midsummer Night's Dream:*
*And as imagination bodies forth / The forms of things unknown,
the poet's pen*
   *Turns them to shapes and gives to airy nothing / A local habitation
and a name.*
   *Such tricks hath strong imagination, / That if it would but appre-
hend some joy,*
   *It comprehends the bringer of that joy; / Or in the night, imagining
some fear,*
   How easy is a bush supposed a bear?[5]

---

2   Jorge Luis Borges, "Avatars of the Tortoise," in *Labyrinths,* trans. James E. Irby (New York: New Directions, 1962; 1964), pp. 202–208, here p. 208.

3   Maurice Merleau-Ponty, *Phénoménologie de la perception* (Paris: Gallimard, 1945); English from *Phenomenology of Perception,* trans. Donald A. Landes (London: Routledge, 2012), p. 304.

4   Andrea Wilson Nightingale, *Spectacles of Truth in Classical Greek Philosophy* (Cambridgee, UK: Cambridge University Press, 2004), p. 3.

5   William Shakespeare, *Midsummer Night's Dream,* act 5, scene 1 (voice of Theseus, Duke of Athens, at his wedding to Hippolyta, Queen of the Amazons).

* * *

If, for Borges, the rational architecture of the built environment incorporates *traces of unreason*, for Merleau-Ponty, by contrast, reason or sanity would entail the maintenance of a sharp and clear *distinction* between one's being as an agent or subject and the palpable, material objects of one's attention or perception. The latter position implies, moreover, a tacit recognition of the *artifice* or the fabrication as well as the contingency of what is taken as materially palpable: that, in other words, the material constitutes a *sign*, a staging of culturally specific relationships between what signifies and what is signified. This maintenance of a sharp difference between the *signans* and the *signatum*, however, is not without a problematic two-fold consequence: the notion (first) that a concept can exist in its own right, independent of its articulation (as spiritualists might claim), along with the notion (second) that material form can itself exist (as materialists may claim) independently of its articulation. At issue is the co-construction and co-determinacy of materialism and immaterialism; the performance and practice of theorizing, of seeing; the marking of a journey from which one has returned to report on what was seen.

* * *

Preface
Making Worlds

Making Worlds or *Worlding* (neologism, v., transitive and/or intransitive). Rather than taking architecture merely as a *what*, it will be more productive to ask *when*: When, amongst the myriad practices and events of world-making or worlding—is (an) "architecture"? *When, where, how, why, under what conditions (and for whom)* can given phenomena—artifacts or mentifacts—serve distinctively *architectonic* functions? Is architecture but one aspect, modality, or function of worlding? Shall we reserve the term for certain kinds of worlding, perhaps those that aim at a comprehensive range of praxis? Are there certain distinctively architectonic actions, practices, and events linking what are commonly staged as distinct (in occidental modernity) "subjects" and "objects"? Particular and distinctive topological or dramaturgical *orchestrations of bodies in space, place, and time*—wherein stagecraft itself is meaningful in a particular way?

In effect, is worlding a *making of the visible*—what is materially palpable—*legible*, thereby potentially delineating or projecting histories, theories, critiques, and historiographies in their own right? Perhaps grouped together under the rubric of "architectonics"?

It has been customary for some time—in much of the occident and in some elsewheres—to believe that works of *art, artistry, or artifice* (however defined) are *historically, critically, and theoretically/philosophically, and perhaps even theologically significant* phenomena; that artifice itself has "a history" or reveals an historical dimension, the astute delineation of which would provide significant insights into the (presumably parallel or in some manner complementary) histories of individuals, communities, peoples, and mentalities—insights that, not least of all, may be legible as providing lessons for our own times. Objects of historical attention being *object-lessons* for our own times. Chronologies as tacitly teleological. The modern professions and institutions of the history of art (art historicism) and of the histories of architecture (architectonics? museography?) were and remain grounded in this enabling assumption, one of whose several corollaries has been that changes in form over time and space may be taken to correspond to changes in beliefs, attitudes, mentalities, intentions, or ideologies, as well as to changes in social, political, or cultural conditions. Or, conversely, that changes in mentality are (or should be) palpably manifested. This—the "fiction of factual representation"—has long been a virtually irresistible occidentalist artifice, having become one of the cornerstones of the edifice of the modernities we have built ourselves into, whose exits have yet to lead anywhere than to other framed images, however many *posts* are posted, pasted, or palimpsested onto those modernities. Postmodernity was never an *elsewhere* but another picture on the walls of the prison-house of museology. Well, of course. Lyotard was right about this. At least in part.

There were myriad sites over the past two centuries where such fictions were ostensified, yet arguably there was none more suddenly and dramatically brilliant than the enormous prefabricated glass and iron building (a *Gesamtkunstwerk* in its own right) in London's Hyde Park in 1851 designed by Joseph Paxton—by profession a landscape architect and designer of garden glasshouses—to accommodate the *Great Exhibition of the Arts & Manufactures of All Nations*: what immediately came to be called the *Crystal Palace*. The first "universal exposition." This most bluntly and radically translucent of nineteenth-century constructions may well have been modernity's most unsurpassable architectural artifact: the lucent embodiment and semiological summa of the epistemological principle of order itself—a structure that was infinitely expandable, scaleless, transparently abstract, whose style consisted of a (seeming) lack of style. A plan referred to it at the time as "a type of what the actual world *should* be." The building was imitated several years later in Paris, thereby setting in motion a sequence of "universal" expositions around the world. The 1851 London Crystal Palace building was virtually duplicated in Melbourne, Australia, a year later. George Cruikshank's 1851 lithograph poignantly portrayed the exhibition's global aspirations:[6] astride the world, the building is shown attracting (absorbing) all the world's peoples and products from every corner of the planet. The earth is bisected from north to south by the British Union Jack: the southern end flies from the Red Fort at Delhi, marking the global reach of the British Empire.

Simply put—to paraphrase Freud fifty years later arguing for his new "science" of psychoanalysis—the Crystal Palace purported to be an "impartial instrument, like the infinitesimal calculus" for making legible the similarities, differences, and the cognitive, aesthetic, and ethical hierarchies amongst all peoples by means of their juxtaposed and plainly seen products and effects, their artistries. Art itself as the pan-human measure of all peoples, a universal module. A *European* universality, of course…

* * *

On the eve of World War II, the Anglo-American poet W. H. Auden famously observed that "poetry makes nothing happen"—a remark which has had multiple parsings, and most commonly these three: first, that a poem (or poetry in general) is ineffectual in the world of daily life, a mere non-threatening or un-dangerous phantasm; second, that poetry is a pastime or a sideline (*parergon*) outside or alongside the main work (*ergon*) and grit of civic life; and third, that the art of poetry creates "nothing" as an entity, a palpable positivity or some *thing* in its own right—like the *zed* or number zero, that brilliant invention of ancient mathematicians in both hemispheres. Auden's is a telling insight into the artistry and artifice of what is promoted or construed as real or natural. This paradox and conundrum is as old as Plato's dilemma about whether to admit the

---

6   See Donald Preziosi, *Brain of the Earth's Body: Art, Museums, and the Phantasms of Modernity* (Minneapolis: University of Minnesota Press, 2003), esp. chap. 6, "The Crystalline Veil and the Phallomorphic Imaginary," pp. 92–115, and fig. 33, p. 115.

representational (mimetic) arts into an ideal society or polity, precisely because of their potential to trouble the souls of its citizens—that is, to make manifest the artifice or fabricatedness of what is taken, promoted, or legislated by those holding or desiring power as true, real, natural, and thereby beyond debate or negotiation. It is proper and necessary to foreground the "danger" and terror posed or instantiated by (what in modernity is distinguished or reified as) "art."

Auden's words were written in a eulogy for another poet who was a well-known political activist at the time, namely W. B. Yeats, and read in part

> *For poetry makes nothing happen: it survives*
> *In the valley of its making where executives*
> *Would never want to tamper, flows on south*
> *From ranches of isolation and the busy griefs,*
> *Raw towns that we believe and die in; it survives,*
> *A way of happening, a mouth.*[7]

In the "surviving" noted there, the reciting of a poem is, among other things, an evocation (a "mouth") that *foregrounds its own artifice*, as well as, at the same time, marking *its context* (the "valley of its own making"). The former is a manifestation of the "poetic (aesthetic) function" of any semiotic/communicative activity, following Jakobson's multifunctional and multimodal matrix of signifying praxis, where that modality of use co-exists and co-signifies along with several other modes—what came to be termed the *referential*, the *emotive*, the *conative* (or exhortatory), the *phatic*, and the *meta-linguistic* or systemic, which foregrounds the speaker or maker's attention to the sign system itself.[8]

The basic point is that signifying practice in any modality or dimension is only rarely singular and is ordinarily co-present with other dimensions or functions, any one of which may be in dominance in a given utterance. Consider simply the multiple connotations possible in a given description of a space and its choreography, or, if you prefer, in the practice of *worlding*. Denotation, in other words, as Roland Barthes and not a few others have insisted, is but one species of connotation, an artifice in its own right. The question to be reckoned with about (what is called) architecture

---

7   W. H. Auden, "In Memory of W. B. Yeats," in idem., *Another Time* (London: Faber and Faber, 1940).

8   See Roman Jakobson, "Linguistics and Poetics," in Thomas Sebeok, ed., *Style in Language* (Bloomington: Indiana Univ. Press, 1960), pp. 360–377. There is a lucid and useful synopsis of this matrix of functionalities by Louis Hébert in http://www.signosemio.com/jakobson/functions-of-language.asp (accessed October 10, 2015).

is not (or less) "What *is* architecture?"—but rather under what conditions
is architectonic practice *legible* (reified) as a "kind" of thing; as one modality or *instance* of fabricating space and choreographing together bodies,
places, spaces, and things; as the enabling and constraining of practice.
Like Auden's poem, it similarly "makes nothing happen." You might wish to
say that architecture (to echo Shakespeare's stunning words in *Midsummer
Night's Dream*) "carves from airy nothing a local habitation and a name"
but it is equally the case that "airiness" and "nothing" are simultaneous
co-fabrications.

I'm reminded of Gertrude Stein's remarks about the city of Oakland
that "there is no *there* there." If architecture (even "Architecture!") is not
any kind of *"it,"* then this is more than a matter of simply replacing things,
reified entities, with events, practices, performances, or processes. We need
to reckon with and interrogate, as much as is feasible without presuming
a globalist, universalist, or "neutral" perspective, our most fundamental
presumptions about how we reckon with our ways of world-making—and
without bringing on board Heideggerean notions about "world-pictures"
and their imagined "ages," back-formations from some Hegelian vanishing
point of final and perfect fulfillment. Oratorios in time-space sounding out
episodic tableaux. Art/Architectural History 101. Dramaturgies staged
from the viewpoint of a trompe-l'œil that is amnesiac with respect to its
own fabricatedness.[9]

But: What is *not* a trompe-l'œil?
Let's begin again from a couple of elsewheres.

* * *

I've been asked to contribute a few words about the Western concept
conventionally called "architecture" for a special academic publication
(the one you may be reading here) devoted to research and reportage
on another contemporary fiction called "visual culture." The following
remarks will likely be construed as heretical within the context of that
discourse, whose theological foundations and presumptions I will also
consider as these remarks unfold. I'm not going to engage with the
problem that is marked by "architecture" historiographically, as I've been

---

9   On which, see Preziosi, *Brain of the Earth's Body,*
     (see note 6), esp. ch. 1, "Haunted by Things," pp. 1–14,
     and ch. 8, "The Limits of Representation," pp. 137–154.
     See also the following note.

dealing with such questions in a critical manner elsewhere, for some time and at considerable length,[10] but I will here attempt to reckon with the issues epistemologically.

Case in Point One:

In her research on the cultural practices of the traditionally nomadic !Kung Bushmen peoples of the Kalahari Desert in West Africa, the late American anthropologist Lorna Marshall once described their settlements as follows:

It takes the women only three-quarters of an hour to an hour to build their scherms [shelters], but half the time at least the women's whim is not to build scherms at all. In that case they sometimes put up two sticks to symbolize the entrance of the scherms so that the family may orient itself as to which side is the man's side and which the woman's side of the fire. Sometimes they do not bother with the sticks.[11]

Case in Point Two:

According to the place-making and worlding practices of certain aboriginal groups in Australia, anything and everything in their material environments may be used to narrate stories, often via journeys over great distances, where such journeys (to paraphrase Michel de Certeau speaking of New York or Paris[12]) constitute a "great poem of [i.e., made by] *walking* (a) city," where the walking is an "architecturizing" of a space, transforming a space into a place. A mythomorphic transformation, in Derrida's terms, creating that of which it speaks.[13] For the Australian groups, the artifice, the "architecture" is the worlding of and with and by a particular given environment, which often may be thousands of square kilometers in area. Worlding problematizes clear distinctions between geography, geomancy, landscape, environment, artifacts, and talismanic relationships amongst phenomena.

Apropos of our encounters and reckonings with palpably fabricated human environments, whether or not conventionally distinguished as

---

10 See for example Donald Preziosi, *Architecture, Language, and Meaning* (The Hague: De Gruyter, 1979); *The Semiotics of the Built Environment* (Bloomington: Indiana Univ. Press, 1979); *The Ottoman City and Its Parts*, with Irene Bierman and Rifa'at Ali Abou-El-Haj (New Rochelle, NY: A. D. Caratzas, 1991); and more recently, *Art Is Not What You Think It Is*, with Claire Farago (Oxford: Blackwell-Wiley, 2012), and most recently *Art, Religion, Amnesia: The Enchantments of Credulity* (London: Routledge, 2014).

11 Lorna Marshall, "!Kung Bushman Bands," *Africa* 30, no. 4 (October 1960), p. 343 (my emphases).

12 Michel de Certeau, *Heterologies: Discourse on the Other*, trans. Brian Massumi (Minneapolis: Univ. of Minnesota Press, 1986).

13 Jacques Derrida, discussing Claude Levi-Strauss's *The Raw and the Cooked*, in "Structure, Sign and Play in the Discourse of the Human Sciences," in *Writing and Difference*, trans. Alan Bass (Chicago: University of Chicago Press, 1978), pp. 278–293, here p. 286.

"material" or "virtual"—and where these are construed more generically
as events and as occasions or solicitations for what could be referred to as
"the choreography of bodies in space and time," and less as "objects"
—what is of interest in the first case in point is Marshall's calling attention
to the *contingency and dispensability* of what in our contemporary world
might commonly be assumed to be the necessary material sites, frames,
or containers *for* (and by extension the expressions, representations,
and marks or markers *of*) behavioral activity. Her account reveals that
the made formation (the hut) is the *circumstantial* product of behavioral
attitudes and routines regarding the topological staging of gendered
relations of kinship. The hut, whose temporary material form results
opportunistically from exploiting various unique local resources at a given
time in the nomadic movements of the group, is at the same time an instrument to strengthen and focus behavior in socially sanctioned ways. What is
notable here, in other words, is the coexistence, the co-determination of
both the (temporary) made formation *and* the topologies of bodily relationships between individuals: who interacts with whom under what conditions,
when and where, and toward what ends.

This brings us to three main implications:

First, what constitutes dwelling for the !Kung people is both a built form
and a set of topological relations structured according to differences
in gender, and that there is no implication of a direct causal link between
the two.

Second, what constitutes dwelling ("worlding") is not exhausted
by a built environment or by the culturally specific concepts of construction,
fabrication, building, architecture, settlement, or cities.

The third and most general and perhaps most interesting implication
to be drawn from Marshall's observations is that settlement or dwelling is
a *multimodal, multifunctional, and multidimensional* behavior which may
(or may not) employ "built" formations. What is reified as the building is a
nexus of functional relationships, which itself exists in space and time
—built spaces, then, both enable and constrain present practices in particular ways with respect to social, historical, and political (dis)placements,
(dis)locations, and disruptions. Worlding, of course, as sociopolitical praxis.

The Palpable Poesis of Palimpsesting

In the task of revealing more precisely the natures, places, and functions of artifacts, buildings, cities, or built environments generally in social behavior, the critical analysis of communicative events or cultural performances in their multimodal and multifunctional totalities is of fundamental importance. Multiple *modalities* of signifying media not only commonly coexist, but each modality incorporates multiple *functions*, in hierarchical arrangements that vary in dominance, often radically, on specific occasions. The point is that the semiotic behavior of worlding is inherently *redundant and indeterminate*, affording fabrications of meanings in multiple dimensions, perspectives, and media both at the same time and over time and space.

I use the term "communication" in the broadest sense to involve manifesting or disseminating information regarding the perception of similarities and differences (of any kind). (The word is etymologically a visual and architectonic metaphor, referring to the juxtapositioning and sharing of walls or boundaries.) Social behavior in general aims at affecting (and effecting) the behaviors, normally in multiple ways, of both oneself and others. The mere insertion or citation within social space of a form, word, gesture, or sound—both materially and virtually, to use conventional (and problematic) distinctions—potentially influences the behavior of others, who are thereby placed in a position of having to react (or pretending to react) or of avoiding (or pretending to avoid) reacting.[14] At the same time, how a formation is received and understood cannot be securely controlled without external direction or modification, leading to an awareness of the essential indeterminacy or semi-determinacy or contingency of semiosis. An indeterminacy *held at bay* by maintaining a "rigorous distinction" between signifier and signified—an insistence that reifies the *artifice of transcendence* as a distinctive realm of being.[15]

---

14 In fundamentalism, whether political or religious (especially in their monarchical/monotheist/fascist variants), every sign is an *index*: that is, it bears a relationship of direct connection between a *signans*, the signing material entity, and a *signatum*, that is, what that entity is purported to point to (see next note). But this works both ways, for it suggests that material "form" itself can exist independent of its articulation. These issues are examined at some length in Preziosi, *Art, Religion, Amnesia* (see note 11), in connection with the co-construction of materialism and immaterialism.

15 "The maintenance of the rigorous distinction [...] between the *signans* and the *signatum*, the equation of the *signatum* and the concept, inherently leaves open the possibility of thinking a *concept signified in and of itself*, a concept simply present for thought, independent of a relationship to language, that is of a relationship to a system of signifiers. [...] leaving open this possibility [...] accedes to the classical exigency of [...] a 'transcendental signified,' which in and of itself, in its essence, would refer to no signifier, would exceed the chain of signs." Jacques Derrida, "*Semiology and Grammatology*: Interview with Julia Kristeva," in *Positions*, trans. Alan Bass (Chicago: Univ. of Chicago Press, 1981), pp. 19–20. See also Preziosi, *Art, Religion, Amnesia* (see note 11), on the problem of the Christian *eucharist*: the made form (wafer) that at a ceremonial moment (and only then) when the priest intones the phrase *hoc est corpus meum*, "this is my body," the piece of bread *is* the "body of Christ."

* * *

In short: *A building is not an index. Neither is a building a symbol, a sign, or an icon.* In fundamentalist religiosities, on the contrary, *every* sign is an index: that is, it bears a relationship of direct connection between a *signans* (the signing material entity) and a *signatum* (what that entity is purported to point to). It was Derrida who astutely pointed out that the maintenance of that duality leaves open the possibility of conceiving of an immaterial realm of existence as having a life of its own. But this works both ways, for it suggests that material "form" itself can exist independently of its "articulation"[16]—the scientism of art historicism.

In worlding—in the ongoing semiotic bricolage of daily life—we orchestrate anything and everything at our disposal (including our own and other bodies, to name but one the stellar constellation Orion) to create and maintain a meaningful environment, to elicit and solicit action. Any sign system is a complexly ordered instrument or modality for cueing such perceptions in given sensory channels and in conventional and culturally specific media. Moreover, meaningfulness or sense is itself inherently time-and-space-specific.

What exactly would it mean, then, to "decode, read, and interpret" the "spatial language" of urban space or human environments more generically if what we are actually confronted with are situations in which a strictly "spatial language" (or the "built environment" from which it is deduced) would itself be only *part* of the picture? This is one of the funda-mental challenges to any visual or material semiology as such. We are faced with the problem of accounting for the totality of multimodal, multifunc-tional, and multidimensional signification.[17] This is a question that more often than not in recent times continues to be reduced to a dichotomy between visual and verbal signification—for example, the somewhat hasty observations of French architect Christian de Portzamparc (in an exchange with Philippe Sollers[18]) in an essay called "Can We Think Without Lan-guage?"[19] where the author claims that this is really a question about

16   See again Preziosi, *Art, Religion, Amnesia* (see note 11), esp. ch. 7, "Semiosis and its (Dis)contents," pp. 84–100.

17   See Roman Jakobson, "Linguistics and Poetics," in Sebeok, *Style in Language* (see note 9), pp. 360–377.

18   See my paper "Museology as Philosophical Conundrum," read in absentia at the International Congress on Museums in the Middle East, Beirut, 2008 (unpublished).

19   Christian de Portzamparc and Philippe Sollers, *Writing and Seeing Architecture,* trans. Catherine Tihanyi (Minneapolis: Univ. of Minnesota Press, 2008), pp. 21–46. On the relationships of architectural theory and criticism to psychoanalysis, see Steve Pile, *The Body and the City: Psychoanalysis, Space, and Subjectivity* (London: Routledge, 1996), esp. ch. 5, "Misplaced: Locating the 'I' in the Field of the Other, pp. 121–144; and Jerome A. Winer, James William Anderson, and Elizabeth A. Danze, eds., *Psychoanalysis and Architecture* [*The Annual of Psychoanalysis,* vol. 33] (Catskill, NY: Mental Health Resources, 2005), esp. the essay by Judith Flower MacCannell, "FreudSpace: Architecture in Psychoanalysis," pp. 93–107.

architecture ("logos" *vs.* the "domain of forms"). Recall Derrida's ironic (after what we've seen here) remark that "architecture no longer defines a domain." For *it* is the *nothing* being addressed here.

This brings us to several implied questions:

(1)   What are the methodological implications for reckoning with inherently multimodal, multifunctional, and multidimensional communication, performance, or behavior? How can we possibly *model* such complexities effectively and efficiently?

(2)   What are the possible effects of such investigations? That is, what could such information be used for, and for whom, and under what conditions would or should they be used?

(3)   Finally, what is now meant by interpretation? Is any new fabrication a potential interpretative artifact vis-à-vis those in its ambient environment, or in the (still with us!) sadly lugubrious "histories of art (and architecture)" more broadly? This is an issue with philosophical implications which are beyond the limits of this short piece to adequately address, so I shall pose it in a slightly more manageable way by reframing the question of *what* is an interpretation by asking instead *When is interpretation? Under what conditions* is some thing (or event) interpretative? Can a building, city, artifact, or painting interpret itself? Is a museum a reframing of its own exterior world? A rethinking of its world? An eloquently raised eyebrow in front of the latest lugubrious exhibition at MoMA? Museology as poetry, the formatting of episodic narrativity, of voice as poesis. Is a city its own interpretation, its own metaphor or allegory? The ideology of chronology…

Emmanuel Levinas once observed that "The whole of reality bears on its face its own allegory […] In utilizing images art not only reflects, but brings about this allegory."[20] As human artifacts, cities themselves may always have "borne on their face" their own allegories. Are "art" and "architecture" essentially, or largely, rhetorical mechanisms designed to bring about that of which they speak? Are they consequently *mythomorphic*? The

---

20   In Emmanuel Levinas, "Reality and Its Shadow," in
      The Levinas Reader, ed. and trans. Seán Hand (Oxford:
      Blackwell, 1989), pp. 129–149, here p. 136.

profession of architecture as a *constative morphing*, a making of the myth of its praxis as *merchandise*, rendering individuals and communities as worshipful spectators in the latter-day religion of starchitecturology.

Is what we're referring to as architecture (or art) staged as a material entity, rather than an event, *the mark of (an) amnesia*? Reification, in linking amnesia inexorably to aphasia and apraxia, is, as Landzelius argues, an inherently political practice.[21] Amnesia is less a negative loss or forgetting than a production, an artifact.

A final point concerns the architectonics, viz., the social semiology, of the trompe-l'œil—something that is arguably at the heart of the discourse on architecture. Citation of which raises the question and the specter of: What is *not* a fool-the-eye phenomenon? If everything is only ever palpable from a particular locus or "standpoint," and since there is no placeless standpoint except for that of a fictional *transcendent* divinity, isn't architecture, isn't worlding, then, the betrayal and the veritable *problematizing of transcendence*—a (fabricated, to be sure) *amnesia* regarding the art, artistry, and artifice of any transcendence? The Platonic dilemma: once you "mark a domain" (Derrida) or build a thing, you can't fully turn off its voice(s). The tale of the Tower of Babel told no less. Plato's solution to the dilemma of artifice was more and better artifice: a cosmic fittingness or decorum, the tethering-together of the here-and-now to the always-already. The Platonic shell-game—not to be confused with the five Platonic solids. But that's another story for another time and place.

The idolatry and blasphemy of reification that architects toy with always, everywhere, recalls what Moses knew when he was railing about that ever-so-shiny calf of gold.

By making *nothing* happen, architecture—architectonic praxis—*worlding*, in short—makes its seeming antitheses very solid indeed. Invariably, endlessly, relentlessly, all that is virtual *melts into place*. The origins of worlding; of architecture.

---

21 Michael Landzelius, "Spatial Reification, or, Collectively Embodied Amnesia, Aphasia, and Apraxia," *Semiotica* 2009, no. 175 (2009), pp. 39–75.

Materialities—Physical States of Artworks
Nadia Schneider Willen and Judith Welter in conversation
with Karla Black, Bruna Casagrande, and Wolfgang Ullrich

NADIA SCHNEIDER WILLEN / JUDITH WELTER   The physical parts of an artwork have—unlike the romanticized concept of the infinite durability of the artwork—a determined duration. Materials have always been subject to aging. Traditional substances like oil paint, stone, or bronze have been scientifically tested and their shelf life prolonged through known conservation approaches; modern, less tested materials, on the other hand, are subject to a faster half-life period. The use of raw and fragile materials changed the question of the conservation of an artwork, as well as the emergence of new artistic strategies that have been challenging a traditional concept of the artwork since the 1960s: the new art forms are based on processes and attach a higher importance to ideas and concepts than to the artwork as an object.

During the 1990s, when the Migros Museum für Gegenwartskunst was founded, process-based, participatory art practices were at a height. The opening of the museum in the industrial spaces of the former brewery marked a turning point of the collection policy: in these pioneering days, the museum acquired artworks that were produced in the context of a particular exhibition and whose materials and conceptual core themes particularly questioned durability.

In the last few years the question of materiality has started to be discussed differently in the academic context. If, before, materiality was studied almost exclusively in the perspective of its iconography, the question nowadays has been reoriented, not least with respect to digitalization. These changes in the perception of artistic practices and materials are crucial for a contemporary notion of the artwork.

A museum that sets its focus, as we do, on installation-based and processual works—which represent challenges in terms of preservation, reconstruction, or reproduction—has to make certain operational priorities. Handling these impermanent works demands expert knowledge as well as high investments of time and expense.

What does the finiteness of artworks signify for art history? We were interested in whether the changing priorities described above also occur in art history. What effect does changeable and ephemeral contemporary art have on the way that these works are documented, described, and analyzed from the perspective of art history?

WOLFGANG ULLRICH   In the museum context, the finitude of artworks can be seen as a provocation—a scandal or deficit. According to the concept of the museum, as it has been developed since the late eighteenth century, art has to be aligned with eternity. It is so tightly related to ideals that are in themselves seen as timeless that to conceive of an artwork as having an expiration date seems to be a desecration. Having said that, transience can be ascribed special qualities: what is transitory, unique, and unrepeatable may therefore have an "aura"—in Walter Benjamin's definition. Transience can also be a conscious protest against the idealization and para-religious overestimation of art. Consider the Fluxus movement, within which multiples were deliberately made from "bad" materials, in order to make artworks as fleeting as everyday consumer products—thereby avoiding the fetishism of timelessness. Within academic art history, it is important to gather and analyze various artistic reasons and concepts for ephemeral works. As is often the case, the attention brought to contemporary forms of art has changed our view of history; in other words, some elements gained prominence that were previously peripheral phenomena at most. This applied, for example, to many forms of art in royal courts, which consisted not only of wall paintings and furniture, but also of gardens and water features, lighting effects and festivities—and thereby a wide variety of ephemeral formats. Another parallel is that courtly art often arose from an economy of waste, as does much contemporary art. It is the task of art history to show such parallels, but at the same time notto neglect views of historical difference. For this reason alone, however, today's ephemeral forms of art are a welcome intellectual challenge for art historians. They make clear that certain concepts of art have long been viewed too narrowly, which is why large areas of artistic practice have been neglected.

NSW / JW   Why today, of all times, in a period in which the compact, highly technologized materiality of all things digital is decisive—in the areas of media consumption and distribution, documentation of cultural practices and products, and, of course, artworks—is the discussion about materiality beyond the digital so pivotal?

WU   Digitization in particular heightens awareness of material impermanence more than ever; data has to be repeatedly transferred onto new media to be preserved. Artifacts have never before been as endangered and threatened by transience as today, in the age of digitization. This casts doubt on the concept of eternity but also, generally, yes, my impression is that there is a new acceptance of transience. This is reflected in many works of art that use risky, untested materials and are therefore a constant reflection on the nature of transience. Ephemeral art is the modern form of a "memento mori," but less melancholy than, say, a seventeenth-century still life painting.

NSW / JW   Bruna Casagrande, from your perspective as a restorer of modern materials and media, is it viable to talk about preserving a work in its original state, or is it more relevant to say that the process of decay is preserved, for example by documenting the dynamics of decay and change?

BRUNA CASAGRANDE   In classical conservation theory, there is an established consensus that visible signs of aging are a fundamental part of a work to be conserved and should therefore be incorporated into preservation measures. What always needs to be negotiated is where signs of aging end and damage starts. This issue is particularly contentious in cases where the materials used are short-lived, the underlying technologies of the work become obsolete within a few years, or the material change is part of the artistic concept. In this case, it is almost impossible to establish a static origin—or the original condition—which is to be maintained. A process of deterioration cannot be preserved, and a dynamic state cannot be fixed. Instead, the aim is to slow down deterioration using appropriate measures and to monitor the process by documenting changes in a work and its various states. In this way, we create a basis of information for its later reception and for informed decisions with regard to the preservation and mediation of a work and its history.

NSW/JW   Purchases from the founding period of the museum are connected to the everyday in both content and aesthetics; they were often intended for use and therefore exhibit a functional aspect. These works from the 1990s were intended to involve the audience or to stimulate reflection on forms of participation. An example of this is the work *Installation Saucisson* (1997) by Atelier van Lieshout. The work consists of sculpturally produced elements of an old-fashioned butcher's shop that refer to a function—namely, the idea of self-sufficiency—without being intended for use. The sausages and conserves displayed on shelves have been produced using traditional slaughtering techniques. Another part of the installation is a guide to the production of these self-same conserves that was published in the artist's catalogue *A Manual / Ein Handbuch* (1997).

You were involved in a preservation project in 2012, which had the aim of investigating how the organic part of the work should be dealt with. It posed the fundamental question of whether the original—but in the meantime greatly altered—meat products should be preserved or replaced with new conserves and sausages that had been created using the original methods and which were potentially edible, as it was originally conceived. What were your considerations and what did you decide to do?

BC   The *Installation Saucisson* project was interesting from a preservation and restoration point of view in several respects. Firstly, it raised the question of how to replace original components of the installation in the course of conserving it and reexhibiting it—a rather rare endeavor in our discipline. Secondly, the museum offered us the opportunity to discuss this question actively in a multidisciplinary context—with curators, administrators of the collection, and participating artists—and to explore and present the results in the context of an exhibition to an interested audience. After assessing the original meat conserves, it was clear that a classic restoration of the spoilt meat would be impossible because canned food should not only look appetizing, but in theory even be edible. The option of reconstructing the canned meat was raised in view of the fact that a manual with detailed instructions for the slaughter of a pig and the canning of meat is an integral part of the installation according to the method originally applied by the Atelier van Lieshout. From the point of view of conservation and/or restoration, a reproduction has the advantage that no changes have to be made to the original structure of the work's components. Original canned food would remain in any case part of the museum's collection. For our considerations, another important factor was that Joep van Lieshout fundamentally agreed with the reproduction. In the end, the strategy of conservation consisted of the process of reproduction—slaughtering, sausage-making, and canning—and an extensive documentation of this in sound, image, and text. The people involved—a traveling butcher and a countrywoman—based their approach as far as possible on the above mentioned manual. We interviewed them about their procedure and documented their know-how, which is in the process of dying out. We also conducted an extensive interview with Joep van Lieshout on conservation issues and the intention of his work. A panel discussion held at the opening of the exhibition, which presented the *Installation Saucisson* again, dealt with the background of the work and inspired an exploration of the issues of collection and conservation. The question of how to deal with matured conserves as a part of this work was considered in the course of the project, but not finally resolved. At the latest, it will be brought up again when the reproduced versions exceed their shelf life. The resulting documentation will then be used as a basis for decision-making in future measures or other reproductions.

NSW/JW   Wolfgang Ullrich, in your opinion, how do the original aesthetic and the functional value of a work go together in this case? Or to put it differently, how do spoiled conserves and sausages relate to potential edibility, as well as the implicit invitation to imitate part of an artwork and produce it oneself? The guide to producing meat products is exhibited as part of the work, thus potentially enabling visitors to acquire the relevant know-how.

WU   This is essentially a "work in progress," as it were. It was developed in 1997, was valid for some years in this form, and then entered a second stage when new conserves were produced and the production process itself partly explained the work. This is a clever way of dealing with transience, using it as an opportunity to give an extra dimension to the work. And why should a work be something finished once and for all? The idea of the original should not lead to the superiority of the original state, nor should every change be regarded as a stage of deterioration.

NSW/JW   Karla Black, your sculptural arrangements often exist only as long as the exhibition is taking place. By working with liquid, creamy, powdery, or other specific materials with certain chemical and physical properties, you enlarge the traditional notion of sculpture by a process-based, performative use of culturally connoted, untypical materials, such as face powder or lipstick. This material is meant for use and is not always easy to conserve. Your sculptures therefore are never in a steady state, but on the contrary they are constantly facing a decomposition. Do you consider the limited life span of the artwork, conditioned by characteristics and use of the material, as part of the artistic process?

KARLA BLACK   No. I have an open process that allows for my own limitations, as well as those of the physical world, but I am incredibly precise about formal aesthetics. I am obsessed by the relations between material, form, composition, and color, and when my aesthetic decision is final, I want it to remain. I don't like it that my sculptures are seen as "impermanent." I don't really think that they are impermanent. My greatest wish is that when I finish a work, and I'm happy with the aesthetics, it would stay exactly like that forever. I know that it's difficult for the materials I work with to do that. I know that if I really want permanence, I should use wood or metal or whatever, but those materials don't have the liveliness and the energy that I want to exist within the work. I want the raw potential that the kinds of materials I use give me but I'm upset and frustrated by their instability. It's just the limitations of the physical world. I still think my work is permanent though. There are different ways of ensuring that, which I continually work on. Maybe a work is reinstalled each time with brand-new materials and therefore can exist forever, or where it's not possible to recreate the aesthetics properly, then careful conservation happens. At a certain point I just had to make a decision about what to do, and I decided I just had to live with the paradox, with the contradiction.

NSW/JW   How important is this contradiction of temporality for the contracts you, or your gallery, conclude when selling one of your artworks? In such precise and detailed documents, the temporality of your own life coincides with the temporality of your artwork. What led you to this kind of contract? Did you have some "historical" or other examples in your mind?

KB   The contracts are a practical necessity. I'm not interested in them as documents. They have no artistic or conceptual value so, in that sense,

they have no relation to the work of someone like, for example, Sol LeWitt.
The contracts that are written and adapted by me and my representative
gallery are required to both protect the work and to ensure it can continue
on into the future.

At a certain point, I had to make a decision about what was most
important about the work. Should all of my sculptures be thrown in the
trash after an exhibition is over? Should I personally reinstall every single
work in every group exhibition or museum installation I am featured in,
or make something totally new every time? Should the work die with me or
should it go on? The aesthetic process isn't open-ended forever, just until
I get what I want; the freedom of process has to stop somewhere. I'm not a
performance artist. I make sculpture. What is most important to me is that
I make something once; from there on, the aesthetics stay as close as is
possible to my original decisions, and I move on and make new work.
As far as I'm concerned, as soon as a piece of work is finished it is totally
rigid. I am absolutely adamant about the precision of how it is handled
thereafter, in order for it to stay the same. The fact that that is pretty much
an impossibility because of the materials I choose to use is another contradiction of my work. It's best for the protection of the work for the beginning
position of any negotiation about it to be one of rigidity.

NSW / JW   Artworks change not only because materials or technical
equipment age, but also because installative or performative artworks are
presented in different ways, depending on the particular architectonic or
site-specific context of the relative exhibition. As a consequence of this
dynamic notion of the artwork, but also as a consequence of professional
processes or modalities of presentation and the sale of exhibition copies,
the concept of the original work has to be rethought. An interesting
example of the museum's collection regarding this question is Gustav
Metzger's *Liquid Crystal Environment* (1965–1966/1998). The installation
consists of large image projections showing the movement of liquid crystals
that are projected to the walls by manipulated slide projectors. The first
prototypes of Metzger's auto-creative art, created in the 1960s, didn't
survive. Therefore *Liquid Crystal Environment* has been reconstructed
for Metzger's retrospective in the Modern Art Oxford. Meanwhile there
are also versions of this artwork in the collection of the Tate Modern
and the Musée d'art contemporain in Lyon (they are dated, respectively,
1965–1966/2005 and 1965–1966/2013). Our version of the artwork is
currently requested frequently as a loan for exhibitions, because it seems

that it is considered to be the "historic" piece, even though it is, from a technical point of view, a reconstruction that has been produced more than thirty years after the original creation of the artwork.

Wolfgang Ullrich, what effect does the variability of works have on the term "original"? How has the definition of this term or the concept of the original changed?

WU   A distinction must be made as to whether an artist included a reflection on changeability from the outset, or whether it takes him/her by surprise. In the first case, changes in the original are part of the work. Consider, for example, garden art. In its heyday—such as the English garden in the mid-eighteenth century—it was natural for the landscape gardener to conceive how the garden should look after ten, fifty, or one hundred years. And so, accordingly, the garden's state in the distant future was just as much the original work of the landscape gardener as its condition immediately after the initial design. And a garden was only a good—even great—work of art if it could be aesthetically convincing at any moment in time. The commissioner of the work wanted to know in advance exactly how the garden would develop in the distant future. I think any kind of art should comply with the same claim. Those who put up a work for sale these days should be able to give information about whether, how, and over which time period it will change. And if an artwork changes, the artist should either be able to identify it merely as a temporary work; or s/he should be able to make a credible claim that through change, an aesthetic experience will be attained that is just as valuable as the work's initial state. Or respectively, that through this, reflections that confirm the quality and identity of the work of art—or even increase it—will result. An artist who is surprised by the changes his work undergoes, however, is an unprofessional artist. Then it is a contingent issue that distances the work from its original state and, as such, invalidates it. You could also put it in the following way: No matter which changes occur in a work, an original is still an original as long as these changes are part of the artistic concept. Because in this case, the changes in the work are included from the beginning—from the origin (*origo*) of the work.

NSW / JW   Bruna Casagrande, what role do the terms "original" or "authentic" play for the life span/death/existence of the artwork? How is the "original" defined from a conservation point of view?

BC   Both terms are controversial in our context and are continual starting points for discussion: Where does the original state end? Where do the signs of aging start? In his *Contemporary Theory of Conservation*, Salvador Muñoz-Viñas concludes that there can be no definitive answers to these questions, because any assessment will always remain subjective and therefore negotiable. Nowadays, the conservation of contemporary art is no longer about having to pinpoint, preserve, or restore a defined original condition. The effort to capture the work in the context of its creation and to make its statement accessible is more important than the search for an authentic state. This is achieved by interviewing the artist as well as a contemporary audience, if possible. Depending on the material circumstances, the information thus obtained can be used to make an informed decision on which of a work's possible states should be displayed. Ideally, the measures taken to reach this state of the work are reversible. In any case, it should be comprehensible and imparted in a way that enables a new decision later if the information, location, or physical situation changes.

NSW / JW   Wolfgang Ullrich, in your essay "Art Handling: Dialektik eines Dienstleistungsverhältnisses" (Art Handling: Dialectics of a Service Relationship) you use the work *Nothing Is A Must* by Karla Black to put forward the hypothesis that art handlers are the ones who bring out this form of art, but who are also responsible for its destruction, because works such as Karla Black's cannot be set up without becoming damaged in the process. The art handlers are therefore forced to become co-authors although they are not declared as such. The production of a work, which is not necessarily completed on its first exhibition, is thus co-determined by other protagonists, but occasionally by other factors such as the architecture, or physical and chemical characteristics of the material, as is exemplary in Karla Black's works. What role does the original play in this complex of the concept of the original? Does being damaged belong to the continual aging process of the authentic, original work?

WU   Yes, damage and aging can be a fundamental part of the original work. Just think of an artistic position such as that of Dieter Roth, who has often worked with perishable objects and regards the deterioration process as an essential dimension. His works are just as time-based as a performance except that they occur over much longer periods. But they share the difficulties of performance in the exhibition process; ultimately, at most they can be documented or repeated although this process risks not living up to the original. In the case of Black, art handlers are the invisible co-actors of the performance, who have an effect on the appearance—in this case, the state—of the work.

NSW / JW   Karla Black, in the contract with the museum for *Principles of Admitting* (2009), which is now part of the collection, you give permission to the museum to install the work without your presence. At the same time the importance of the precise, almost ritual gesture that is necessary to convert the roughly 2,800 kilograms of plaster powder and pigment into a sculptural arrangement is evident in the installation manual. What role does your physical presence as artist play during the installation of one of your artworks? Does the artwork that has been installed by yourself have the same status as the one that has been installed by art handlers?

KB   I have worked for years on developing contracts and guidelines with rigorous instructions, diagrams, and photographs to create a system whereby works can be reinstalled. It's important to me that the sculptures have a permanent life, and I feel like this is the only way to do it. The freedom of process, through which I create the work, only needs to happen once. It happens when I first make the work, after that it is finished and is, therefore, transferable. Like a painting would be. It's a complicated process, and I am very involved in it. In a way, it's like the work never leaves my hands. All reinstalls are done in close liaison with me.

The powder floor works easily retain their freshness because new powder is used every time. Often, the materials that the works are made from can't help but continue to show a freshness of gesture, it's just in their nature. I will often "puff out" or slightly reform hanging works when they're reinstalled and if I can't be there I'll explain how to do that to someone else. My two studio managers Ronnie and Susie do a lot of reinstalls. They have worked with me for a long time and they are in direct touch with me during the process, but they also have a lot of experience of the work and so they know what to do.

Usually I am always part of installing the work and therefore I see it. If my studio managers install something, I usually only see it in photos. As long as it's installed correctly, then it's fine. If I'm not there, I'll be involved all along the way via photographs and emails and so on. When I'm dead, all of this will be done by my estate, and I imagine that I will always have skilled assistants to reinstall work that will trace back through time to me. The studio managers that I already have, along with myself, will train a new generation of assistants before we get too old to pass on the processes. It will never just be left up to "art handlers."

NSW / JW   In the guidelines you write: "The state at which the work becomes unacceptable for display and when replacement parts are needed will be judged by the artist." How much transformation do you accept for your artwork to still accept it as "the original artwork"? And which factors are crucial for you to decide that the artwork cannot be exhibited anymore, or that it is destroyed?

KB   This is another example of how the work never really leaves my hands. And, again, it's the best protection for the work to begin any negotiation from a position of such rigidity. This decision would be different for every artwork. Color is a very important aspect; if the color of the powder was mixed wrongly then the work could not be allowed to be displayed, but that could be rectified through negotiation. Despite this guideline, there probably isn't any state that would totally prevent the work from being displayed, but the solution to any problems would have to be found in negotiation with the artist/gallery/estate.

NSW / JW   From the point of view of the restorer, Bruna Casagrande, is it even possible to speak of an artwork no longer existing when it has been documented and "only" its physical presence has come to an end? Can a work die or completely disappear?

BC   As a conservator, I am responsible for the preservation of the physical presence and readability of a work. Much of my work is to understand and document the work in the context of its function and effect and, on this basis, to be able to make informed decisions concerning conservation strategies. A work is never limited to the current, existing material; the conservation or restoration first fully develops in its temporal and cultural context. Very short-lived works can be survived by their documentation; this preserves them for posterity, can be representative or, at the very least, is proof of their existence. In this case, we conservators can regard material manifestations of contemporary art entrusted to us as "cultural sediments." As experts of our time, we collect as much knowledge as possible about them. So it is more about sharing and passing down works in one form or another, and less about life and death.

NSW / JW   Works that consist of ephemeral materials, or that are created by arranging many individual parts in a space, need the exhibition situation to be created in the first place—to enter into force as a fixed physical aggregate state. Could it be said that exhibiting a work always represents an aspect of conservation?

BC   Yes, I am thoroughly convinced of this. If we think of the material manifestations of artworks as mutable, exhibitions are instants in the career of the works where they are repeatedly renegotiated, defined, understood, and described. The conservation and/or restoration of contemporary art uses the term "iteration": the repeated installation/presentation/performance of a work, and the "iteration report," which documents a particular manifestation of a work. Using the *Installation Saucisson* as an example, this means that the background to the exhibition should be made comprehensible: Why were the conserves reproduced? How were they produced and presented? In their chronological sequence, iteration reports are sources of the history of an artwork and contribute as such to a type of conservation that passes works on.

NSW / JW   What kind of relationship is there between work and documentation? Are there works where documentation is part of the work or could it be said that documentation forms another aggregate state of the work?

BC   Conservation documentation includes metadata and images of a work in various media forms, which contribute significantly to its understanding on a material and functional, as well as a cultural and historical, level. It can represent a work, for example, in the form of a video of a performance in an exhibition. It can be essential for the reception of a work, such as in the form of information about material indicated on a sign. The conservation documentation, however, is not part of a work, nor does it replace its material manifestation. Much more, it is a constant companion, and sooner or later, proof of its existence.

NSW / JW   The museum leaves many of the final decisions about art conservation to the artist. This procedure can lead to conflicts: for example if a work displays signs of aging or irreversible damage to the extent that the institution no longer feels it to be in a fit condition for exhibition, whereas the artist considers this to be an integral part of the work. In practice, the artist's opinion is central—Wolfgang Ullrich, what status does the authority of the artist over his or her work have in the art-historical framework of interpretation?

WU   Because an artist does not live forever, sooner or later a time comes when others need to decide how to deal with a work that has changed—especially when it involves changes that were not necessarily part of the artistic concept. As long as it is possible, the artist should, of course, be consulted—but the action that s/he proposes should not automatically be carried out. Rather, an artwork is part of public discourse, and its meaning is therefore always being newly defined, interpreted, and evaluated. Issues of preservation that reflect this public discourse should also be taken into account in further dealings with a work, and not only the interests of a single actor—namely, the artist. In other words, from the moment a work is in the public domain, its originator no longer has the sole power of definition.

The conversation was realized via e-mail in June 2016.

Conservation
Reflecting the focus on "Tomorrow" in the essays collected in this chapter, the works in this image series incorporate fragile or rapidly perishable materials.

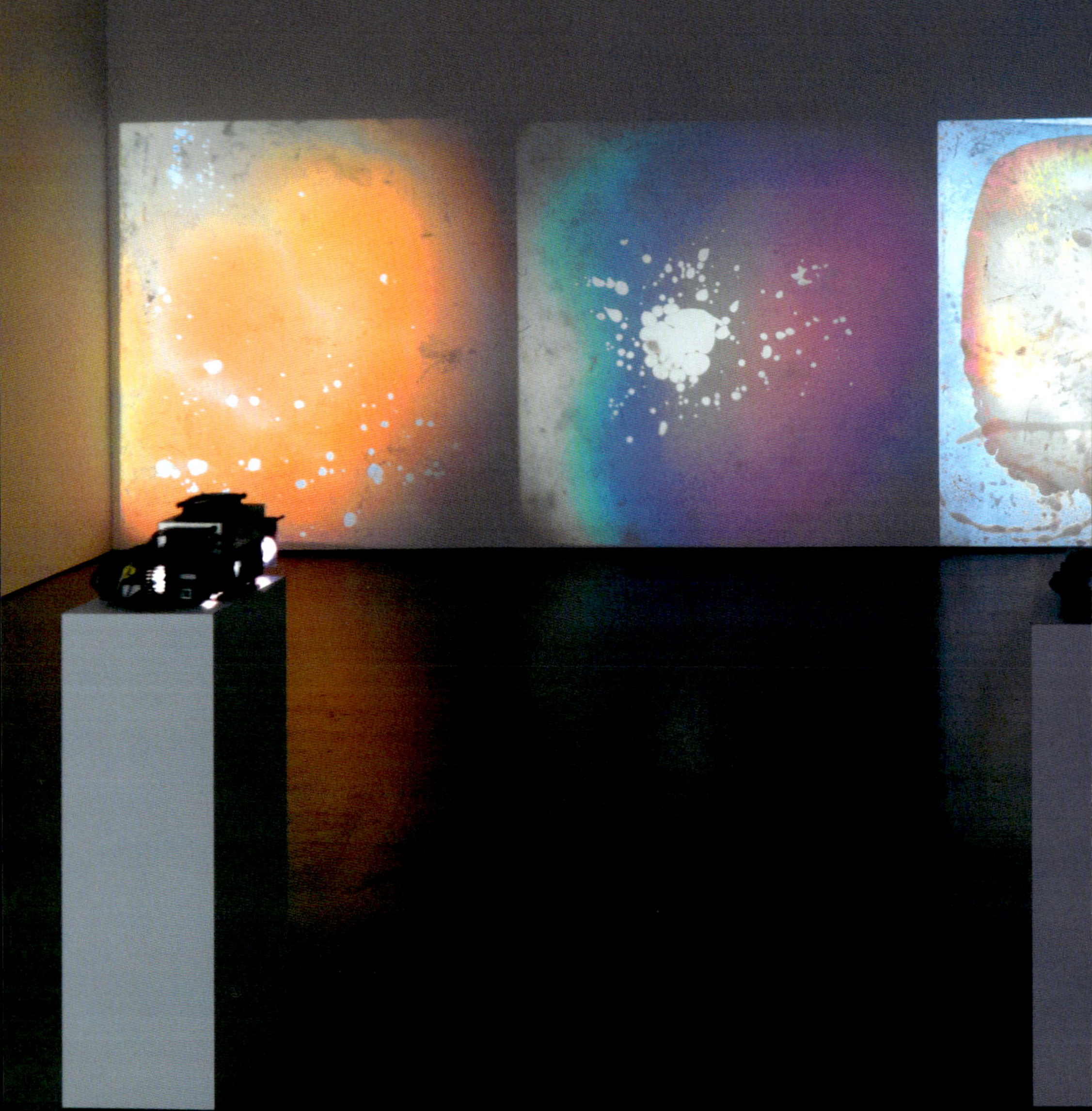

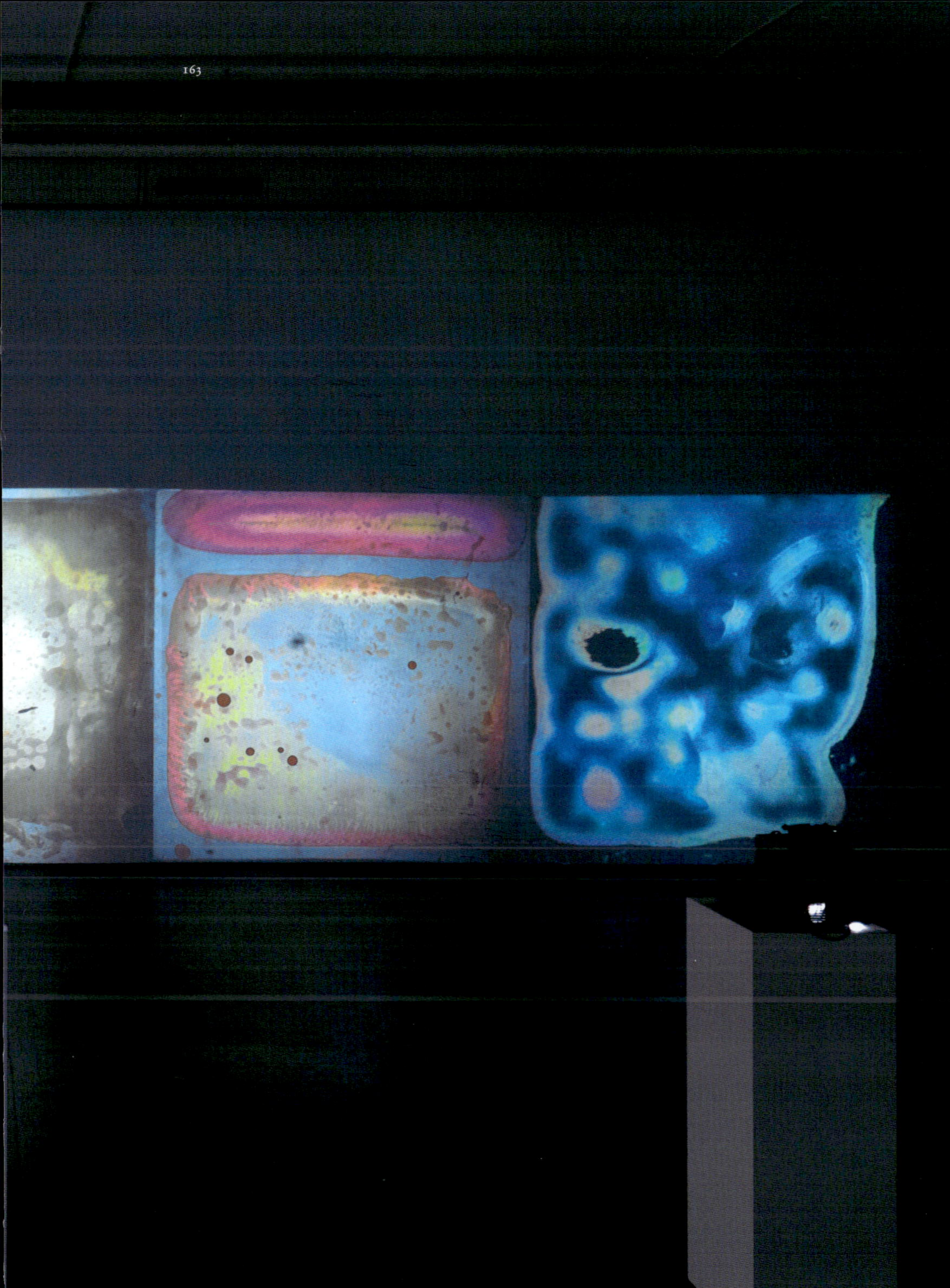

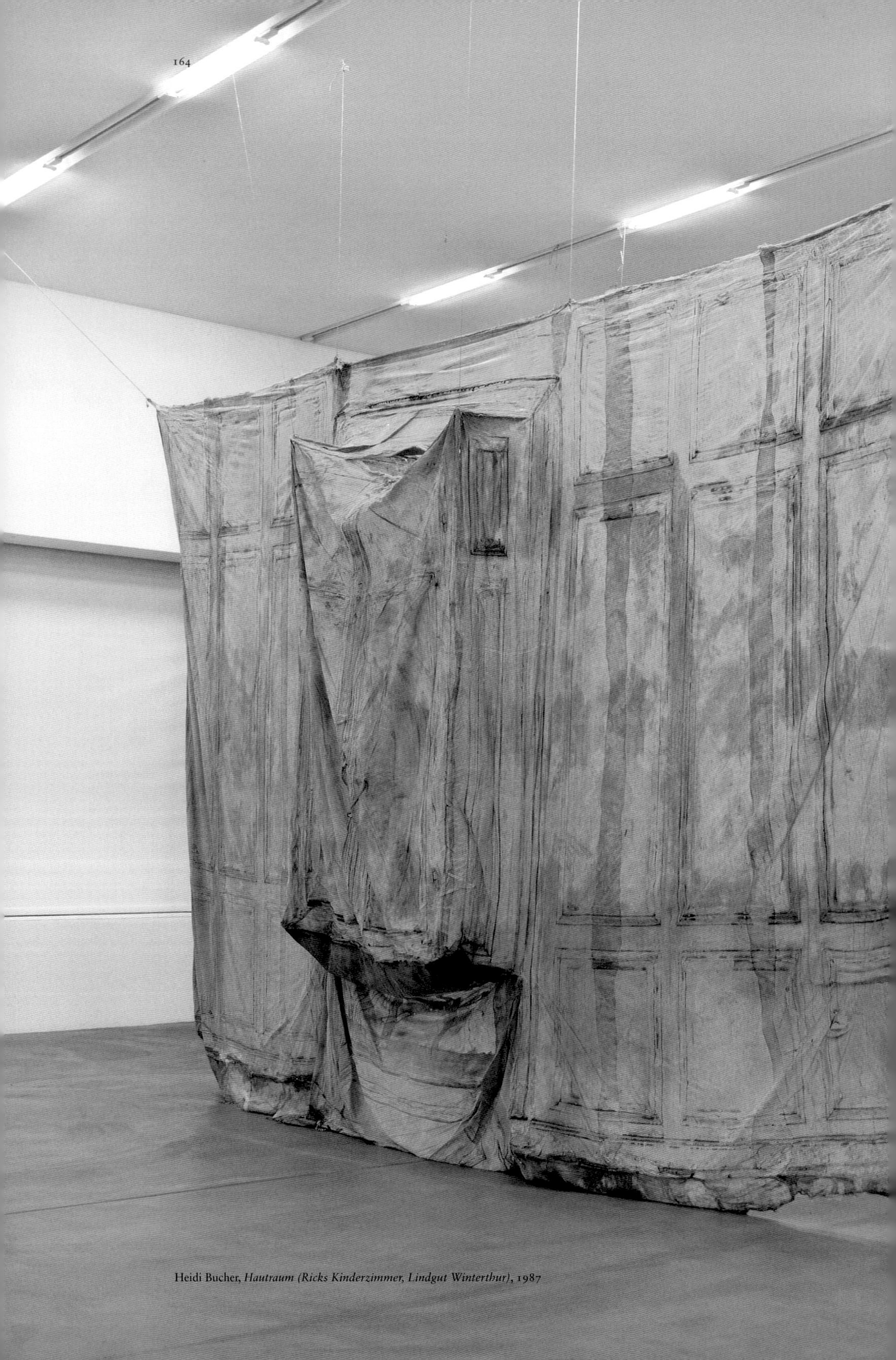

Heidi Bucher, *Hautraum (Ricks Kinderzimmer, Lindgut Winterthur)*, 1987

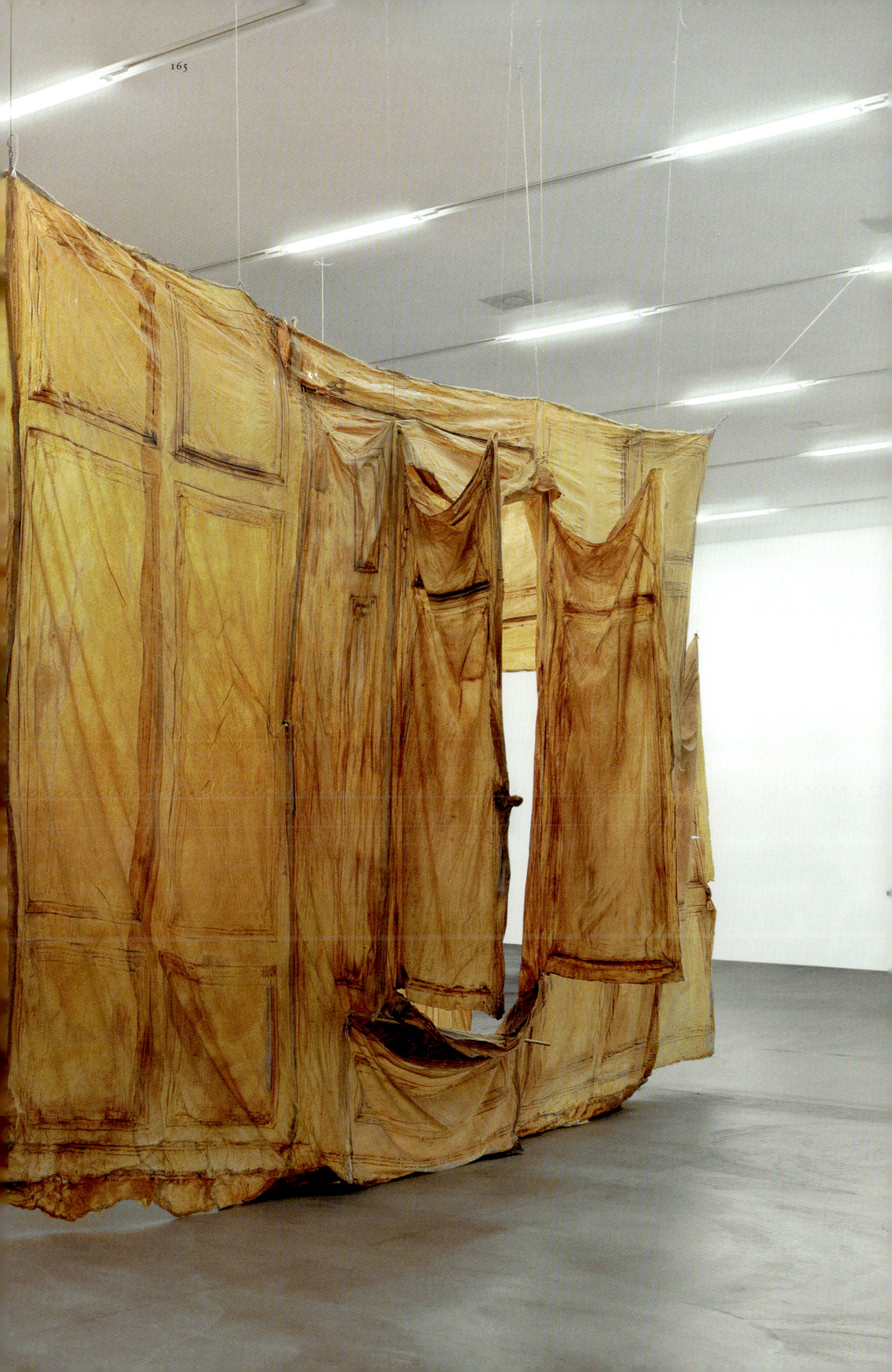

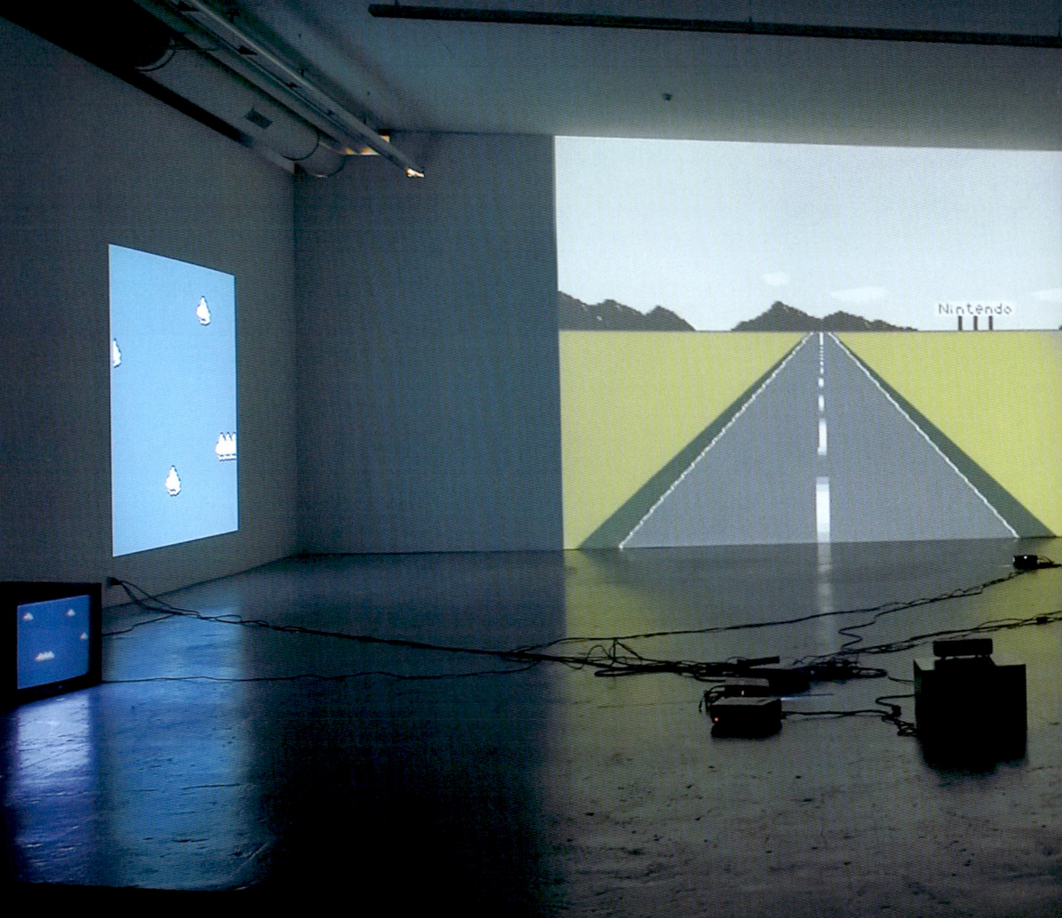
Nintendo

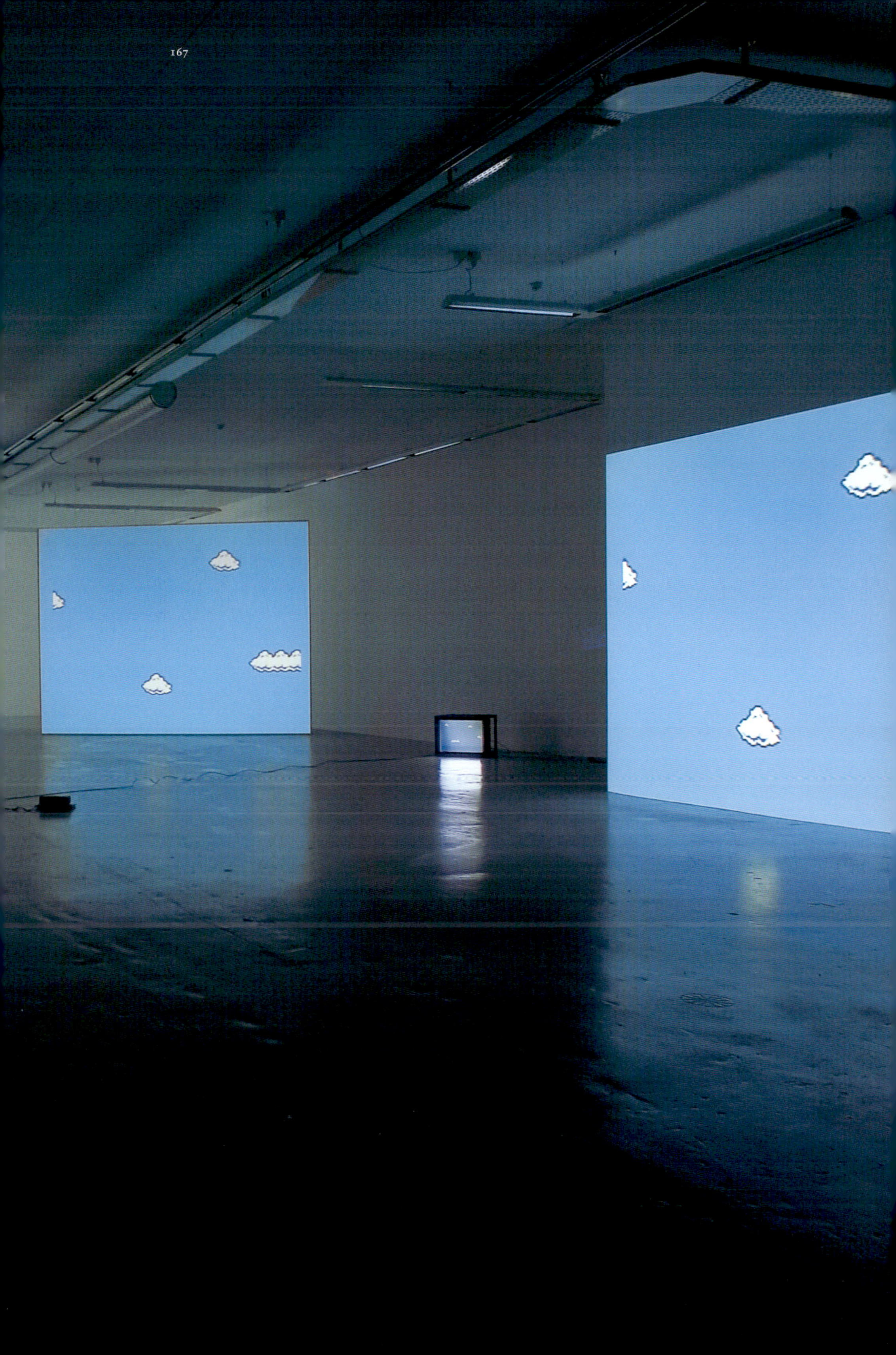

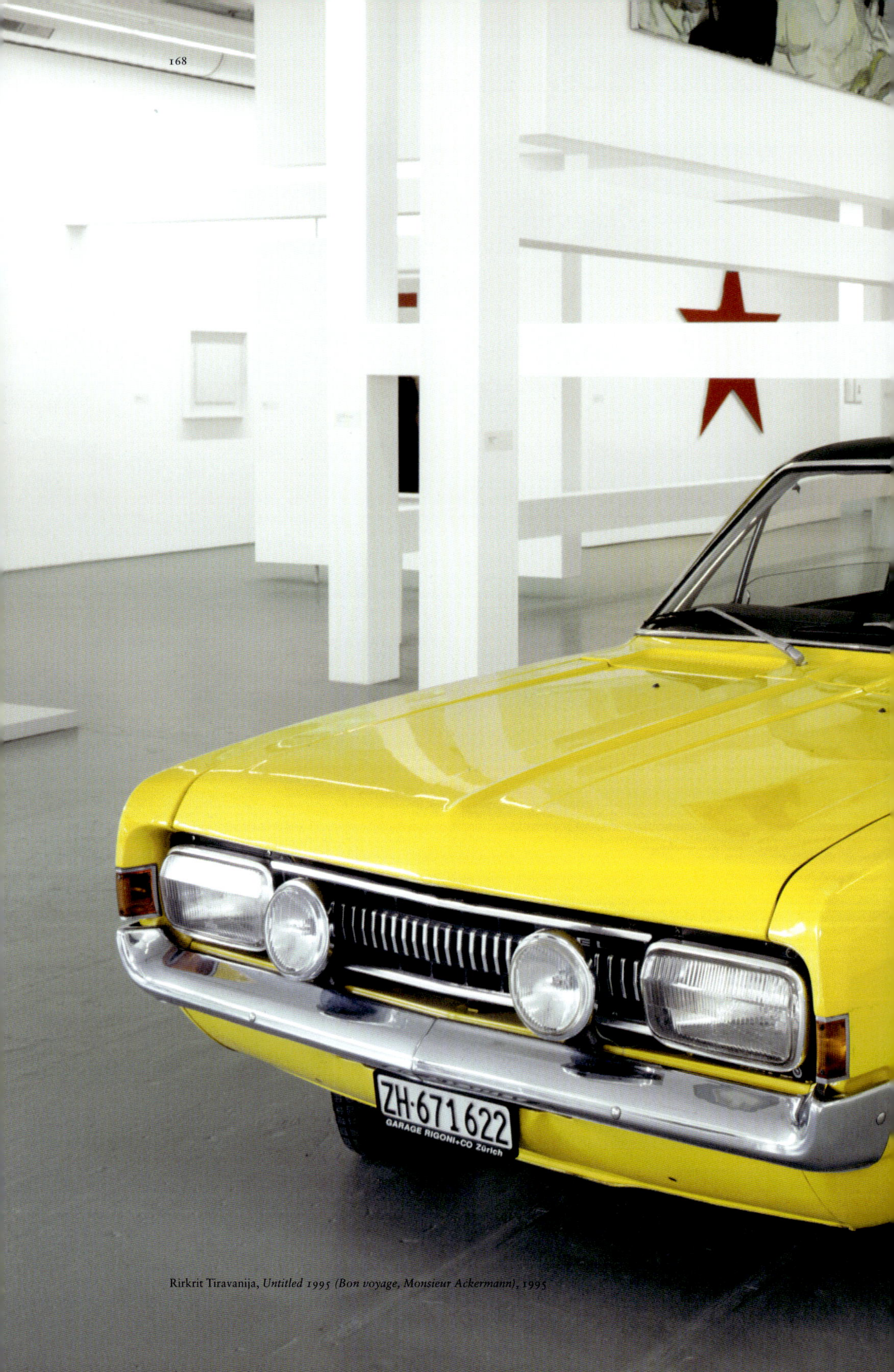

Rirkrit Tiravanija, *Untitled 1995 (Bon voyage, Monsieur Ackermann)*, 1995

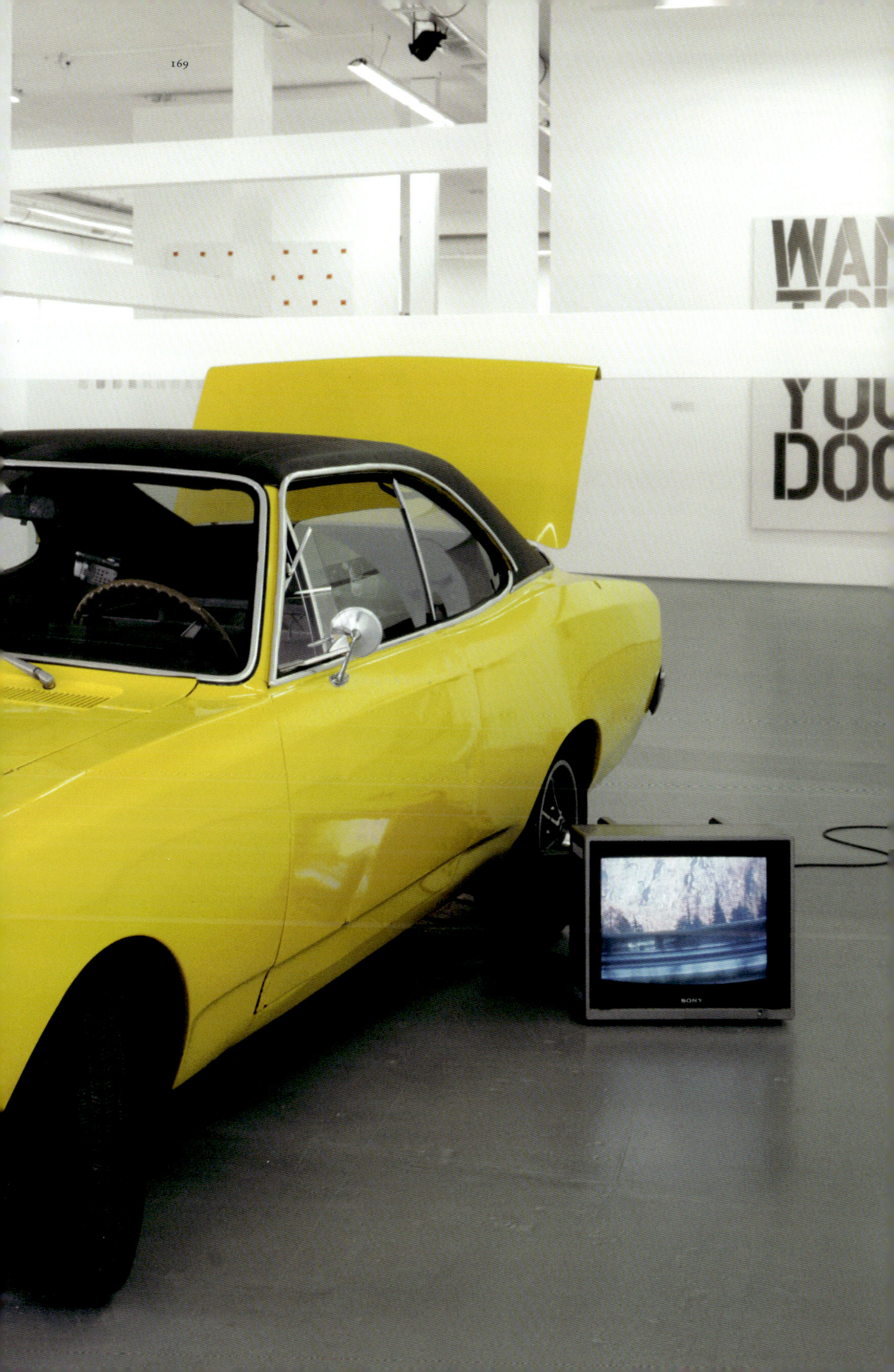

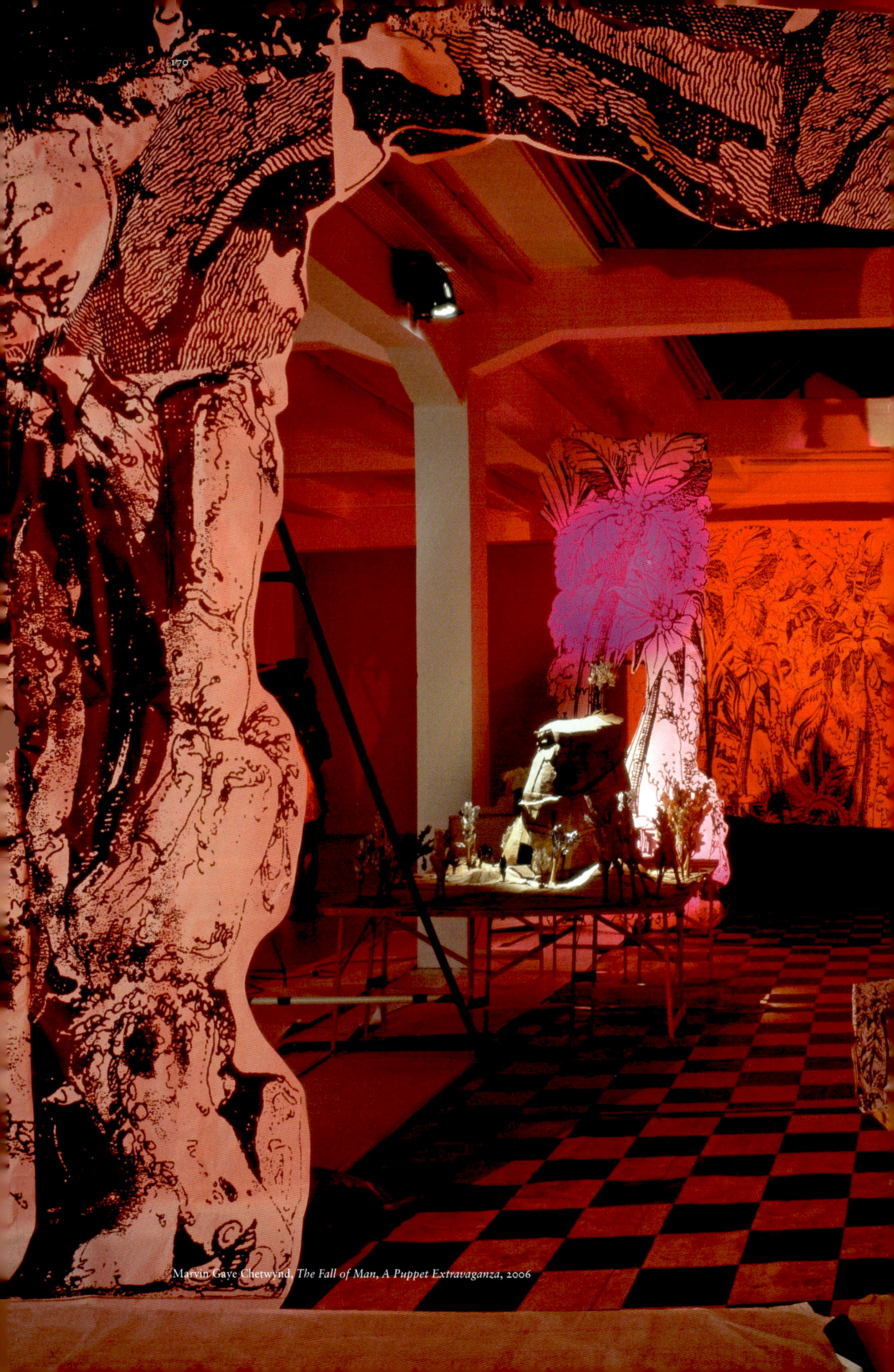

Marvin Gaye Chetwynd, *The Fall of Man, A Puppet Extravaganza*, 2006

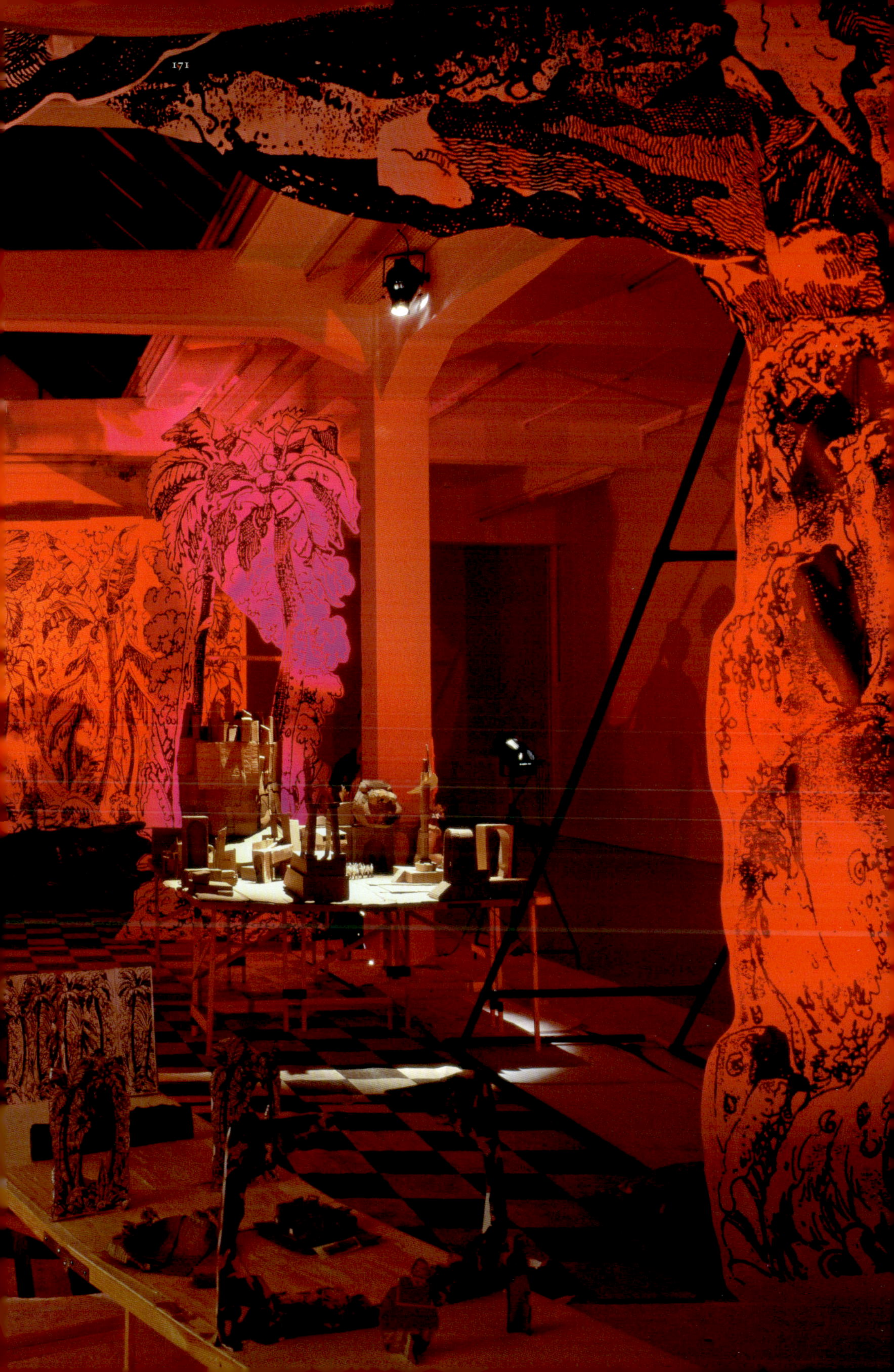

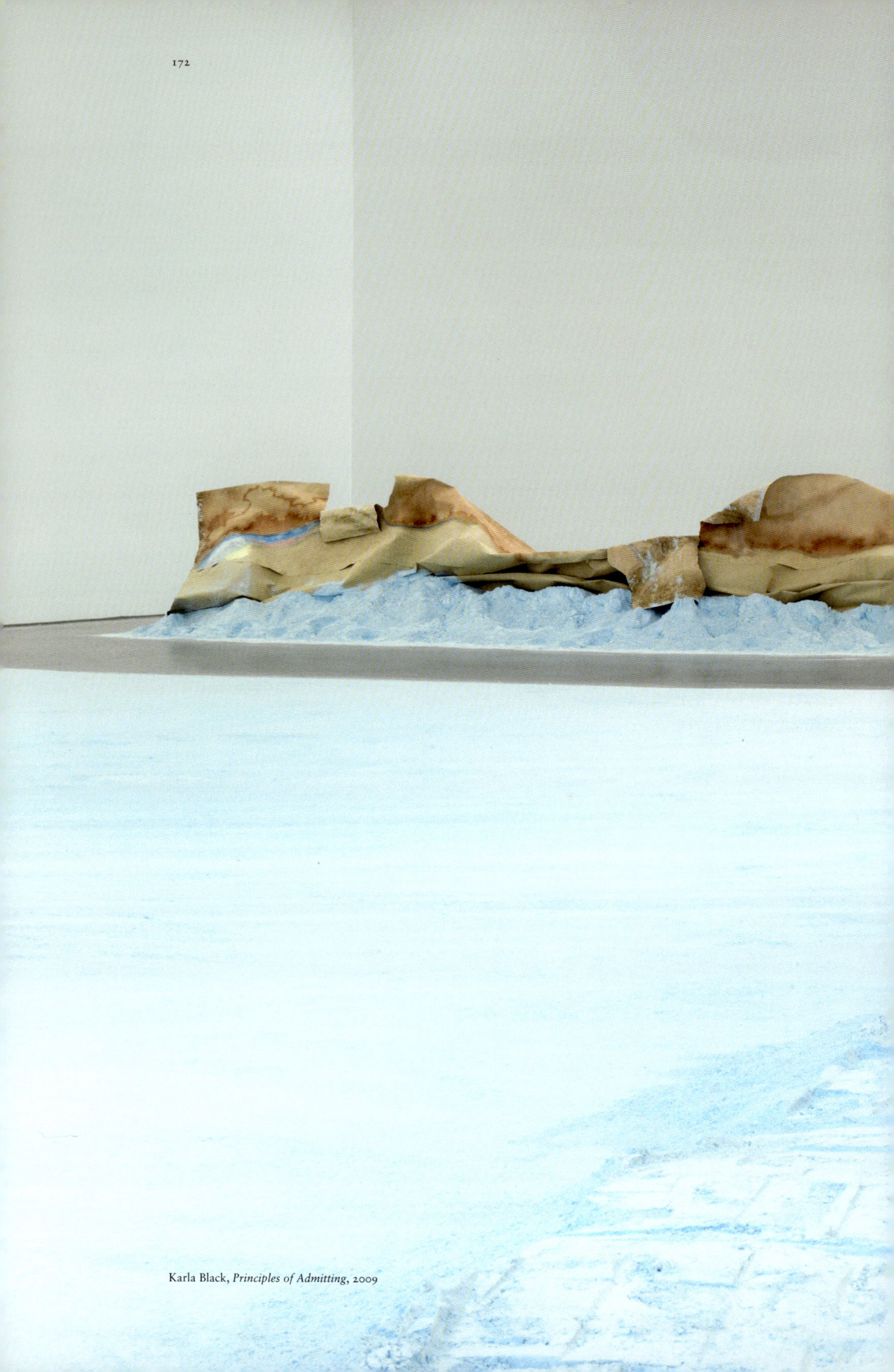

Karla Black, *Principles of Admitting*, 2009

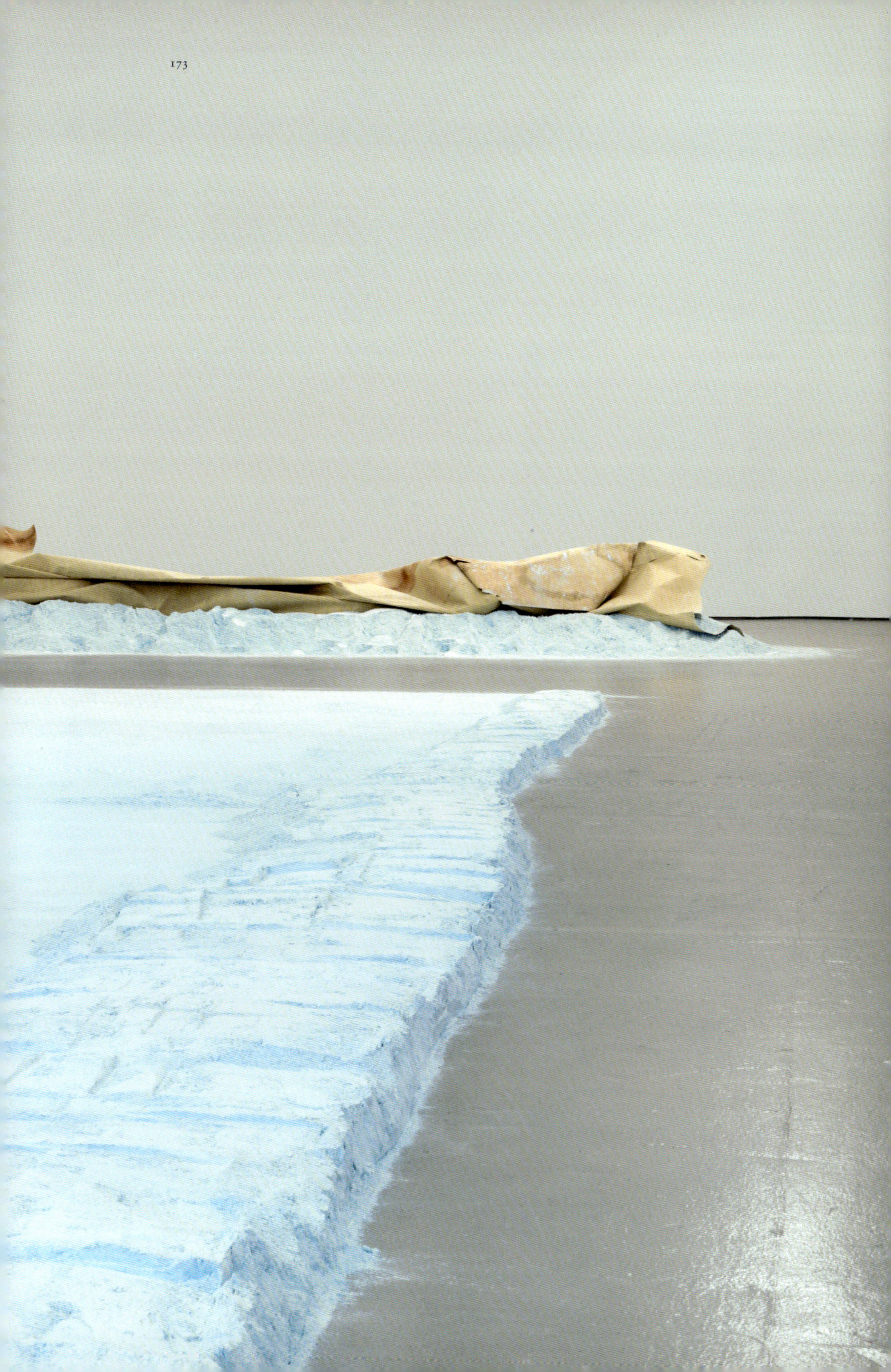

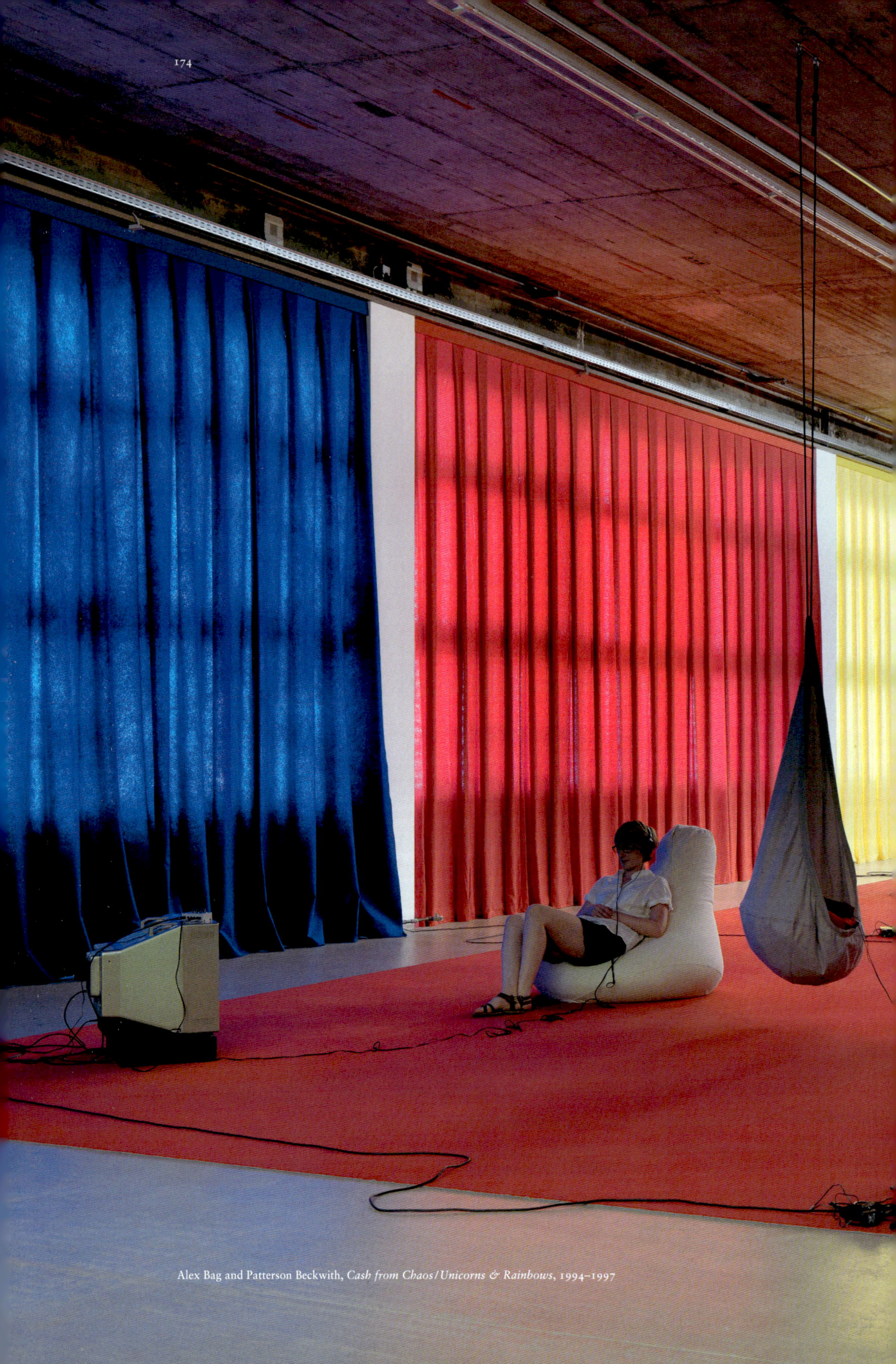

Alex Bag and Patterson Beckwith, *Cash from Chaos/Unicorns & Rainbows*, 1994–1997

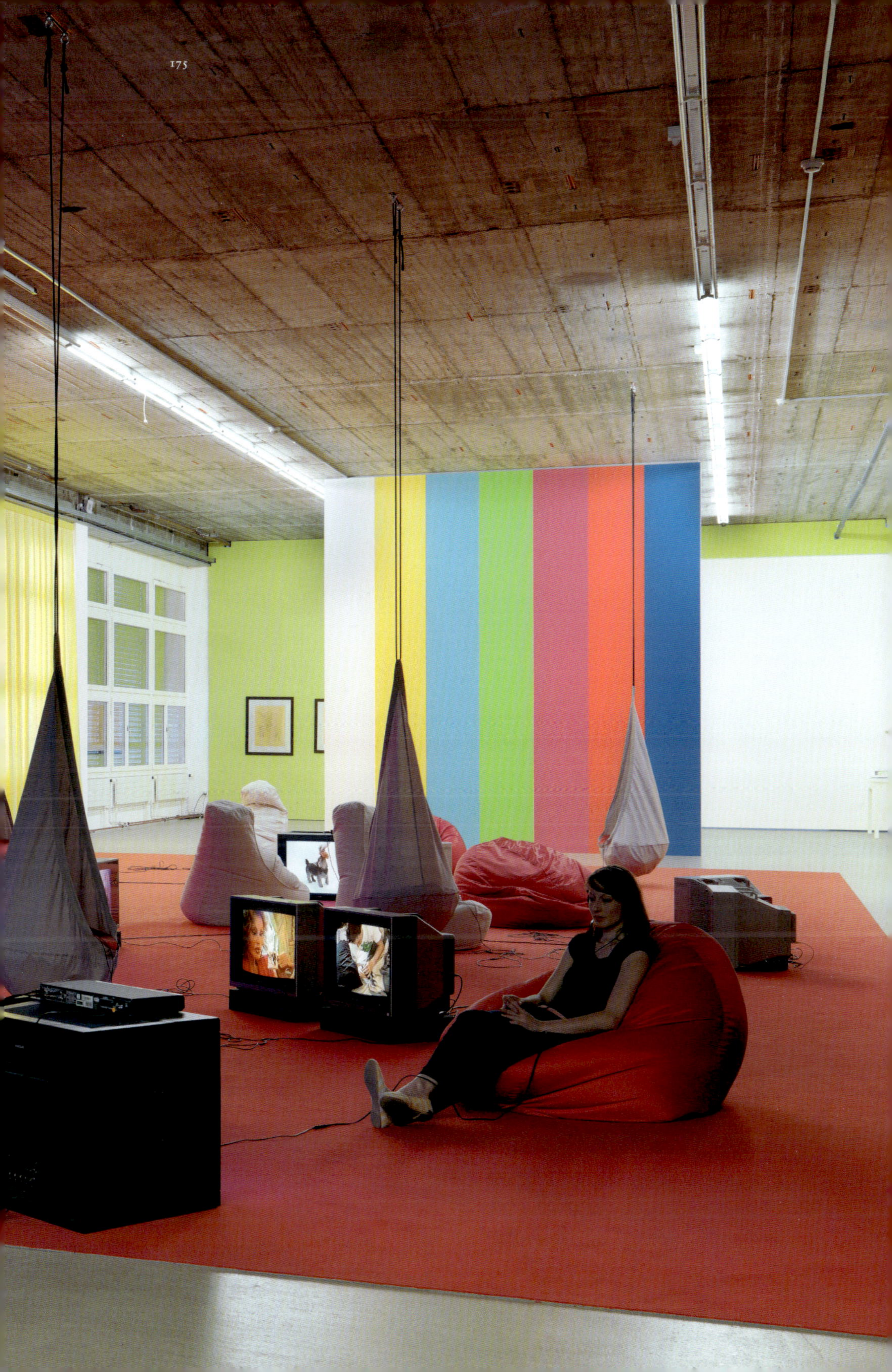

Flux

Cracks: Artistic-Political Activism and the Institutions of the Art Field

Oliver Marchart

A well-known diptych from Jörg Immendorff's Maoist phase seeks to illustrate the relationships between art and politics as well as art and the public. In Immendorff's picture, an artist-agitator barges into an interior, obviously a studio, yanking the door wide open and calling out to his fellow painter: "Wo stehst du mit deiner Kunst, Kollege?" "Which stand do you take with your art, colleague?" His left hand gestures out toward the street, where a protest march is passing by. In the interior, by contrast, a lonesome artist is sitting before his easel. Immendorff stages the decision art is challenged to make in a political situation. The question it is asked concerns its position; it is a question of partisanship: "Which stand do you take with your art, colleague?" Yet Immendorff's theatrical production reduces the range of options to a binary model. It is not a coincidence that the work is a diptych. The seam between the diptych's two parts is precisely aligned with the door hinge separating the interior on the left from the public sphere on the right—or, given that it is a door *hinge*, joins the one space to the other. So the agitator summarily demands a decision. Meanwhile, he has already breached the studio's seclusion to let in the light of the public sphere. The door is open; the moment is ripe for the painter to choose between the public and privacy, between the street and the studio, between collectivity and individuality, in short: between politics and art.

This last point, however, merits closer scrutiny. Immendorff's question is not just: *Which stand do you take* with your art? It is also: Which stand do you take *with your art?* The question of the artist's affiliation with a political collective goes hand in hand with the question of the specificity of artistic practice. The cause in whose service the artist makes his work not only determines its politics, it also determines the kind of art he makes. Immendorff, it would seem, has ruled out certain artistic practices, movements, and schools—a note pinned to his studio's wall lists "Pop art, New Realism, Concept art, Land art, Op art, etc." The artist in the picture is seated before an easel, brush in hand. The public on the other side of the divide is similarly characterized by an inscription, on the banner the protesters are carrying. It reads "Fight against Wage Exploitation—Workplace Hounding—Inflation—Political Oppression." The flag of the Communist Party of Germany is flying above the crowd. So the time has come for a decision between these two series: the succession of "Western" art styles and the array of social ills to be redressed through political struggle.

The picture was painted in 1973. The political slogans have changed in the intervening decades; so have the artistic practices. But the global wave of protest triggered by the occupations of public squares in 2011 seems to have initiated a return of politics into the art field. Questions of artistic-political activism are once again a subject of broad-based debate. And yet a certain skepticism remains palpable in most art institutions and media. It is likely rooted in the assumption that exponents of artistic-political activism are bowing to the Immendorffian model. When an artist steps outside the institution and puts his art to the service of a political cause, the reproach that he makes propaganda is not far off. For does not art that seeks to become political turn into propaganda? The function of propaganda is indeed to create legibility through simplification. In the art field, which prizes sophistication, simplification is taboo; in the political arena, by contrast—and in this regard the charge hits the mark—it is an indispensable feature of effective articulation. Does not every political articulation ultimately confront us with a binary question: Which side are you on? Ours or theirs? Are you in favor or against? Do you belong to the one percent or the ninety-nine percent? Are you part of the problem or part of the solution? In the final analysis, there can be no politics without a line of demarcation being drawn and a position being staked out. Does that mean, however, that one must subscribe to a simplistic politics—a politics that knows only black and white? Might there be an inverse strategy, a sort of *complex simplification?* Or would that be a contradiction in terms?

It is important to recognize that it is the rare case in politics when a *single* line of demarcation is drawn. When we are politically active, we move amid a multiplicity of intersecting lines. Whenever we stumble over one such line, we are compelled to take a position, even if that position may contradict other positions taken vis-à-vis other lines of demarcation. This conversely implies a considerable qualification of the first position and effectively necessitates strategic juggling of several and even many positions.

A performance by the Israeli collective Public Movement illustrates this observation. The piece—the very title, *Positions*, suggests its pertinence to our context—reconnoiters the uneven terrain of political subjectivation. The setting is minimalist: a cord is strung across a public square. One member of Public Movement announces a series of binary oppositions: "left/right," "male/female," "Israeli/Palestinian," etc. The participants are requested to take a side, gathering on one or the other side of the cord according to their decision. This protocol, though perhaps simplistic, highlights the *complex* nature of the political. Political action may reduce complexity to a binary decision, but it at once engenders its own form of complexity: the complexity of intersecting antagonisms. That is why politics is such a complicated business, because in reality, we are rarely faced with only a single decision between two options (the revolutionary situation would be the exception). Like the participants in the performance, we realize upon brief reflection that our own political positions (the plural is crucial) are far from consistent. Like them, we are perpetually compelled to switch between the sides of the line. For example, some who may have moved to the "left" side will take the Israeli side in the next step, while others will cross to join the Palestinian side. Their movements reflect the fact that there is no unified position on this conflict universally accepted by the left. Experience with the performance has generally shown that the groups will split up again and again, facing up to the possibility of an uneven, complex political terrain riven by internal contradictions. And so the observer will often see the participants beginning to hesitate. They rarely reach a point where there cannot be any debate which side one should be on. The difficulty is compounded by the presence of a public audience; it takes courage to reveal one's own political opinions, withstand peer pressure, and accept a certain political interpellation in the first place. No less important a complicating factor is the "objectivity" of the lines of decision that, once they are superimposed, keep the public engendered by *Positions* wavering.

The simplicity of the political field is a *complex simplicity* in this precise sense of a network of contradictions. By contrast, the "complexity" the art field usually takes pride in—and this explains the resentment with which large sectors of the field view artistic-political activisms—is a *simplistic complexity*: a form of complexity, that is to say, that lacks all internal contradiction and conflict. This amorphous complexity renders all so-called "artistic positions" interchangeable insofar as they can be put up side by side on a gallery wall or share an art fair booth without consequence or risk. The art field is governed by the law of fractional differences, which boil down to trademarks whose very uniqueness makes them fungible. Unlike in the political field, there are no decisions that are ultimately incompatible and mutually exclusive, the kinds of decisions compelled by real conflicts.

The moment an actual political line crosses the art field—the moment a real antagonism emerges in the field—panic seizes its institutions. For wherever *the political* irrupts in the form of an antagonism, a space of contingency opens up within the institutional framework. What suddenly comes into view is the mutability of institutional strictures and routines, the possibility that the institution might function differently, or might cease to function. A shocking thought to strike the mind of a functionary whose sole interest is in the smooth operation of routines. (I use the term "functionary" in the literal sense: someone who is interested exclusively in the functioning of his institution.) This may be one reason why many art-field functionaries harbor such resentment against activist art practices: the "artist-activists" are evidently the antagonism's emissaries, confronting the institution with the need to take a position—but taking a position would disrupt the institution's smooth operation.

But as the reigning doctrine would have it, art is political only when it refuses to take an unambiguous position. The "true" politics of art, we are told, resides in its (as we would now say: simplistic) complexity, its opacity and the wide berth it gives political praxis strictly conceived. The less explicitly political art is, this reasoning suggests, the more political it is—and so, the functionary concludes with irrefutable logic, there is no need at all for explicitly political art. As I have noted, this notion of what we might call a primordially political art—the notion that art is always political and, hence, that political art is superfluous—has become the reigning doctrine in the art field. Its undisputed master is Jacques Rancière, who has furnished it with philosophical legitimacy (which explains his immense popularity in the field), a role played, a few decades earlier, by

Adorno. It follows that any unambiguous stance, any unequivocal message or clear position, is taken to be an index of "bad art," since "good art," by the standard of this reigning doctrine, is distinguished by equivocation, ambivalence, and "complexity." The best art, in this view, is one in which anything that is political blurs into a haze (a vague intimation of political content can enhance its marketability, as long as it remains vague). Being apolitical is how art fulfills its political destiny.

By being anything but vague about its concerns and stakes, by naming urgent problems and voicing political demands, artistic-political activism defies this depoliticizing doctrine of the art field. This does not make it popular with the field's functionaries, but it lets it breach the walls of the art institutions and open them up to the political. It connects the art institution's interior to the world around it, creating—as activism that is both artistic and political—"door hinges" that connect the two spaces by articulating the separation between them. It need not do so in the straight-forwardly propagandistic manner of Immendorff's 1970s art Maoism. Still, the critical yardstick of artistic-political activism is not the simplistic complexity of the art field doctrine but the complex simplicity of the political. That is also why artistic-political activism does not simply tear the art institution's walls down but instead covers them with a fine web of cracks, as in the Leonard Cohen lyrics: "There is a crack in everything/ that's how the light gets in."

Martin Cordiano and Tomás Espina's installation *Dominio* (2011), which is in the collection of MAMCO, Geneva, neatly captures this sort of institution in an emblematic image. We come upon a scene that is reminiscent of a middle-class living room. At first glance, there is nothing out of the ordinary about it, but then we gradually realize that absolutely every object in the room is fractured or honeycombed with cracks: the table, the mirror, the tableware, the books in the bookcase and the book-case itself. The social space we all inhabit is no different. It may appear solid at first, but when we look closely, we find that its surface is not at all as smooth as it seems. It is crisscrossed by cracks that are nothing other than the offshoots of social conflicts—class conflicts, status conflicts, gender conflicts, ethnic conflicts, etc. They all traverse society, from the political system right into our living rooms. Crucially, they are caused not by history's "objective laws of development" or by a determinative eco-nomic basis, as orthodox Marxism believed. They are caused by political action: which is to say, by *activism* in the broadest sense of the word.

This activism, then, is by no means constrained to the political space narrowly conceived. It can make itself felt in any social domain and in any functional system, including the art field. And it can manifest itself in any dimension—from a general strike to individual protest. John Holloway, the in-house philosopher of Mexico's Zapatista Army of National Liberation (EZLN), has even argued that social change is the result of virtually invisible changes in people's everyday behavior. In his view, there can be something subversive about sitting in a park on a quiet afternoon and reading a book, especially when—here he takes up a suggestion in Horkheimer—that book is not useful for anything, making the act of reading an escape from the demands of instrumental reason. It produces no more than a tiny and barely perceptible *crack* in the edifice of capitalism. Yet innumerable such cracks are incessantly being produced. As Holloway sees it, the social world is a surface furrowed by millions of cracks. They provide a foothold for transformative action. They may be widened, and new cracks may be driven into the surface: "The opening of cracks is the opening of a world that presents itself as closed."[1] The resulting openings can be spatial or temporal in nature. Students demonstrating against the introduction of tuition fees—one of Holloway's examples—can head out into the streets or the park or take instruction into their own hands for a limited period, driving a crack into the university's walls. Cities teem with spatial fractures, he writes, with occupied buildings, autonomous centers, community gardens, etc. These spaces are "cracks, the sharp ends of social conflict."[2] Even if they eventually close up, they leave an impression that may live on and motivate the formation of new cracks.

That is why, Holloway argues, political activists need to take two essential characteristics of these cracks into account. One is their fluctuating and mobile quality. A crack, he writes, moves in unpredictable ways, spreading with varying speed, narrowing, closing, disappearing, or returning to the surface. A worker, to cite another of Holloway's examples, can water his garden today and demonstrate against Monsanto tomorrow. The residents of a building may simply live side by side today and join forces against the landlord's attempt to raise rents tomorrow. Cracks are in motion: "*Movement is what matters. The possibility of the cracks is in their moving.*"[3] The other essential characteristic is that cracks run from the visible into the invisible and back. Holloway suggests that we look at a wall and find a crack:

1   John Holloway, *Crack Capitalism* (London and New York: Pluto Press, 2010), p. 9.

2   Ibid., p. 49.

3   Ibid., p. 72.

At one end it is clearly visible, at the other end it is so fine, so tiny
that we have to strain our eyes to see where it ends. But the crack
extends and widens along that fine line that we can barely see.
If we focus just on the end that is clearly visible, then we understand
nothing about the potential of the crack, about how it can extend.
There is a line of continuity between the obvious and the barely
visible.[4]

The clearly visible end of the crack might be the Zapatista uprising or
a major anti-capitalist protest, whereas at its fine and almost imperceptible
end, a woman sits by her kitchen table, reads about the protest, and feel a
surge of enthusiasm, or someone in a park simply reads a book for pleasure.
Holloway acknowledges that one can never tell in advance whether such
hairline cracks may be widened into a major fracture. But that question
is exactly at the heart of the political struggle—the only way to answer it,
in the end, is to continually scan one's own environment for fractures and
drive forever new cracks into it.

And that is precisely what artistic-political activism does. It reminds
us, to the extent that we play the social role of an institution's functionary,
that we must not lose sight of the contested and fragile nature of all social
realities. In this way it produces a shift of perception within the institution.
Where we used to see a middle-class living room we now find nothing
but a web of fractures and cracks provisionally patched up with duct tape.
It heightens our awareness of the contingency that resides within the
institution: in other words, our appreciation of the fact that the institution
might just as well be organized differently. And it heightens our awareness
of conflict: our appreciation of the ubiquity of social struggles.

The implication for the institution is that it must enter into a
reflective relation to the logics of its institutionalization—including the
institutionalization of the public sphere that it is. What might such a
reflective institutionalization entail—especially in light of the demands
"artist-activists" bring to institutions of art? A public sphere in this sense
would initially require nothing more than infrastructure that makes things
possible. There is no forcing things, but institutions that are cognizant
of their own contingency and contested status can open up a space of
possibility. There can be no certainty that this space will not close up again;
but that is merely to say that, as always in the field of the political, such

---

4   Ibid., p. 73.

work cannot rely on any guarantees. And this in turn means—another aspect of reflective institutionalization—that the structure of the space must be subject to continual rethinking, realignment, and revision with a view to its potentiality. For instance, such a space must take on functions of public spheres that close down elsewhere. When, say, media do not live up to their mission by barring certain issues from public discussion, substitute publics are needed that assume the function of a quasi-medium. One responsibility of art institutions might thus be to make room for debates that are cut off in the major public media and to multiply information that is stifled in the general public.

On the one hand, such lasting engagement with the outside world would tie the institution to a larger political project that transcends the narrow interests of the cultural sector; on the other hand, it would entail a reassessment of the artistic practices the institution accommodates. The two are interconnected. And it is this connection between an institution's interior and its outside that the practices of artistic-political activism model in exemplary form. To denounce such practices as "insufficiently complex," "propagandistic," and "artistically inferior" is to fundamentally misunderstand both the essence of the political and the nature of one's own institution.

Hard to See: Race Relations in Contemporary Art Museums in the United States

Christian Kravagna

This essay situates the question of the significance of the museum of contemporary art in the temporally and geographically specific framework of the current debates over race in the United States. Without aspiring to more general conclusions, the discussion in the following pages will examine some aspects of how contemporary art museums engage with national and regional race issues and how their work relates to thematically relevant presentations in other museums within their respective local environments. A comparative study of a synchronic cross-section (spring of 2015) sets projects in contemporary art museums in Miami and New Orleans in relation to the presence of race issues in the inaugural exhibition *America Is Hard to See* concurrently on view at the new Whitney Museum of American Art in New York. This approach allows me to shed light on some ways in which contemporary art museums can contribute to the discussion of present-day dynamics of social inclusion and exclusion and the underlying history.

In the spring of 2015, I went on a four-month research trip to seven states in the American South as well as the cities of Chicago, New York, and Washington, DC. The question that guided me was: How did museums represent slavery, race relations, and the African American Civil Rights Movement? What was primarily a topic of historical research when I began my trip became unexpectedly topical while I was in the United States.

My trip coincided with the celebrations commemorating the 150th anniversary of the end of the Civil War and the abolition of slavery, as well as the 50th anniversary of the voting rights marches from Selma to Montgomery in March 1965. The signature achievement of the latter had been the passage of the Voting Rights Act, which enfranchised African Americans who had been largely barred from voting in the Southern states. The nation's postwar reunification and the partial successes of the Civil Rights Movement of the mid-1960s had bookended a century of freedom without equality, as described by James Baldwin in *The Fire Next Time* in 1963.[1] If it had taken a full hundred years from the emancipation of America's slaves to effective enforcement of their right to vote, the remembrance of the protest marches and Selma's "Bloody Sunday" in the spring of 2015 also raised the question of what to make of contemporary dimensions of discrimination and racism in the light of the challenges, struggles, and achievements of the 1960s. When Barack Obama, speaking at the celebration in Selma, noted that "we just need to open our eyes, and ears, and hearts, to know that this nation's racial history still casts its long shadow upon us," he was certainly referring to the growing number of incidents of lethal police violence against unarmed blacks, but also to the disproportionately high rate of incarceration among black men and the discrimination of African Americans in the American educational system.

The spring of 2015 would bring further police killings and the racist attack on a black congregation in Charleston, SC, as well as a growing debate in the media about structural racism and new forms of racial segregation in housing and education. A raft of publications would declare the demise of the illusion of a post-racial society.[2] Meanwhile, for several years, the protest movement spearheaded by Black Lives Matter had created a rich visual culture of anti-racism that frequently invoked slogans, motifs, and aesthetics of its historical predecessors in the Civil Rights and Black Power movements. The sway of the past over the present in contemporary race relations—what Obama referred to with the image of the "long shadow"—was also a running theme in popular music, from D'Angelo's *Black Messiah* and his widely publicized meeting with the former Black Panther Bobby Seale to Kendrick Lamar's *To Pimp a Butterfly* and his band's chain gang performance during the 2016 Grammy Awards ceremony and on to Beyoncé's *Formation* video and her 2016 Super Bowl halftime

---

1   James Baldwin, *The Fire Next Time* (New York: Dial, 1963).

2   Ta-Nehisi Coates, *Between the World and Me* (New York: Spiegel & Gray, 2015); Houston A. Baker Jr. and K. Merida Simmons, eds., *The Trouble with Post-Blackness* (New York: Columbia University Press, 2015).

show, which took inspiration from the style and symbolism of the Black
Panthers.

In most American museums dedicated to black history, historic
manifestations of racism, and the African American liberation movements,
the presentations give short shrift to the contemporary situation. The
narratives of their permanent exhibitions, most of which were installed
quite some time ago, usually end with the successes of the Civil Rights
Movement or Obama's inauguration as the country's first black president.
At the National Voting Rights Museum in Selma, for example, the sequence
of rooms concludes with an Obama Gallery celebrating the president's
election as a belated triumph of the various forms of civil rights activism in
the 1960s. By contrast, developments between the 1970s and the first
decade of the twenty-first century that played a major part in shaping race
relations today go unmentioned: think of the "War on Drugs," zero-
tolerance policies in schools and neighborhoods, and the commercialization
of the penal system in the Prison Industrial Complex. Taken together,
these policies have led to the mass incarceration of African Americans,
with social repercussions affecting families and entire neighborhoods.[3]

Exhibitions in art museums, especially ones with a focus on contemporary art, usually have a different rhythm than presentations in historical
museums. Their greater flexibility does not necessarily imply that they
engage with volatile political issues. Nor is my purpose in the following to
examine contemporary art museums under the aspect of their serving to
compensate for the gaps in historical museums. The significance of contemporary art and its presentation does not primarily derive from its ability
to respond rapidly to political and social grievances of the day. The above-
mentioned works of popular culture and the revival of ideas of the Black
Power movement in the context of Black Lives Matter on the one hand,
and the debate over the meaning of the Confederate flag prompted by
the Charleston shooting and Donald Trump's stance on the Ku Klux Klan
on the other, exemplify the antagonism between disparate politics of
history today. In this political climate, the contemporary relevance of art,
or of an institution's exhibition programming, may in fact hinge more on
which perspective on history it proposes. In connection with its radical
opposition to the concerns of political correctness, the glorification of the
past over the present expressed by the Republican slogan "Make America

3   Michelle Alexander, *The New Jim Crow: Mass
     Incarceration in the Age of Colorblindness* (New York:
     New Press, 2010).

Great Again" also speaks to a yearning for the recreation of a white and masculine America. While one side's understanding of the present moment and its struggle against racism is informed by a retrospective awareness of the Civil Rights Movement as an unfinished project, America's reactionary other side eagerly looks forward to the end of the first black president's incumbency as the close of an era and the rise of a society in which the conceptions of anti-discrimination policy that emerged from the movements of the 1960s are a thing of the past.

New York

In May 2015, the Whitney Museum of American Art opens its new home, a building designed by Renzo Piano in New York's Meatpacking District, with the exhibition *America Is Hard to See*. Coming in the late years of the Obama era—the country is getting ready for the primary campaigns in the run-up to the 2016 presidential elections—and with the contradictions sketched above dividing American society, the title is appealing, promising insights into how artists reflect on the social conflicts of their time. It quotes a poem by Robert Frost by way of a documentary film on Eugene McCarthy's 1968 presidential campaign in which the filmmaker Emile de Antonio explored the possibilities of an alternative politics. These political echoes are apt to stoke the expectations for an inaugural show the Whitney has conceived "as an opportunity to reexamine the history of art in the United States from the beginning of the twentieth century to the present." Which position will the museum's presentation of modern and contemporary American art stake out in the field of conflicting racialized politics of history? Visible from afar, the neon letters spelling "negro sunshine" of Glenn Ligon's *Warm Broad Glow* (2011) send a strong signal. Some forty out of the roughly four hundred artists with works in *America Is Hard to See* are African Americans, a comparatively large proportion[4] that suggests the Whitney's answer to the question of a revision of American art history: heightened attention to historically marginalized groups (of artists) also implies an expansion of the spectrum of themes and aesthetic practices. That goes for the more recent past, whose diversity the exhibition illustrates with a look back at the controversial 1993 Whitney Biennial, and even more for the decades through the 1970s, whose reflection in art is presented

---

4   Victoria L. Valentine, "At Whitney Museum, 'America Is Hard to See' Acknowledges African American Contributions to Recent Art History," *Culturetype*, September 27, 2015, http://www.culturetype. com/2015/09/27/at-whitney-museum-america-is-hard-to-see-acknowledges-african-american-contributions-to-recent-art-history/ (accessed October 15, 2016).

as an almost exclusively white domain in many museums even today.
America Is Hard to See seeks to integrate black positions into the stylistically or thematically focused sections without making a fuss about it; this lets it highlight—often with the help of descriptive wall texts—aspects of American history that art museums tend to gloss over (slavery, segregation, racial violence, and the struggles for equal rights) and at least hint at the art world's institutional racisms. Moreover, the presentation on three floors—long stretches of which are in fact fairly conventional—is punctuated by political interludes. Closely spaced small-format works of political art more narrowly conceived form a recurrent counterpoint to the dominant narrative of artistic styles and tendencies. One can be of two minds about this curatorial gesture, which effectively draws a distinction between museum art and activist art, but at one point it gives rise to the show's most conspicuous contribution concerning the nexus between the history and the present of racist structural violence: a selection of graphic art (by Isamu Noguchi, Hale Woodruff, and others) taking a stand against the lawless executions of blacks, a practice deeply rooted in the culture of the American South. The works were on view in the 1935 exhibition *An Art Commentary on Lynching* at the Arthur U. Newton Galleries, New York, in connection with a nationwide campaign by the NAACP calling for anti-lynching legislation. The curators might have related the conjunction of art and propaganda in these works from the 1930s to examples from the rich visual culture of today's anti-racist movements, especially since the latter is explicit about the parallels between lynching as the historic manifestation of "white terror" and the police shootings of black men in recent years. Without actually making that comparison, the note accompanying the excursion into 1930s political art brings the works squarely into the present by describing them as "unified in their insistence that—to use the language of our moment rather than theirs—black lives matter." Not coincidentally, the lynching motif recurs in a small work by Betye Saar on view in the interlude on politics in the 1960s.

Miami

Miami has two museums of contemporary art that, though different in size and orientation, are equally distinguished: the Pérez Art Museum Miami (PAMM) and the Museum of Contemporary Art North Miami (MOCA). The centrally located and well-resourced PAMM is a big player in the international art world, whereas MOCA, despite its international program, shows a greater commitment to catering to local audiences in North Miami, a city with a black and Latino majority. In its mission statement, it describes itself as "dedicated to making contemporary art accessible to diverse audiences—especially underserved populations" and acknowledges "the need to enrich the cultural life of the community." The high proportion of African American, Latino, and Caribbean artists in the museum's program of exhibitions and events reflects this ambition.

In March 2015, MOCA presents *Under the Bridge, Beyond the Beach and above the Muck*, a show of pictures and sculptures by the artist Purvis Young, a longtime resident of Miami's black Overtown neighborhood who died in 2010. A screening of David Raccuglia and Shaun Conrad's film *Purvis of Overtown* rounds out the exhibition. An autodidact, Young started painting in prison in the early 1960s. Beginning in the 1970s, he made gestural-figurative works on found boards, plywood panels, and similar supports that he publicly installed on walls in his neighborhood. Drawing on the materials in his immediate environment, Young created political, social, and religious imagery that brings the black experience into focus; recurrent motifs depict themes of incarceration, exclusion, and liberation as well as mass scenes of protesters, arms raised and carrying banners, that gesture toward high points of African American history such as the Civil Rights Movement as well as local issues like the large-scale real estate development projects threatening Overtown. Adjacent to downtown Miami, Overtown—called "Colored Town" during segregation—became hip after World War II, with black music clubs that drew comparison to Harlem. In the early 1960s, new highways cut through the neighborhood, driving out thousands of residents and largely destroying its economic structure, and then decades of neglect turned it into an infamous ghetto. More recently, Overtown has faced a wave of gentrification. "The combination of bad people and good land"[5] has lured powerful developers, whose encroachments have elicited increasingly fierce resistance.[6] So the exhibition at MOCA is timely, with a particular relevance to contemporary race issues that derives from Young's deep familiarity with Overtown and its history, which the museum chooses to highlight at a time when the underprivileged black population of its own neighborhood is once again threatened by expulsion as Miami sets about transforming itself into a global city.

5   Tony Roshan Samara and Grace Chang, "Gentrifying Downtown Miami," *Reimagine: RP&E Journal* 15, no. 1 (2008), http://www.reimaginerpe.org/node/1807/ (accessed October 17, 2016).

6   Michael E. Miller, "Overtown Anger Bursts into Flames as Construction Site Is Targeted by Arsonist," *Miami New Times*, February 3, 2015, http://www.miaminewtimes.com/news/overtown-anger-bursts-into-flames-as-construction-site-is-targeted-by-arsonist-6548845/ (accessed October 17, 2016).

In light of this nexus of race issues and questions of urban development,
a comparison between MOCA and the Pérez Art Museum Miami (PAMM)
is illuminating. The former Miami Art Museum was renamed in 2013
in honor of Jorge M. Pérez—a billionaire, Miami real estate kingpin, and
major art collector who donated $40 million, half of it in works of Latin
American art—and reopened in a building designed by Herzog &
de Meuron. A part of the staff as well as the larger public protested the
renaming, arguing, among other things, that it was out of proportion
to Pérez's donation given that Miami-Dade County had contributed the
centrally located land as well as $100 million. PAMM is of particular
interest for our context because its collecting and exhibition policies
emphasize the intention to improve the standing of Latino and African
American artists in an effort to paint a picture of contemporary art to
match South Florida's multiethnic demographic composition. The show on
view at the museum in March 2015, *Global Positioning Systems*, a survey
of themes of history and memory in contemporary art, features numerous
outstanding works by artists such as Fred Wilson, William Cordova,
Walid Raad, Paul Chan, Allan Sekula, and Carrie Mae Weems that address
the black experience, anti-colonial resistance, neo-colonialism, or the social
effects of capitalism and racism from a variety of angles.

After walking past the donor plaques prominently displayed in the
lobby right next to the entrance to the exhibition, the visitor touring the
show finds himself wondering more than once how the critical potential of
the works fares under the museum's specific conditions. One need not
share the view that only art that engages with the immediate realities of its
institutional framing can legitimately be regarded as political to take a
doubtful view of the status of critical art in this museum; compare the
skepticism Adrian Piper has expressed toward what she called "global
political art," a kind of critical art that situates the political primarily on
the plane of reference.[7] How, for instance, should we read the photographic
piece by Paul Chan (2007) documenting a performance during which
African American residents of a New Orleans neighborhood badly damaged by Hurricane Katrina staged Beckett's *Waiting for Godot* on an
intersection? How does this intelligent critique of the linkage between
urban zoning and the concrete suffering of an ethnic-social group play in a
museum that bears the name, and is sustained by the capital, of a developer

---

7   Adrian Piper, *Out of Order, Out of Sight*, vol. 1: *Selected
Writings in Meta-Art 1968–1992* (Cambridge, MA, and
London: MIT Press, 1996), p. 234. By "global," Piper does
not mean art that is disseminated throughout the world

but universal art, as distinguished from one that addresses
the relationship between work and beholder in the context
of the institutional conditions that inform it.

who plays a major part in Miami's transformation, with the attendant gentrification sketched above? Can PAMM's visitors draw a connection between Fred Wilson's already classic *The Colonial Collection* (1991), which highlights the colonial violence that was instrumental in the accumulation of some Western collections, and a museum whose purchasing power derives in considerable part from the profitable investment of global capital in local real estate projects? Other museums of contemporary art raise similar questions, but here they take on a particular nuance: PAMM aims for a global perspective while also underlining the city's and region's social realities in the arguments propounded by its projects. The two works by Purvis Young included in the presentation certainly have a very different effect than similar pieces on view in the concurrent show at MOCA. Where the latter portrays Young as an important artist whose social themes make his work very much topical in Miami today, his inclusion at PAMM has the feel of a tribute to a local autodidact, while what his art has to say is marginalized by the power of the global art-capital axis.

New Orleans

Two exhibitions are on view at New Orleans's Contemporary Arts Center (CAC) in the spring of 2015: a solo show of work by Radcliffe Bailey and a thematic group show exploring the influences of carnival traditions on contemporary performance art. Although neither presentation expressly refers to current events, the two exhibitions taken together make for a compelling example of how an institution of contemporary art can stake out a position for itself in regional culture and history as well as its city's ensemble of museums. In *EN MAS': Carnival and Performance Art of the Caribbean*, CAC gestures toward the processions, masquerades, and costumes that are omnipresent practices in New Orleans's Mardi Gras culture. In the French Quarter, the Louisiana State Museum Presbytère presents that culture in the perspective of a public institution, complemented by a black-community museum take at the Backstreet Cultural Museum in Treme. Where the political dimensions of carnival culture are sometimes lost from view in the city's tourist marketing today, the works by nine contemporary artists featured in *EN MAS'* highlight the "connections between masquerade and political criticism, spectacularity and social invisibility, and public space and national citizenship."

Among the works included in *Radcliffe Bailey: Recent Works* is the Atlanta-based artist's installation *Windward Coast*: a pile of thousands

of loose piano keys evokes an agitated sea from which, in the distance,
a single black head—a painted plaster bust dusted with glitter—emerges.
Like many other works by Bailey, the piece, which originally dates from
2009 and was recreated for the eighth time for the show at CAC, examines
the significance of the black Atlantic for American history and culture.
Each realization of the installation brings new variations, a creative
evolution Bailey describes as analogous to musical principles. When the
keys are taken to stand for European classical music, the passage across the
Atlantic carries Africans to death and enslavement. But the piano parts not
only represent the sea, they also read as driftwood, suggesting that the
glittering head bobbing on the waves may be interpreted as signaling the
resurrection of black culture out of the debris of colonial-era European
culture. In New Orleans, the violent force of the swells inevitably brings
the devastation of Hurricane Katrina to mind, in which the city's African
American population suffered more than other groups due to structural
disadvantages already present before the storm as well as less access to aid
and assistance during and after it struck the city. At the Presbytère, the
detail-rich exhibition *Living with Hurricanes: Katrina and Beyond* offers
more information on the disaster, but the centuries-long history leading up
to it subtly hinted at in Bailey's piece is absent from the presentation.

In a side gallery, *If Bells Could Talk*, a sculpture created for the show,
modulates the musical motif into a register that strikes closer to home in
the self-described birthplace of jazz. An oversized music stand supports
a platform on which an agglomeration of trumpets and trombones project
from an antique birdcage as though the liberating energy of this miniature
brass band had forced the doors open; a recording of the jazz trumpeter
Hannibal Lokumbe is playing. In *Congo* and *Clotilde*, large-format paintings incorporating objects, Bailey similarly assembles tokens of enslavement,
colonial violence, and liberation, covering them with a layer of black sand
as though an archaeological excavation were required to make them
accessible for closer examination. *Clotilde* takes its title from a slave ship
that reached the American coast near Mobile, Ala., not far from New
Orleans, fifty years after the transatlantic slave trade was outlawed—the
same interval that separates the achievements of the Civil Rights Movement
from today's debate over issues of race. The attentive visitor can draw
a multitude of connections between Bailey's work and sights in other
museums in the city. His references to the Middle Passage and the transatlantic transfer of culture, the Congolese symbolism in several works, and
even the archaeological aspect of the mixed-media pictures correspond

to themes of the exhibition *Kongo across the Waters* concurrently on view at the New Orleans Museum of Art, which traces the lingering echoes of African steps and rhythms in black dance and music styles across the South and presents objects found beneath the floors of old houses to spotlight the often clandestine persistence of African spiritual practices in America, pointing out the need for more work in the young field of African American archaeology. Bailey himself has one picture in the show that critiques the despoliation of Africa's artistic wealth, much of which ended up in Western museums.

The synchronic cross-section from the spring of 2015 I have outlined in the preceding pages is intended as a snapshot and not a sufficient basis for a substantial assessment of the museums I have mentioned. A look at their programming one year after my visits, however, suggests the continuity of the positions these institutions have staked out in today's debates over race. For instance, with strong references to African American and anti-colonial resistance movements, the Black Arts movement of the 1970s, and Black Lives Matter, the exhibition *Adam Pendleton: Becoming Imperceptible* at the Contemporary Art Center in New Orleans may be regarded as an extension of the discussion of politics and aesthetics initiated, with different historical and cultural references, in Radcliffe Bailey's show. Meanwhile, the Museum of Contemporary Art North Miami's distinctive interweaving of local and regional perspectives with national discourses, described above in the example of Purvis Young, Overtown, and gentrification, is also evident in the group exhibition *Intersectionality in South Florida*, which addresses the concurrence of repressive regimes of normalization of the body (racism, sexism, homophobia, classism, etc.), again tying the current debate back to the (African American, feminist, etc.) struggles for emancipation of the 1960s. Undertaking projects like these and presenting art of the first rank, the museums I toured propose compelling answers in the debates over race raging in the United States today and intervene into the struggle between controversial politics of history with stances anchored in their local environments.

"What Does 'Everybody' Mean?"—Radically Democratic Museum Education and Its Contradictions
Büro trafo.K

"What does 'everybody' mean?" This question marks the point of departure for our work when we develop projects as Büro trafo.K,[1] our Vienna-based collective for art, pedagogy, and critical knowledge production. We raise it because we do not want to let go of the ambition to address "everybody," while also knowing that this ambition is always impossible to achieve and must be renegotiated in each instance in light of the economies of attention and the exclusions that institutions generate. Since the 1970s, if not even before then, public museums have striven to be "for everybody," but as numerous social struggles and new museologies have illustrated, museums continue to produce structural exclusions.[2] "Culture for everyone" was a premise that entailed, more than anything else, the insistence that new audiences should be introduced to "high culture." Despite their democratic aspirations, museum officials usually harbored a paternalistic vision of knowledge regarded as valuable being imparted to visitors to museums and exhibitions whom they imagined as less knowledgeable. At the same time,

1 Büro trafo.K works on research and educational projects at the interface of education and the production of critical knowledge. In our projects, we embark on collective and emancipatory processes in which different perspectives come across each other and new spaces of agency come into being. trafo.K are Ines Garnitschnig, Renate Höllwart, Elke Smodics, and Nora Sternfeld. See www.trafo-k.at/ for more information.

2 See Tony Bennett, *The Birth of the Museum: History, Theory, Politics* (London and New York: Routledge, 1995); Carol Duncan, *Civilizing Rituals: Inside Public Art Museums* (London and New York: Routledge, 1996); Peter Vergo, ed., *The New Museology* (London: Reaktion, 1989); Alexander Alberro and Blake Stimson, *Institutional Critique: An Anthology of Artists' Writings* (Cambridge, MA: MIT Press, 2009); Andrea Fraser, "From the Critique of Institutions to an Institution of Critique," *Artforum* 44, no. 1 (September 2005), pp. 278–283.

the focus on the audience shone a spotlight on a field that had hitherto languished in obscurity: the practice of museum education. Starting in the 1980s, however, the desire to address "everybody" almost fell into disrepute; it is now widely regarded as naïve and imprecise. In their "public relations work," projects and museums have increasingly carved their audience up into various "partial publics" to be molded in accordance with a specific "target audience": if you walk into a museum, you have always already been identified by its advertising department and presented on the market of attentions, to be picked up—from the wall texts by the entrance to the evaluation form—where you have been placed. The associated birth of museum education as a professional field is very much tied up with this logic: its rhetoric, too, continually produces affiliations, groups, and differences. As we confront the privatization of an increasing number of institutions of art and education and the growing power of economic pressures, it would seem to be important once again to frame public demands and bring them up to date. What, then, is a museum's public?

In light of the contradictions and developments sketched above, we want to devote the following pages to a reexamination of the attempt to address "everybody" and reclaim it for a radically democratic politics. Museum education today is no longer merely about an affirmative introduction of new audiences to an existing and stable store of knowledge preserved in museums. Since the 1990s, proponents of a critical educational praxis in museums have generally acknowledged that calling in question the status of institutions such as the museum as sites of the canonization of truth production is an integral part of their work. This entails probing and displacing the boundaries of these institutions and involving all parties in efforts to bring about substantial and structural changes. In this process, old premises are time and again confronted with new questions: Who is everybody? What happens when the knowledge, and the wishes, of the "others" do not conform to the expectations of institutions and educators? Discussing exemplary projects selected from the work of Büro trafo.K, we want to reflect on educational approaches that propose a radical-democratic redefinition of the ambition to address "everybody": approaches that grapple with the exclusions institutions effect and the strategies designed to open them up to new contents and structures; that do not deny conflicts; and that articulate the ambition to stake out a position while leaving room for the unexpected and unforeseeable.

"Just because you exclude us doesn't necessarily mean we want to
get in!"

A sketch the designers Toledo i Dertschei developed in collaboration with
us shows the question "What does 'everybody' mean?" crossed out by a
drawing by the artist Petja Dimitrova.[3] The gap between the two letters "l"
in "alle" ("everybody") becomes an interstice or opening within the concept
itself. Two individuals strike out and demand a place inside the definition
of the universal.

If the question "What does 'everybody' mean?" stands at the beginning of each of our projects, it is because we are trying to become conscious
of the explicit and, more importantly, the implicit exclusions and distinctions that any context implies. It serves us as a methodological device that
generates awareness of the specific ways in which every project generates
an outside: we strive to see its blind angles, to recognize what it is trying to
avoid, we ask ourselves what it is the curators or we ourselves have not yet
thought of. In so doing, however, our interest is precisely not to then
address this imaginary "outside" as a target audience. Rather, we aim to
devise interventions that are capable of destabilizing the boundaries
between inside and outside. Interestingly, such boundaries often appear to
be invisible to the project's own structure. The point, then, is to render
boundaries—rather than marginalized groups—visible; and to reallocate
the distribution of what can be said, shown, and seen. For the latter is
indeed crucially determined by who was hitherto meant when we spoke of
"everybody" (or by the notion of a target audience), and so is amenable to
expansion and deconstruction. In other words, every new project takes on
the challenge of redefining what is understood when we say "everybody."
At stake are the possibilities and limitations of an alliance with the position
Jacques Rancière has called "the part with no part." What does he mean
by that?

The part with no part in Jacques Rancière

"Politics exists when the natural order of domination is interrupted by the
institution of a part of those who have no part," Rancière writes in his

---

3   Toledo i Dertschei's collective practice revolves around the question of how society can be shaped. Their work reflects on visual politics and regimes of representation while also developing "formally practicable" perspectives for action. See www.studiotid.com/. Petja Dimitrova is a visual artist and activist. Her practice is situated between visual art, political activism, and participatory cultural work. She lives and works in Vienna. See petjadimitrova.net/.

FIG. 2

book *Disagreement*.[4] The reference to the "part of those who have no part" highlights the fact that politics is inherently rooted in an equation that does not compute. The logic of the police, by ensuring the regulated distribution of the parts, produces not only winners and losers, but also parts the regulations do not provide for—parts that have no part. In a certain sense, the idea of equality Rancière draws on, in conjunction with the Enlightenment, had created a self-conception that made the entitlement to rights and a part in the social distribution conceivable. A revolutionary idea of the "everybody" who would share in freedom, equality, and solidarity emerged. However, this modern politics (which presumably found its most prominent expression in the French Revolution) engendered not only a model of equality but also new forms of inequality. Not everybody was "everybody": not everybody had the right to the same rights, a fundamental defect that has been debated extensively with a view to the issues of slavery, the rights of women, but also the unequal distribution of rights according to property relations.[5] After the French Revolution, the social parts had been redistributed. Yet their distribution continued to be policed and was based on a count that produced an uncounted remainder, a part with no part. When this part with no part lays claim to its part, politics happens. In politics, in other words, we are dealing with an equation that rests on a disproportion, which it thwarts by bringing it into the contestation. Rancière's term for this disproportion is the "incommensurable on which politics is based." The struggle over the social distribution, that is to say, is not merely a fight for larger or smaller pieces of the pie, it is a struggle over the core issue, the right to share in the distribution. Politics, for Rancière, is the disruption of the agreement among the shareholders who distribute the pie—more or less fairly, more or less agreeably—among themselves. "Disagreement" is Rancière's term for the political process of the demand to become part of the distribution and thus fundamentally dismantle it, the reclamation of the necessary reallocation of the agreement in favor of the incommensurable.[6]

Handbook: Working in the cultural field

Now, to think that the "part with no part" would even be interested in reclaiming a place in an institution defined entirely by others is a fairly

---

4 Jacques Rancière, *Disagreement: Politics and Philosophy*, trans. Julie Rose (Minneapolis: University of Minnesota Press, 1999), p. 11.

5 See Nora Sternfeld, "Whose Universalism Is It?" trans. Mary O'Neill, *transversal* (June 2007), transversal.at/transversal/0607/sternfeld/en (accessed October 6, 2016).

6 See Nora Sternfeld, *Das pädagogische Unverhältnis: Lehren und lernen bei Rancière, Gramsci und Foucault* (Vienna: Turia + Kant, 2009), pp. 36–39.

FIG. 3/4

strong—and quite possibly fantastic—assumption. To reflect on this point, we turn to the example of "Handbuch: Arbeiten im Kulturbereich," a project in which we sought to inquire into professional fields in the arts and culture sector with a view to their exclusions, while also building awareness of our own fantasies about opening up the field. Our emancipatory ambition was to contribute to a critique of society by examining privileges as well as exclusions, address inequalities, expand opportunities and the range of choices for the individuals, and make more room for migrant perspectives in the domains in question.

When we raised the question of "everybody," and hence of opening up the institutions, in this project, our first purpose was to undertake a critical reflection on the idea as such. In recent years, efforts to address so-called marginalized groups have led museums to launch a growing number of projects with a focus on migration; such projects have received targeted public and private funding support. In many instances, an emphasis on museum education is meant to underscore a project's relevance while also reaching out to new audiences. Conceptions such as "interculturalism" and "intercultural dialogue" are still in the ascendant. Yet these conceptions cannot avoid the question of where and in which places they actually pursue an "opening" of the institution rather than mere "audience development"—and in particular, whether they might be effectively obscuring the structures of discrimination. Furthermore, many museum education programs take for granted, and so reproduce, a fixed difference that is always already in place. Carmen Mörsch has put this point succinctly, writing that "the focus on 'culture' and 'hybridity' contributes towards a situation in which factors that define this power imbalance—for example, the unequal distribution of resources such as money, education or definitional power, the varying ability to capitalize on different knowledge (as well as spoken languages) as well as the ubiquity of everyday and structural racism—remain unnamed and unchanged."[7] What might a museum education practice look like that, rather than reproducing differences in paternalistic fashion, aims to redistribute both the power of interpretation and resources? That is a question museums face, and so do various forms and practices of cultural education outside the institutions that, like cultural institutions themselves, are part of the hegemonic order and "inevitably involved in the creation and confirmation of social norms and

---

7   Carmen Mörsch, "Beyond Access: Retrospective introductory thoughts on the convention on 'Art Education in a Migrant Society,'" in Institute für Auslandsbeziehungen, Institute for Art Education at the Zurich University of the Arts, and the Institute for Art in Context at the Berlin University of the Arts, eds., *Art Education in a Migrant Society/ Reflexions on a Convention* (2011), 11, via www.ifa.de (accessed July 31, 2016).

values, inclusion and exclusion, power and market, although potentially also in their subversion and modification."[8]

Building on these considerations, the next step of the project was devoted to a study of exclusions and spaces for action in the migration society in the example of professional fields in the arts, culture, and media sector that are often invisible and not addressed transparently even in the debate over labor and equality in the migration society. It quickly became obvious that the arts and culture sector is generally largely inaccessible as a potential professional field for working-class youths, with access particularly difficult for migrant youths. As noted above, apprentices and refugees are at most addressed as visitors or objects of research; they may work in exhibition installation, as attendants, or on the cleaning crew; but they rarely ever penetrate into fields where their authorship would be taken seriously and a career in the cultural sector would come into view as a possible choice for them. To address this issue and at least initiate change, we set up an online platform designed in a participatory process involving its potential future users.[9] Our goal was to chart and develop dedicated forms of access and discuss central exclusions in the field and its institutions while also implementing processes of appropriation. And when we speak of youths, migrant groups, or marginalized individuals, we speak of structural conditions that shape the world and condition individual paths. In other words, these people are not a homogeneous group, and the institutional construction of a specific group of youths—whatever label is chosen for them—as a "target audience" plays a significant part in the failure of strategies intended to promote participation.

So who are the agents, for whom should modes of access be established, and to which purpose? The desire for the inclusion of "everybody" confronts us with a multiplicity of questions and contradictions: "Just because you exclude us doesn't necessarily mean we want to get in!" The pointed statement boils down the critique of an inclusion not attended by a simultaneous change in the relations of power over the definition of

---

8   Jacques Rancière, *Disagreement: Politics and Philosophy*, Carmen Mörsch, "What is Cultural Mediation?" in Institute for Art Education der Zürcher Hochschule der Künste, ed., *Time for Cultural Mediation* (2012), 38, http://www.kultur-vermittlung.ch/zeit-fuer-vermittlung/download/pdf-e/TfCM_o_Complete_Publication.pdf (accessed July 31, 2016).

9   The digital handbook offers information on themes, practices, and professional fields in the cultural sector. Who works in the cultural sector? What does its everyday operation look like? How are candidates for jobs selected? And how can access to the field be created? Youths and young adults conduct research into the fields of visual art, book publishing, theater, media, and cultural projects. They interview protagonists and communicate their experiences and perspectives. The digital handbook offers insight into training and job opportunities. The platform is a networking hub connecting youths, youth workers, and professionals in the cultural sector. It also addresses current issues in law and labor in the migration society. See www.herein.at/ (accessed July 31, 2016). The handbook is part of the project INTERMEZZO implemented by maiz in cooperation with Somm and trafo.K, with funding support from the European Social Fund and the Austrian Federal Ministry of Education.

the terms of the debate. How can we engage afresh in each instance with the paradox that we demand access for migrants to a hegemonic discourse and thereby in a certain sense normalize and reproduce that discourse? In other words, how much room is there for youths to be politicized or empowered in a way not desired by us? Which possibilities do they have to stake out their own positions?

We were very quickly confronted with the fact that the permeability from the outside in that we called for is at odds with the concerns of the youths themselves, many of whom quite deliberately crossed a career in the cultural sector off their mental list of what they might do. Meanwhile, the arts, culture, and media sector itself (re)produces largely homogeneous structures that impede access due to numerous (often unexpressed) social distinctions and barriers; last but not least, there are very few jobs available in the field. One specific feature of the arts and culture sector is particularly relevant in this connection. The significance of cultural as well as social capital is considerably higher here than in most other social domains.[10] As educators and project authors, we must not overlook the fact that we, too, are part of the exclusionary mechanisms. Then again, this acknowledgment does not remove the need for all agents in the field to question their positions and do more than merely adopt critical positions that enhance their own value in the market. Or as Tom Holert has put it for the field of visual art: "The casual ease with which people adopt a posture of institutional critique obviously raises the question whether such 'criticality' is really all it's cracked up to be when the institutions at most modernize and upgrade their theoretical toolkits but refuse to make deeper cuts or engage in more caustic self-examination. We might also ask whether aesthetic reflexivity does not thus become—dialectically speaking, inevitably become—yet another source of economic and governmental optimization processes."[11] The point of art education, however, might also be to obstruct such inevitability, making acting in this way radically un-hip and unaffordable.

Such questions were very much on our minds as we developed, in the project "Handbuch: Arbeiten im Kulturbereich," an online platform that not only reflects on and avoids these contradictions, but also

---

10   See trafo.K, *Ausschlüsse und Handlungsfelder in der Kunst-, Kultur- und Medienarbeit: Ergebnisse der sozialwissenschaftlichen Begleitung des Projekts Handbuch: Arbeiten im Kulturbereich* (Vienna, 2014); Pierre Bourdieu, "The Forms of Capital," in John G. Richardson, ed., *Handbook of Theory and Research for the Sociology of Education* (Westport, CT: Greenwood, 1986), pp. 241–258; Pierre Bourdieu, *Distinction: A Social Critique of the Judgement of Taste*, trans. Richard Nice (Cambridge, MA: Harvard University Press, 1984).

11   Pascal Jurt, "Tom Holert im Gespräch über die Hürden der Kunstkritik: 'Man traut der Kunst vielleicht zu viel zu,'" *Jungle World* 34 (August 21, 2014), jungle-world.com/artikel/2014/34/50456.html (accessed July 31, 2016).

deliberately names and harnesses them. It pursues five questions, each of which operates on several and indeed sometimes contradictory levels:

1. How can individuals pursue their own paths and build the associated skills and knowledge in connection with work in the field of arts, culture, and media? (Level of self-definition)
2. Where do youths, apprentices, and migrants actually find work in the cultural sector? (Level of information)
3. How can institutions in the field be motivated to be more open toward youths, apprentices, and migrants? (Level of institutional critique)
4. How can we reflect on our various positions in the field of artistic, cultural, and media work and what would a dismantling of accepted knowledge look like? (Level of reflection)
5. And how can strategies and stratagems be developed to break through exclusions in the field? (Level of subversion)

"It's a fine building. One should occupy it."

When we were commissioned to curate a cultural-historical exhibition titled *Die 70er: Damals war Zukunft*, we similarly asked ourselves: In a blockbuster show at the Schallaburg exhibition center—possibly as many as 100,000 visitors or more were expected to see it—who might be "everybody"? It was important to us to develop a conception that, while appealing to a mass audience, would address marginalized stories, stage encounters between different forms of knowledge, and allow for conflict.[12] We accordingly sought to design the exhibition with a constant view to its educational implementation and leave room beyond the opening for the unexpected and unforeseeable actions.

We intended the display to become a space of possibility that would accommodate a negotiation of recent history relevant to the contemporary moment. This led us to develop a conception organized in seven chapters, each of which took a demand from the 1970s as its point of departure and concluded with questions topical today. Five debate spaces designed as contact zones and forums are an integral part of the exhibition. Each of

---

12 *Die 70er: Damals war Zukunft*, Ausstellungszentrum Schallaburg, March 18–November 6, 2016. Curatorial team: Büro trafo.K—Renate Höllwart, Elke Smodics, Nora Sternfeld, Ines Garnitschnig—and Hannes Etzlstorfer; scholarly team: Monika Bernold, Robert Foltin, Bertold Molden, Magdalena Rest, Dirk Rupnow, the artists; debate spaces: Lisa Bolyos, Claudia Hummel, Martin Krenn, Sophie Schasiepen and Ezgi Erol, Stefanie Seibold, and museum educators; architecture: Gabu Heindl; exhibition graphic design: Toledo i Dertschei.

these spaces was developed well in advance of the opening by an artist in collaboration with trafo.K, the architect, and Schallaburg's museum educators. Starting out from questions about the future, we engaged in a shared process of negotiation to design—and reject—strategies to involve the visitors, review the relevance of the curators' thematic choices, and sought to chart spaces of possibility between participatory ambitions and institutional routines.[13] In particular, we strove to intervene into habitual production flows and demarcations between curatorial and educational work and to use placement within the exhibition to disrupt its narrative arc. The show's final debate space raises the question that appears in the title of this essay: "What does 'everybody' mean?"[14] It marks the conclusion of the section on the theme of "The Museum of the Future"[15] and turns the focus on the Schallaburg as the exhibiting institution. In cooperation with the artist and art educator Claudia Hummel, a space was created that resists the customary neoliberal fashion of "participatory lounges" and functions as an intervention. Very much contrary to what many of them expect, the visitors—having reached the end of the exhibition—find themselves in an empty room. A single poster that reads "Es ist ein schönes Haus. Man sollte es besetzen."—"It's a fine building. One should occupy it."—and a wall text challenge them to become involved in the debate over the "history of museum occupations and the associated demands for the redistribution of resources such as money, spaces, access, attention," and to fill the room with their own things and demands.[16] In other words, the question of the future of the museum as first raised in the 1970s remains open. Our contemporary answer gestures toward the history of political occupations, reclamations, and activisms; and if we hope to go beyond the museum discourse of the 1970s by acting not merely "for everybody" but in an actual shared and divided space, it must be negotiated anew in each instance.

---

13   Whose education? What to fight for? What to set in motion? What does that have to do with me? How to live together? What does "everybody" mean?

14   Conception: Claudia Hummel in cooperation with Büro trafo.K; the architect, Gabu Heindl; and the educators at Schallaburg, Helmut Borek, Karin Bünger, Georg Clam-Martinic, and Johann Reitbauer.

15   The title alludes to Gerhard Bott, ed., *Das Museum der Zukunft: 43 Beiträge zur Diskussion über die Zukunft des Museums* (Cologne: DuMont Schauberg, 1970).

16   The poster quotes "an erstwhile squatter's remark about a building appropriated as an exhibition venue by the 6th Berlin Biennale (2010)." Claudia Hummel, debate space "Was heißt alle?" in *Die 70er: Damals war Zukunft*, exh. cat. (Schallaburg: Schallaburg Kulturbetriebsgesellschaft, 2016), p. 287.

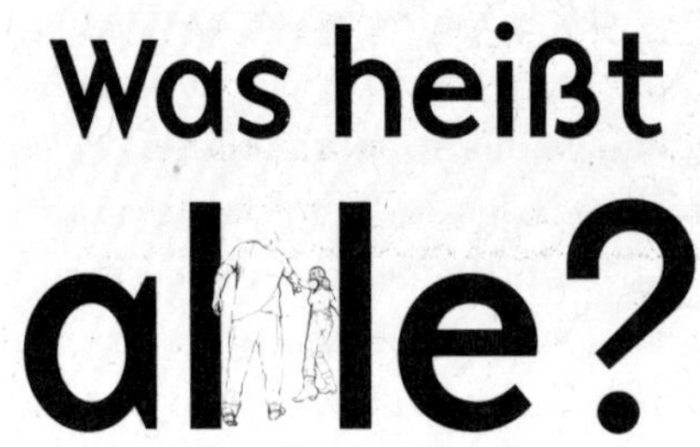

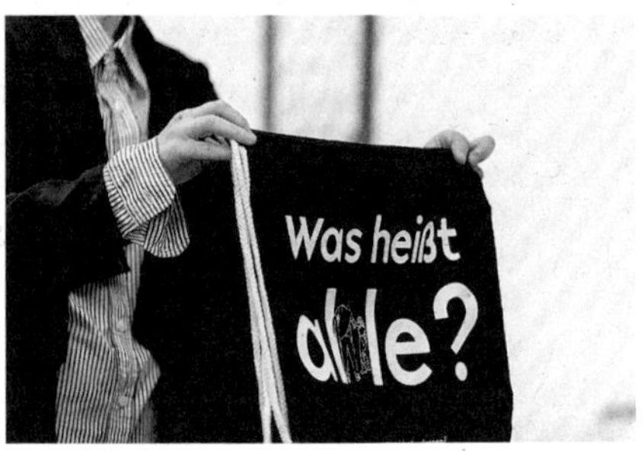

FIG. 1
Motif: Petja Dimitrova and Toledo i Dertschei

FIG. 2
Motif: Petja Dimitrova and Toledo i Dertschei

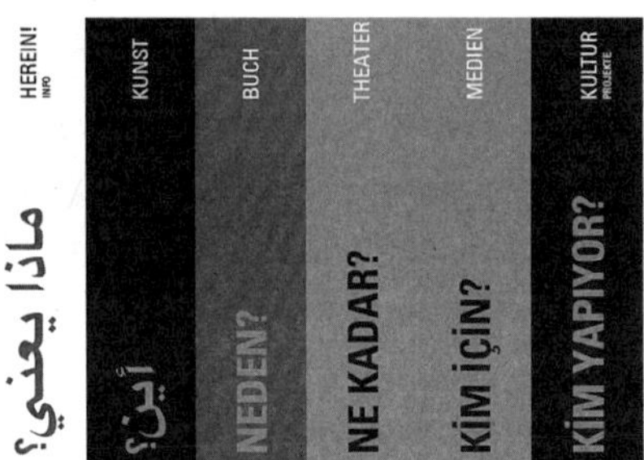

FIG. 3
Handbook Working in the Cultural Field, screenshot:
www.herein.at

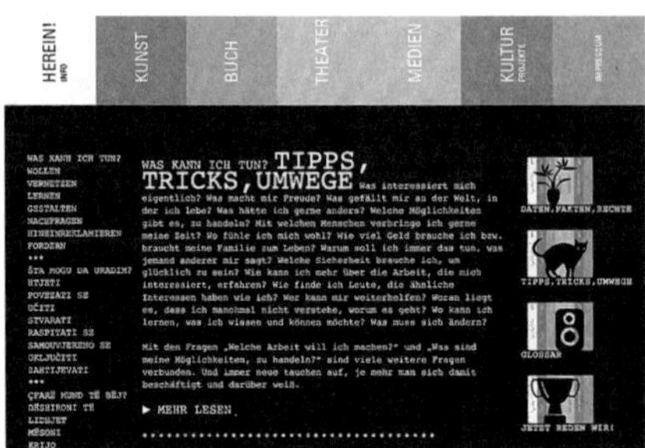

FIG. 4
Handbook Working in the Cultural Field, screenshot:
www.herein.at

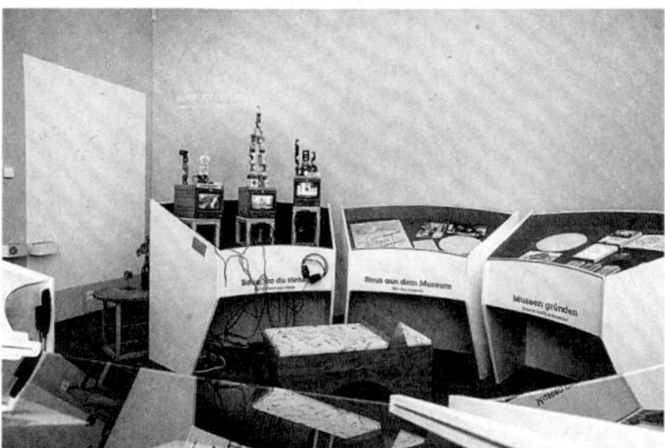

FIG. 5
Exhibition view, *Die 70er: Damals war Zukunft*, Schallaburg,
2016, photo: Sandra Kosel

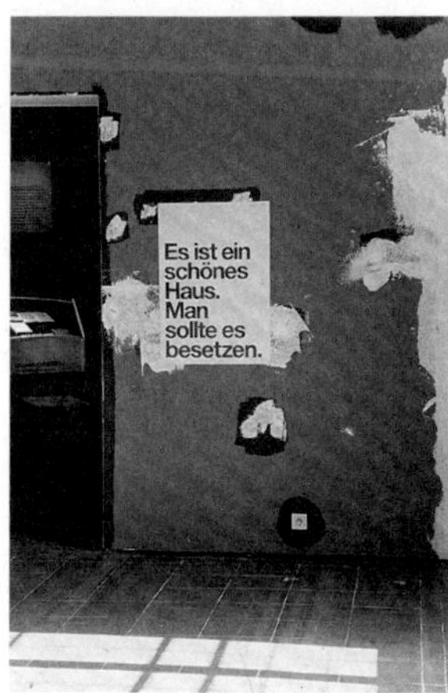

FIG. 6
Exhibition view, *Die 70er: Damals war Zukunft*, Schallaburg,
2016, photo: Sandra Kosel

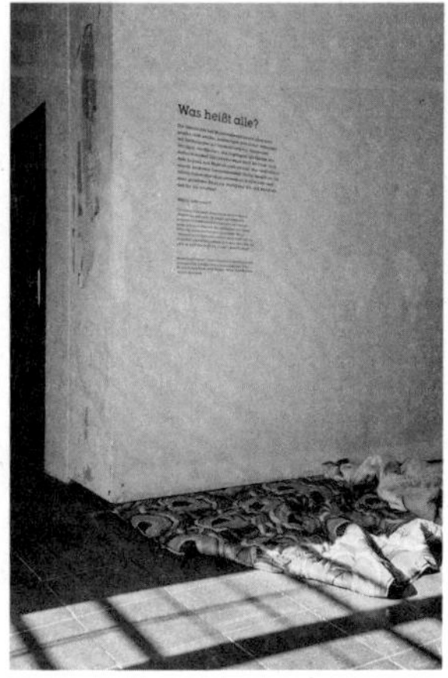

FIG. 7
Exhibition view, *Die 70er: Damals war Zukunft*, Schallaburg,
2016, photo: Sandra Kosel

The Applied Social Arts
Artur Żmijewski

Does contemporary art have any visible social impact? Can the effects
of an artist's work be seen and verified? Does art have any political
significance—besides serving as a whipping boy for various populists?
Is it possible to engage in a discussion with art—and is it worth doing so?
Most of all, why are questions of this kind viewed as a blow against
the very essence of art?

Yearning to Be Done with All This Consequence

Art had long struggled to gain autonomy, to free itself from politics,
religion, authority, and everything else that sought to use art for its
own ends. Independence was to have made art more important: every
avant-garde movement saw art as being equal in stature with such
reality-shapers as science, knowledge, politics, or religion. Aleksander
Lipski wrote:

> Non-figurative art has struck at the inviolable core of the traditional
> artistic paradigm requiring the depiction of figures. The global
> artistic revolution is therefore the culmination of the emancipation
> of art. The process whereby art severed all ties and allegiance to
> externalities such as politics, religion, philosophy, technology, and

the mores of the day was complete with the abandonment of one last principle—that of signification.[1]

The desire to be an active agent creating a social and political environment came up against a hidden enemy, however. That enemy was—and still is—shame. Politically committed art has often come to a tragic end. Artists supporting totalitarian regimes, like the Nazi sculptors Josef Thorak and Arno Breker, or filmmaker Leni Riefenstahl, compromised the very possibility of art becoming an instrument of politics. Polish art owes its sense of shame to its fling with socialist realism.

Guilt and shame associated with the past alongside the desire for art to be an active, contributing presence in public life has produced a paradoxical effect. All consequences attributable to art are now suspect; every visible change occasioned by its commitments has come under fire. Even the unseen authority that comes from the co-creation of symbolic realities that lend structure to our shared world, whether we like it or not, is being challenged. That tangle of shame, fear of appropriation, and the desire for influence has led to alienation. Shame has set in motion the mechanisms of repression and denial. Instead of drawing enjoyment from the outcome of their actions, the visual and performing arts are content merely to dream of such outcomes: fantasy has supplanted reality.

The autonomy of art has therefore made it "inconsequential." The actions of art no longer have any visible or verifiable impact. The deficit that Peter Bürger once discerned in bourgeois art has made its way into high culture: "the exaltation of art above day-to-day experience [is] typical for the status of a work of art in a bourgeois society. [...] Aestheticism is also a manifestation of art's failure to produce social consequences."[2] Naturally, social consequences have occurred, but not necessarily the ones that were most desired. Over the last fifteen years or so, these consequences have included: 1) Scandals breaking out over the topics art proposed to introduce into public debate. 2) The continuing brutalization of public debate has been attributed by *Gazeta Wyborcza* journalist Anna Zawadzka to the violent language used by art in the 1990s and the resulting media backlash. 3) Players from the realm of politics "learning" how to use subversive strategies that had once been proper to art. Subversive strategies "are the best example of Benjamin's proposed shift of emphasis from

---

1 Aleksander Lipski, *Elementy socjologii sztuki: Problem awangardy artystycznej XX wieku* [Elements of the Sociology of Art: Issues of the Artistic Avant-Garde of the 20th Century] (Wrocław: Atla 2, 2001).

2 Peter Bürger, *Theory of the Avant-Garde*, trans. Michael Shaw (Minneapolis: University of Minnesota Press, 1984). Originally published in German as *Theorie der Avantgarde* (Berlin: Suhrkamp, 1974; 2nd ed. 1980).

'content' to 'apparatuses of production' that enable one to use 'foreign' representations in making one's own work."[3] One instance of such subversive action was when right-wing deputies to the Polish parliament Witold Tomczak and Halina Nowina-Konopczyna removed the stone (meteor) from the prone figure of Pope John Paul II (Maurizio Cattelan's *La Nona Ora*) during an exhibition in Warsaw's Zachęta National Gallery of Art in December 2000. Tomczak and Konopczyna demonstrated they could "read and understand" the strategies of art, and were capable of using them. Once Tomczak and Konopczyna learned how to perpetrate a transgression, and violate the taboo associated with gallery spaces, they simply responded "in kind," using the language of gestures and visual action, the language of performance. In 1997, Katarzyna Kozyra used a hidden camera to film women in a Budapest bathhouse, and did the same in a men's establishment two years later. The resulting film was shown at the Venice Biennale, causing the inevitable uproar in the Polish press. Repetition and media coverage helped bring this "denunciatory" strategy into the mainstream. In 2002, newspaper editor Adam Michnik secretly recorded film producer Lew Rywin when the latter came asking for a bribe, while in 2006 member of parliament Renata Beger filmed her privately conducted negotiations with other politicians and released the recordings to the media. Kozyra, Michnik, and Beger all engaged in similarly questionable behavior while emphasizing the ends justifying their choice of means. Transgression has thus become a valid political strategy. Since then, a whole series of "negative" transgressions or violations of democratic taboos have been perpetrated by education minister Roman Giertych. 4) Violating one set of taboos leads to the emergence of other taboos (Joanna Tokarska-Bakir); perhaps art contributed to redrawing the map with its focus on some parts of the body politic, as a result of which others became taboo.

Art has therefore struggled to retain its power to act, but it should have remained as perpetually neutral as Switzerland in its exercise. And what would constitute fair use of that power? Let me quote an exhibition invitation sent out over the Web: "A profound interest in the physical and mental limitations of human beings has become the wellspring of Żmijewski's artistic inquiries, leading to questions his bewildered viewers ineffectually seek to answer." The foregoing provides a simple definition of what artists should make viewers: bewildered recipients ineffectually

---

3   Łukasz Ronduda, *Strategie subwersywne w sztukach medialnych* [Subversive Strategies in the Media-based Arts] (Krakow: Rabid, 2006).

looking for answers. Evidently, art produces states of helplessness and generates questions to which there are no answers. The word "ineffectually" bespeaks the alienation art has unknowingly lapsed into. Asked what made him become an actor, Jeremy Irons, known for his portrayal of tragic lovers (*Swann's Way, Lolita*) answered that he wanted to be "outside of society."

Duty and Rebellion

The consequence of the trauma of "being used" is refusal. Guilt and shame have been encoded in art as a "flight from"—an ongoing process of inner negotiation well-expressed in the title of an exhibition Grzegorz Kowalski and Maryla Sitkowska mounted on the centenary of the Academy of Fine Arts in Warsaw: *Duty and Rebellion*.[4] Even though the exhibition concerned the academy as an institution, its title was indicative of a present split within art. A split that allows art to "work for" the state and the national economy, to serve society as a shaper of environments, producer of visual information systems, designer of interiors and industrial goods, in short—to do its duty. On the other hand, art is kept from lapsing into dependence on the authorities by its rebelliousness, because it insistently challenges the taboo, nurtures dreams, proliferates freedom, and produces social knowledge (art can be said to be an open university of knowledge). Art constantly offers and denies its services to the powers that be. In doing its duty it usually does not cross a certain line marked by shame. The deadlock between duty and rebellion does not permit identification or affinity with other discourses that are somehow associated with authority. At most, art can impersonate or lampoon them: imitate the language of politics and religion, lampoon the language of the media, go for the grotesque. A sense of duty attenuates all attempts at rebellion, while outward rebellion compromises duty. This sets the frame for art, confined within the bounds of duty and subject to an ethics of, necessarily noble, rebellion delimited by shame. Thus does art erect a cognitive barrier for itself. Shame acts as an inner "parole officer" making sure rebellion is not taken too far. Art may be political as long as it stays away from politics— it can act politically in galleries but not in real-life debates unfolding in a different communal space, such as the media. It may be social as long as it does not produce social consequences. In the Nieznalska affair, for

---

4   *Powinność Bunt: Akademia Sztuk Pięknych w Warszawie 1944–2004* [Duty and Rebellion: The Academy of Fine Arts in Warsaw], Galeria Zachęta, Warsaw, September 17–October 24, 2004.

instance,[5] the accusations in the media, the indictment, and the hearings in court were treated by Dorota Nieznalska and her circle as a calamity rather than an opportunity to practice art "by other means." They balked at the prospect of exerting social impact.

Having an effect implies some kind of power, and having power is what art is most afraid of. The problem being that it already has power. Art has the power to name and define, to intervene in the workings of culture, exert pressure on elements of the social structure by turning them into artifacts (artworks). And every artifact is after all an apparatus for actively modeling fragments of reality. If politics is the power to name things, art has that power—perhaps even in spite of itself. Even a love story is an agent of cultural power because it can induce or channel emotional needs.

Let's get back to the freedom associated with rebellion. Is rebellion in art a manifestation of freedom? No, because it is limited by duty. Rebellion has its limits, and these are reached much earlier than the ones laid down by civil and criminal law. Rebellion has been harnessed to achieve a dialectical rupture. Where there is no rebellion, duty reigns, and art is reduced to the ancillary function of satisfying social needs and supporting the authorities. Rebellion must be present to offset the performance of shameful duties. That is why it is part of the package with its illusion of autonomy. Rebellion is, so to speak, "a duty."

Since the 1990s, art has been growing increasingly institutionalized. Institutional critics, now in charge of defining the remit of art, have been moving to mitigate art's "ideological turpitude." Fantasies about the alleged "needs" of the marketplace are also discouraging more radical forms of expression. Defiance can only be taken so far nowadays, and besides: the art market will also commodify rebellion. Art is becoming more and more anodyne.

The Idiot Savant

Shame constitutes a deep emotional substratum of art. Shame at having been implicated in power relations and endorsing totalitarian regimes prevents it from engaging in politics or explicitly creating discourses of

---

5   In 2001, Dorota Nieznalska showed a cruciform lightbox
     at the Wyspa Gallery in Gdansk. In the center of the cross
     was placed a photo depicting male genitalia. The object was
     accused of offending religious sentiments, and a lengthy
     court case ensued.

knowledge. Anything political and scientific can only be a by-product of art. Owing to this reluctance to "take ownership of knowledge," attempts to call attention to social problems or discuss areas society would otherwise be indifferent to are accompanied by opposition and even hostility towards discourses appointed to handle these problems and issues, i.e. science and politics. Autonomy in art has gone so far as to become a measure of ideological purity, an acid test of "artistic integrity." Symbolic power, strength through knowledge, openly political attitudes are simply rejected.

On top of it all, one has to contend with the ignorance of artists. As Marcin Czerwiński wrote back in the 1970s, artists do not have "the ability to translate intuition into discursive language" and thus rely on "the germs of truth scattered across reality that have the potential to develop into either ideas or images."[6] That is one of the reasons why art has been called a social symptom. The euphemism refers to the unwitting, intuitive way it performs an assigned task. Artists as creative individuals are, according to this view, unwitting mediums of social processes. Willingly or not they visualize its crucial junctures in a perfectly mindless way. That makes the artist an idiot savant of sorts: someone with interesting and important things to say but no idea how these things came to them or what use to put them to. Czerwiński calls such a state "ideological abstinence," while Joanna Tokarska-Bakir has this to say on the subject:

> The artists of today might in a somewhat nineteenth-century way be perceived as secularized high priests who, acting "through the symbolic medium that is the physical human body," try to act out ritually a certain form of unexplored social relations that has come to dominate the world. The problem being that the relations they want to express through art are understood neither by themselves nor by the societies they want to reveal them to.[7]

It might, in fact, be in the interest of society to keep artists ignorant to some extent. The cognitive procedures of art based on risk and intuition seem threatening. The lameness of theoretical education in art schools might be a symptom of unconscious reluctance on the part of the community to enhance the intuitive tools of art.

6   Marcin Czerwiński, *Samotność sztuki* [The Solitude of Art] (Warsaw: PIW, 1978).

7   Joanna Tokarska-Bakir, "Energia odpadków" [The Energy of Waste], *Res Publica Nowa* 3 (2006).

Overcoming Alienation

Is there a way out of this trap? Is it possible to stop defining what does and does not befit a client of the authorities, of business, and even a rebel? Art has already made a step towards doing away with this dialectics. It has assumed the position of a judge, an evaluator—the paradoxical position of an "involved observer." It has elaborated strategies of social critique—a hermeneutics of the "socially evident." With her action where she peeled potatoes in Warsaw's Zachęta gallery, Julita Wójcik encouraged us to read that commonplace activity as a statement about the shifting battlefield, a nod at things that are really hidden and outside the pale of high culture. Wójcik contributed to changing the protagonist: the nature of reality is determined by an "invisible majority," not by exotic exceptions. Critique along these lines can involve either artistic identification with "the causes of evil" or interventionist and remedial action insofar as that is possible. These are the constituents of a paradigm shift involving explicit support for processes of modernization or discourses of knowledge, sometimes even agreeing to undertake topical intervention and negotiate on behalf of vulnerable groups. One can say that this has partly helped overcome the alienation of art, its shying away from consequence, its refusal to exert any real and verifiable influence. But there is more at stake: regaining control over the ideology that leads to the unthinking generation of autonomy and is the cause of continual regress, and limiting the audacity and scope of artistic action.

The Ignorant and the Illiterate

One of the reasons for the alienation of art is that it relies on the language of images. Despite their immediacy, images remain unclear to representatives of other disciplines. Pictures are not texts, they are read "all at once"; all their meanings are taken in with a single glance. Such a suspension of linear reading, and the fact that meaning reveals itself in a flash and opens up a whole range of associations is tantamount to "cognitive violence." There is less scope for "proprietary images" than reading a text provides. Texts stimulate the imagination: when we read we see images—a mosaic of visualizations emerging from the memory and "superimposed onto" the text. Therein lies the blankness of words: a word is not the things it names. Images are bolder in the way they refer to the object depicted. "In the image, [...] the object yields itself wholly, and our vision of it is *certain—*

contrary to the text or to other perceptions which give me the object in a vague, arguable manner, and therefore incite me to suspicions as to what I think I am seeing."[8] Confronted with a picture, the imagination works not to fill in the blankness of words, but to determine "what is it that I see?" Yet what else can the thing I see be, since it is already "everything there is?" The inability to read images is surely a form of illiteracy, and experts from other fields could do with a few remedial classes. The ignorance here is twofold: artists are seen as ignorant by experts in other fields and vice versa; experts in the field of, say, science or politics are as helpless as children when it comes to "reading" images. Anthropology, for one, holds the view that art's involvement in various kinds of social criticism brings unclear effects:

> Documentary practice has moved closer to fine arts photography—relying on more subtle and abstract forms of photographic expression—at the same time that much fine arts photography has evolved to a kind of diffused social criticism, much more suggestive than evidential or literal, emerging more from the photographer's *view* of society than from a sustained analysis.[9]

The findings that artists put forward are seen as too ambiguous and not verifiable in any scientific way. But this only shows how bungling science is when faced with an intuitive medium, how prone it is to "cognitive fundamentalism." The result is another ideological debate in which opposing arguments are derided as being unclear, vague, ambiguous, etc. The passage quoted above also tells us that science has learned "more subtle and abstract forms of photographic expression" from art. Now that it has "become aware" of the cultural ubiquity of images, does science not want to dominate over the ways they are read? Just as it has dominated our thinking about knowledge, by peremptorily persuading us it is the only credible source of that knowledge?

Furthermore, the knowledge that emerges as the product of artistic activity is obstinately reduced to the status of a merely aesthetic proposition by experts from other fields. Even though art literally "shows" what it has come to know, and its knowledge is discursive and lends itself to reasoning,

---

8 Roland Barthes, *Camera Lucida*, trans. Richard Howard (New York: Farrar, Straus and Giroux, 1981), p. 106. Originally published in French as *La Chambre Claire* (Paris: Editions du Seuil, 1980).

9 Douglas Harper, "On the Authority of the Image: Visual Methods at the Crossroads," in *Handbook of Qualitative Research*, ed. Norman K. Denzin and Yvonna S. Lincoln (Thousand Oaks, CA: Sage, 1994), pp. 403–412, here p. 409.

the cliché that art is merely a producer of aesthetics is so ingrained that it produces an "indifference effect" among experts from other fields. The knowledge art has generated remains inaccessible to them—they are unable to read it. Meanwhile it was none other than an anthropologist who wrote the following passage:

> In this language [of film] individual images/frames are words, shots and camera angles are the inflectional elements, while editing provides the syntax. [...] A series of images, arranged—organized—according to a certain convention (the grammar of cinema) into a collection of takes directly linked to one another in terms of meaning, makes up a phrase of editing. [...] Depending on the way images and shots are spliced together, on the phrases used in editing, the idiom of film may be used to construct "epic phrases," declarative sentences of sorts, depicting a slice of life, an action sequence, fragments of an event. One can also compose (edit) so-called "reasoned phrases"—through the skilful arrangement of semantically unrelated visual and/or sonic (verbal, musical) fragments—thus evoking associations, bringing out analogies, and even constructing metaphorical sentences. In effect, a cinematic text may assume forms resembling discourse, and thus satisfy the basic requirement made of a scientific language.[10]

Virus or Algorithm?

As I have indicated, art has, of its own accord, rejected consequences, and turned its back on effects. Nonetheless, it still manages to come up with useful cognitive procedures. Existential algorithms, the use of which makes it possible to "keep your eyes open" when exploring social structures, allow one to enter into hidden places and true relations. In the cognitive equation we construct out of known and unknown qualities so that we may, in solving it, make the world a more transparent place, art has replaced speculation with existence. Existence speculates, thinks, and comes to know itself. Rather than drawing graphs, art becomes involved in real situations. Its cognitive strategies do not place reality in brackets like science does. It goes beyond the bracket—knowledge emerges within life, it springs out

---

10   Ryszard Vorbrich, "Tekst werbalny i niewerbalny"
     [Verbal and Non-Verbal Text], in *Antropologia wobec
     fotografii i filmu* [Anthropology of Photography and Film]
     (Poznań: Biblioteka Telgte, 2004).

of emotion, visions, and sensations, out of real experience. It is all these
things at once. It is suffused with contradictions and anxiety, mistakes and
hopes, good and ethical deficiency, authoritarianism, and timidity. In order
to know reality, art does not patronize but becomes one with it. "Impossible," science would protest, "the observer must be external with respect
to the object under observation. S/he is placed outside by the very act
of observation." Art, meanwhile, claims that this need not be the case.
The bracket and its observer intermesh in a total cognitive experience.
The observer emerges out of it through the image which becomes both the
gateway to knowledge and its source—a referent, an address, a hotlink.
Images as an extremely capacious form of writing in which contradiction
and incoherence may be inscribed without detriment to the discourse,
convey total knowledge—everything there is to know. But there are, in that
simultaneity, orders of reading, layered like a theater stage: upstage,
center-stage, downstage, wings…

The problem has to do with the language of critical practice whose
associations make it possible for art to be defined as inimical to society.
One example is the language used to define the concept of an "artistic
virus." Art, it claims, produces artifacts: social and cultural events that
"infect" various parts of the social system just like viruses infect an
organism. They "damage" or "alter" it. The infected system must change:
heal or be cured. The problem is that the associations produced by the
word "virus" are all negative: poison, disease, parasite, enemy. The concept
of art as a virus infecting and operating in various parts of the social
system leaves no room for verification: What is the impact of the infection?
Does it ever occur at all? How do we check what an "artistic virus"
has done? Can the impact be anything other than just infection? Infection
which is in itself an achievement because it sets in motion fantasies of
change and influence.

Why must we talk about viruses, and not algorithms for instance?
In mathematics, computing, linguistics, and related disciplines, an algorithm
is a procedure (a finite set of well-defined instructions) for accomplishing
some task which, given an initial state, will terminate in a defined end-state.
"In mathematics and computer science algorithms are finite, orderly sets
of clearly defined actions necessary to perform a task in a limited number
of steps. [...] Algorithms are to guide a system from a certain initial state
to a desired final state."[11] Such rigorous procedures would, of course,

---

11   Wikipedia, "Algorytm" [in Polish], http://pl.wikipedia.org/
     wiki/Algorytm.

be dysfunctional when applied to art. But if a virus can be a metaphor
for action, so can an algorithm. Algorithms imply something operational
and positive, a mode of purposeful action. I am not proposing that we
artificially replace one term with another, but that we change the meanings
of language. One that would allow us to consider the possibility of impact,
to see art as a "device that produces impact." As guiding the system from
a certain initial state to a desired final state.

Restore Effectiveness

Neither the immunity of art nor its stature have any effect on science, and
neither science nor politics are afraid of art. What ought to be done, now
that too much autonomy has led to the alienation of art, so that it is "not
heard" and most of the knowledge it generates is being squandered?

1. The first way could be for art to instrumentalize its own autonomy and
thus regain control over it. Instrumentalization would mean reducing the
role of autonomy to that of a tool like other tools. Autonomy would then
once more become useful for the carrying out of plans and would no longer
be a means of controlling our (the artists') "ideological purity." Instrumentalization is a "choice of dependency." Art could once again serve as an
instrument of knowledge, science, politics.

2. The second way would be to encroach upon other fields, such as science
or politics, as a way of proving oneself. The point is to work with people
who are not in awe of art. Stature is what protects artists and critics from
being "called." There is the famous story about Duchamp submitting a
urinal he signed R. Mutt for an exhibition. The qualifying committee
rejected the work, with only Duchamp himself voting in favor. The piece
could only be shown once Duchamp admitted it was his work. What made
the difference was the stature of the author.

The stature and immunity that protect art are unknown in sciences such as,
say, anthropology or sociology. There, an artist's statement is a verifiable
hypothesis that can be refuted with the aid of other, more convincing
arguments. Experts from other fields are substantively better prepared to
debate the claims art makes. Since art is interested in social issues, what
better interlocutor for it than a sociologist or social psychologist? I do not
want to overestimate specialists in other disciplines— they too are limited

by the invisible assumptions of their fields. Nonetheless art reviewers lack competence. They need sociological, philosophical, and psychological expertise. Karol Sienkiewicz in *Sekcja*, an Internet magazine run by art history students at Warsaw University, sums up the discussion around *Repetition* [dir. Artur Żmijewski, 2005] as follows:

> [L]ess relevant are the artistic merits of the project—"project" because it cannot be brought down to a forty-odd-minute-long film. I am not referring to the editing, the aesthetic categories, or whether this or that critic was bored during the screening—such categories are irrelevant when trying to judge or interpret *Repetition*. Perhaps art history and criticism with all their tools are still helpless in the face of [the work]. An art historian wanting to take part in a discussion among sociologists and psychologists can only assume the role of a homespun connoisseur.[12]

Critics often do not know enough, and this lack of knowledge can lead art back to aestheticizing. In the archaic, circular mode of communication where critics mediate between the artist and the viewer, lack of knowledge on the part of critics "forces" artists to simplify their message. It forces them to return to a reduced art—one that is restricted to the bounds critics have set for it, an art their competence is able to "handle." For what the critic cannot understand cannot be expressed and never makes it into the circuit of knowledge, is not revealed within the work. That, too, is one of the effects—and causes—of alienation.

It would be interesting if a work of art were "defeated" in the course of a genuine discussion, a clash of arguments. At the moment, a discussion with such an ending is not possible: art overwhelms its opponents. You could say that the ability to defeat opponents is embedded in a work of art. Embedded in the tangle of its ambiguity, stature, and immunity. Opponents find this knot nearly impossible to disentangle; and it perpetuates the symbolic violence encoded in art. Usually there is no dialogue in the first place, only a monologue where the artist provides a single canonical interpretation, and if there are any battles at all, they are waged to maintain the supremacy of that interpretation.

---

12   Karol Sienkiewicz, "Bezradność krytyka: Uwagi na marginesie dyskusji o *Powtórzeniu* Artura Żmijewskiego" [The Helplessness of the Critic: Comments on the Discussion about Artur Żmijewski's *Repetition*], *Sekcja* 1 (2006). [The publication is no longer found online.]

3. It is also worth trying to keep statements by reviewers from being treated as decrees. Since the turn of the century we have been witnessing a clear ideological asymmetry—the voice of artists is growing fainter. It is being drowned by successive teams of reviewers proclaiming the emergence or obsolescence of certain subjects in art. Such was the case with the new banalists, with art meant to be helpful, with art addressing issues of globalization. The most notorious statement to that effect was made by Magdalena Ujma on the website of the Bunkier Sztuki gallery, when she said that taking an interest in power has become "passé." The following year sociologist Jadwiga Staniszkis published *O władzy i bezsilności* [On Power and Powerlessness],[13] a book taking up the issue of new forms of power, its changing image and means of control, and last but not least, its networked nature. Would Staniszkis also regard an [academic] interest in power as being "passé"? In a world where the authorities fall back on "the terrorist threat" in order to reassert their prerogatives, where the government eavesdrops on law-abiding citizens, and changes the meaning of language, can power be so naively dismissed? Magdalena Ujma's comment brought out a crucial problem, that of the loss of an acquired competence. Encroaching upon the study of power relations gave art valuable competence in that field. But such competence has no chance of holding its own against the asymmetry of strength and frequency that obtains between statements by critics and artists. Artists "keep quiet"—they are reluctant to defend and explain their actions, and leave that task up to reviewers. What art will and will not be interested in can be determined by the skillful management of fads, by terming this or that "passé," and by alternately praising and wounding the narcissist within every artist. This is where something I would call ideological amnesia and the amnesia of competence come in. Art becomes skilled in carrying out certain cognitive procedures; when these become useful and universally applied, they are compromised. This is what leads to ideological amnesia, or the loss of an acquired competence. Just as art accumulates knowledge about modes of visual action: composition, color, spatial relations, so could it, in theory, verbalize and accumulate knowledge about the cognitive and critical procedures it applies.

Does that mean that extending the scope of freedom in art is not merely an illusion? "The decrees of reviewers" have left us with an internal hegemonic discourse where pluralism should have been. A true area of freedom could

---

13   Jadwiga Staniszkis, *O władzy i bezsilności* [On Power and
Powerlessness] (Kraków: Wydawnictwo Literackie, 2006).

be obtained by simply using the plural—if we had areas, fields of freedom:
a variety of fields of interest and, above all, if we kept and developed the
competencies we had once acquired.

The Applied Social Arts

Instrumentalization of autonomy makes it possible to use art for all sorts
of things: as a tool for obtaining and disseminating knowledge, as a
producer of cognitive procedures relying on intuition and the imagination,
and serving the cause of knowledge and political action. Naturally, art may
still perform its classical function and express "the most poignant moments
of the human condition." Control over autonomy is not the only kind of
control that should be achieved. There is still the problem of originality and
opaqueness. These too should be tools that can be used freely when the
need arises. One would have to strip originality of its judgmental function,
that is its propensity for control and exclusion.

I think that art could try and restore the original meanings of words.
The term autonomy would then mean the right to choose a sphere of
freedom instead of being an extreme personality trait. Originality would
be a sign of creativity and not novelty at all costs. And, finally, opaqueness
would be indicative of the difficulty of a message, not its illegibility and
inability to communicate.

Will dependence on other discourses, such as politics and science,
not lead to an ideological reduction of content to what is useful from
the standpoint of a group's political interests, for instance? Such a risk does
exist but there are at least two reasons why it should be taken up: 1. Art
manages very well in risky areas, while the "uselessness" artists feel can
encourage risky behavior. Wilhelm Sasnal said he sometimes feels like a
"gallery louse" in collaborating with an art world that produces tautological
references. Dependence on clearly "utilitarian discourses" is in all likelihood
a subconscious desire on the part of artists expressed in fantasies of change
that could occur through the agency of art; 2. Politics, science, and religion
can do what art no longer can: achieve a connection with reality by producing useful tools—tools for the implementation of power and of knowledge.
By becoming once again dependent, art may learn how to be socially useful,
even at an operational level (it already knows how to challenge reality
and can count on support for its proliferation of rebellion). A good example
of an artistic activity not afraid of entering into various forms of dependence is film. Film is literally "used" by various discourses. Film is a way to

intervene, fight for something, inform, educate, update knowledge, tell fairy tales, persuade, call attention to problems, critical junctures, etc. And film is very close to the realm of art. Today, the camera is the artist's best friend.

In a text about Elżbieta Jabłońska's work, critic Dorota Jarecka asked: "Whom should art serve today, and for what purpose? [...] [Should it] engage in political discussion that will always be inadequate when placed against the discourse of philosophers and sociologists?"[14] Yes, it should engage in such discussion. Art will enhance that discussion with its ability to use different strategies, its familiarity with intuition, imagination, and premonition. Unfortunately, art also has severe weaknesses and tends to dismiss its own importance. It has infused its discourse with self-compromise, amnesia, and recurring ignorance. Theoretical subjects in art school are taught as if they were merely a device for expanding the memory rather than exercises in thinking and discovering the world. There is doubtless some political interest in keeping art weak by forcing it to flounder between ignorance and knowledge, by having it perpetuate seemingly useful clichés regarding beauty and the artsy types who produce it. In the collective circuit of power, art is never "charged" as its "inventions" are not accepted. Arrested on the verge of the rational, it makes its actions out to be nothing more than vivid yet irrational fantasies. In the 1990s it played the rube, paying its share of the bill for the changes happening in the country (that would partly account for the scandals around art in recent years)—knocking on a weak discourse pays off in the economics of national frustration. In any struggle for power somebody has to play the useful idiot—and art with its naïveté and lack of defensive strategies was often used for such a purpose, notably by the LPR.[15] We all lost out by our failure to use the cognitive procedures developed by art to any greater extent. Procedures based on intuition and imagination, procedures based on denying one's righteousness and giving up judgementalism.

Intuition and the imagination embrace repressed and denied fantasies, desires and needs, and help search for ways to satisfy them. Renouncing the role of judge will reveal our collective and individual complicity in the injustices of the system. Then it will no longer be "them" but us who will share responsibility for the way our shared reality looks.

This text originally appeared in Krytyka Polityczna *[Political Critique], no. 11/12 (2007).* Krytyka Polityczna *is an important left-wing Polish journal published by a group of philosophers, political activists, and artists of which Żmijewski is a pivotal member (www.krytykapolityczna.pl). Translated from the Polish by Marin Wawrzynczak.*

---

14 Dorota Jarecka, "To już fanaberia Jabłońskiej" ["A Bee in Jabłońska's Bonnet"], *Gazeta Wyborcza*, April 7, 2006.

15 The League of Polish Families, a political party established in 2001 following the merger of several Catholic-national factions.

Art Education in Contemporary Art Museums
Alena Nawrotzki in conversation with Sepake Angiama,
Zachary Bowman, and Bernadett Settele

ALENA NAWROTZKI   In 1970s Germany, Hilmar Hoffmann championed
"culture for all"; today the Swiss government's arts funding guidelines call
for culture to be open to participation by as many people as possible.
For a long time, people have been asking who should have access to culture.
In a social-democratic conception of culture, the call for unlimited participation makes perfect sense. This means not just maximizing museum
visitors, but also enabling people to become part of the institution and its
discussions through participatory projects, and to influence that institution
in a relevant way. But how does the art system itself see these claims?
What happens to interpretive authority over art when the discourse can be
influenced by new groups of interested people (who do not necessarily
have specific knowledge of art history and theory)?

BERNADETT SETTELE   In my opinion, the point is not to involve as many
as possible but to involve a few in an unconventional but positive way,
or to involve an unconventional range of groups or individuals in the affairs
of art. There's a direct correlation, by the way, between the production
of different interpretations and the hegemonic definition of the power of art.
When Hilmar Hoffmann was the head of Frankfurt's cultural affairs
department, he argued that museums should be free of charge, as many big
museums in the United Kingdom are.

ZACHARY BOWMAN   One of my goals is to accurately represent the artist's vision and the curatorial framework while validating the often contradictory interpretations of the viewers. I don't believe in "interpretive authority" because there's always a limit to control over interpretation. I attempt to create a myriad of access points to the information provided by the artist and the curator, as well as a number of ways to extend that information outside the experience of viewing the artworks in a museum setting.

Another goal I have may be in conflict with the first: to help viewers work through their own experiences with works of art via dialogue with other viewers in the context of inquiry-based tours. This form of educational tour questions the notion that only art professionals have the correct information about art. On inquiry-based tours, the educator is present to stimulate interactive discussions and shape them based on his or her knowledge. Inherent in inquiry is the idea that all people who visit the museum bring with them a wealth of experiences that help to inform the discussion and the works themselves. Allowing viewers to define their experience with works of art gives them a confidence in viewing. Lack of confidence is most often what keeps people from understanding, or attempting to understand, works of art. I truly believe that the more diverse the audience and the greater its participation, the more ability art has to impact the public. Whether we focus on the artist's vision, the curator's vision, or the viewer's experience, we must always try to be as faithful to each of these as possible.

AN   Bernadett, you worked for documenta 12 (2007) and the 5th Berlin Biennale (2008). In Kassel you enabled an interesting intersection of art education and sociocultural projects. What have you learned about redistributing the power of interpretation and involving diverse groups of visitors or nonvisitors?

BS   I learned that the point of artistic or critical art education is often to *not* fulfill expectations. But let's back up. We should distinguish between two different spheres of activity: (a) working with art and third parties (who may or may not be amateurs), and (b) working on contextual dispositions and parameters. So I distinguish working on art from working on its institutions, as my colleagues and I did in the 2012 book *Kunstvermittlung in Transformation* (Art Education in Transformation).

In my practice and research, I've found that art education involves many different types of knowledge: activist approaches, didactic methods, theories of education, participatory tactics, openness, authenticity, and distance/proximity. Educational praxis is full of nuances: from opening up fields of discussion and challenging systems to constructive approaches—and of course, provocation and disappointment can be part of it as well. When you're conceptualizing the art education program for a biennial, there are many things you can learn from, including art, institutional critique, the sociology of organizations, and group dynamics—especially when you arrange these topics around political questions and principles.

AN   Zachary, what is your view on the conflict between maximizing the involvement of local residents and leaving the curators their interpretive authority? And what have you learned about these relationships in the United States? You work at PS1 in New York—what are your peer groups there in terms of art education programs? And how have you tried to achieve relevance in society? Is one of your aims to involve "everyone," or at least as many as possible?

ZB   PS1 doesn't have an education department, so it's difficult to identify a peer group. Luckily, as part of the Museum of Modern Art, we've had access to many resources through its robust education department. Being a person who cares deeply about education, working in an institution that does not prioritize education, I focused less on achieving relevance in society and more on creating access for underserved communities. In my time running the school programs at PS1, I realized that contemporary art is the best art to introduce to people who are undereducated in the arts. Instead of trying to get kids to relate to work made before they were born, before their parents were born, before the Internet, before Beyoncé—kids can relate so much more to work that speaks directly to their experience of the world.

AN   Experimental art education challenges the public: take away the consumer mindset and the passive immersion, and involvement and participation will come. That means that instead of going on a guided tour through the museum space and having the artworks explained by experts, visitors think, join in, decide for themselves. Is this really a need of a major part of the public? What does a "mature" visitor need in order to be "mature"?

BS   I once explained it this way: a truly shared or collective enterprise entails the possibility of becoming active—not just in the sense of doing something or being allowed to do something, or even being an essential part of the undertaking, but of being responsible for the action, taking on part of the liability and perhaps doing some of the planning as well. This requires a shift from attendance to participation. Merely attending an event means using it in a predetermined way. Participating means that there is also an opportunity to change the situation, some kind of agency. Allowing attendees to participate means giving them a role in determining structures, aims, and methods. Ultimately, that means being involved in deciding what happens, and it includes a different chronology and a different form of preparation. A participatory public is involved long *before* they enter the museum's space—so the false opposition between guidance and involvement falls apart as well.

With regard to the collective verbal work we do with art: of course the type of discussion I can have varies—as does the level of involvement possible—from group to group, from person to person. And I think art education creates maturity precisely by understanding this and taking it into account. For that, you need professionals—and institutions get those through permanent job positions, budgets, opportunities for reflection and research, qualifications, and peer consultation.

ZB   All a visitor needs to bring is an open mind and a desire to think deeply. Knowledge comes from a process of working through ideas, not an explanation of facts. Spending time looking at and thinking deeply about a single work of art and discussing your observations with a group of people is truly rewarding. Instead of dismissing a work or observation at first glance, the idea is to examine where the work came from and what it means, where our observations stem from and what they can reveal about us.

SEPAKE ANGIAMA   I believe it's a question of "preparing" the public or asking, "What is our future public?" It's important to think of museums, biennials, and public galleries as things that evolve and grow. Will the role of the mediator always be necessary? Will the public's reception develop, grow, and change as artistic production and spaces for art evolve? When I first went to galleries on my own, I didn't join guided tours. As a young adult I became more involved in the museum's group programs, and I enjoyed the social aspect of meeting with others. Gradually museums and galleries became a place you could also go at night, with more thought given to the inclusion of music and dance in the programming.

So for me it's more about thinking about how the programs will mature to support visits. For the visitor, maturing relies, perhaps, on a certain level of independence. How well are we able to communicate our programs? Do we explain them in language that can be understood by a broad public, or do we feel it important to maintain art jargon? To be effective at cultural education, we need to recognize that learning is a social activity.

AN   Bernadett, you've been dealing with extended art-education formats for a long time. In your view, how can the public be successfully involved in a way that meets their needs as well as the museum's?

BS   That's a good question, and everyone has to answer it for themselves. Institutions are made up of individuals, and so is the public. In art education we have to think less about formats and more about which form of education or gathering facilitates communication about art. In my view, art education means working artistically and pedagogically not just with art, but also with *Bildung* itself—meaning both *education* and *formation*—in changing constellations. Political questions can arise as well, but *Bildung* is always at the center. This term is quite difficult to translate into other languages. The English word *education* (from the Latin *educere*, meaning "to lead forth") was taken up by critical education theory because it highlighted the instructional aspect of *Bildung*: you can guide someone out of something, but they have to do the walking themselves. I think museums should foster education as a form of culture. Not every museum; that would be asking too much. Depending on their needs and capacities. Sometimes it's unavoidable that the responsibility to educate others is subordinated to marketing needs, availability of space, budget, and so on.

AN   Aside from giving access to as many social groups as possible, some argue that the public should participate and be involved not just intellectually but also creatively. Why does art education need this component, this practical, hands-on approach of "reenacting" artistic methods?

BS   That's the wrong way of asking the question. We should ask: What facilitates hands-on activities in art institutions, and what impedes them? In a country as rich as Switzerland, why aren't introductory art courses free for every interested and talented person? Why aren't art schools attended by a wider range of population groups? Because they're oriented toward the fortunate few after a certain age. But a broad segment of the population is clearly interested in creative activity. The myth of "art" is working. The question is, what do you do about it in terms of cultural policy?

ZB   The process of making art can create new forms of thinking. Associations may form where they didn't previously exist. In participating in creative production, people may reveal to themselves or the group some information or way of approaching information that they were unaware they possessed. Art making is generative and regenerative for many individuals.

I think what's important is not for visitors to understand a particular artist's method by mimicry, but to use the process to see what they can reveal to themselves, and perhaps to form an affinity for the work by understanding the motor skills involved in making it. To understand how others used their bodies (including their brains) to produce something can bring us closer to identifying with certain works.

SA   Of course, it's hard to say whether there's a need to be creatively active as a public. However, I do see a benefit in learning through doing. Some people enjoy the process of engaging with artwork creatively, especially where language is a barrier. For some, it might bring a closer understanding of work they've seen. But producing a creative response doesn't necessarily mean making visual art; exhibitions can stimulate writing, music, and other forms.

I also think it's important to move away from the notion that it's only children who need creative activity. Sparking creativity can create a totally different social dynamic that cannot be generated through conversation alone.

AN   What are your views on the opportunities presented by the trends toward digitizing the museum's holdings and including social media in the museum's work? Is it possible for the museum to interact in a broader way with the public, and do these new strategies enable even more participation? Or are they just marketing ideas—for example, giving an award for the best selfie, or raffling off the next exhibition catalogue?

BS   As I said above, it depends what museums do with it. No medium, no approach, is good or bad in itself. Can you formulate your critique more precisely?

AN   I ask because we've been spending a lot of time discussing how we can use the "new" digital media. Incorporating it takes a lot of effort, staff, and money, and since the results often lack relevant content, they never go beyond pseudo-involvement for the visitors—the visitors can't "learn" anything or have fun in a playful way or be creative. I think we have a lot of work to do before we can make proper use of digital media in the museum world (even though there are a lot of good examples already).

ZB   Digital communication is increasingly the most popular form of communication, and museums should absolutely participate. One of the best outcomes of engaging people with social media is that it helps to demystify the institution by using a form of language that is easily comprehended, especially by younger people. Building and nurturing a digital audience is necessary for museums to remain relevant. Also, marketing is never bad. The more people there are involved with the museum, the more people the artwork can reach.

SA   It's important to make a distinction here between pure communication and marketing, on the one hand, and education on the other. Social media is a communication and marketing tool. I haven't yet seen it used effectively for education, but that doesn't mean it doesn't have the potential to do so. When I was in Saint Petersburg, I realized that a huge number of young people were using art as a backdrop for their next Instagram or Facebook profile. Initially I was shocked—people were showing their interest in a work by turning their backs to it! So I'd say we shouldn't underestimate the power of social media, but we must ask: "To what end?"

AN   The educator stands in the middle of a charged field of conflict. She or he has to explain ideas, discourses, and artworks to outsiders while simultaneously representing the institution. She or he is also expected to think critically, be adaptable, include the public, and take visitors seriously. How important do you think the art educator is during the encounter with an artwork? Are educators, perhaps, obsolete? Are they only there to smooth over tensions between the public and art, to prevent misunderstandings that might result in a rejection of art in general?

BS   Art educators perform art—in their speech; in the explanations they give or do not give; in their references to different disciplines, forms of knowledge, art discourses, and institutional patterns of behavior; in the disclosure of sources; in speaking and in stumbling. Again: art educators perform art. And in doing so they can make things smoother or rougher— and much more.

ZB   I have great faith that all visitors can comprehend complex ideas on their own. In most cases, visitors don't need an educator to make the ideas more accessible—they need them to bounce their observations off, and to instill in them a confidence in their own ability. There are certainly visitors who refuse to accept the validity or importance of certain artistic pursuits. Sometimes it helps to contextualize, and sometimes it helps to ask people to explain why they dislike something. It's much easier to dismiss wall text than a person. And it's more difficult to dismiss something if you have to explain why you're dismissing it.

SA   Alena, I think you're referring more to the role of the mediator here—a role we all play while working for cultural institutions. In my experience, many people have commented on having spent much more time with art that they would not necessarily have gleaned much from if left alone. Manifesta very much appreciates the role of the mediator and understands it as a fundamental part of the education program. I've always been very interested in more performative ways of mediating an exhibition.
       Educators or mediators don't necessarily smooth over tensions; if anything, they sometimes do the opposite, shaking visitors up as a way of initiating dialogue. When you feel strongly about something, you're more likely to share your viewpoint. For me, mediation doesn't bring you to a place where you feel as though the work is resolved, but rather to a place where you critically reflect on the questions and ideas that arise from looking at and talking about art together.

AN   Sepake, how is the art education department integrated into the documenta team? What are your obligations, and what freedoms do you have?

SA   I have to say that the situation is quite unique. Art education at documenta 14 is shaped by the notion that education is not the program we provide but the residue that remains after the fair has come to an end.

The working title of this documenta is *Learning from Athens*, so embedded in the title is this notion of learning. Education may come in different forms: through the hospitality of others, the production of an artwork, a conversation with an artist, the engagement of a local advisor, the cooking of a meal—it might even be on the dance floor!

I think of education as something personal and unique to all who take part in documenta 14—from the staff to the artists to all those who engage in their programs. We all come into the conversation with our own experience and understanding of art, and we'll all leave with someone else's perspective. So who is learning? It's important to constantly be aware of the processes by which an institution learns in order to share that learning with others. That way education or learning is an ongoing process that continues to reveal itself, from when Adam first had the idea of bringing documenta to Athens right up to the last visit to the exhibition. In that sense, documenta 14 will formally and informally begin, through education and public programs, before the exhibition opens, and it will continue in discussions long after it closes.

AN   Many of the points we've been discussing have been issues in the art world for decades. Olafur Eliasson and Yoko Ono claim that art and museums have become more and more elitist. On the other hand, Philipp Herzog von Württemberg, the chairman of Sotheby's Europe, says the art market has enabled art to spread throughout the world, so that it's no longer an elite luxury good. Have we failed to make art more democratic, or are we indeed part of a movement that opens art up for everyone?

BS   Let me turn the question around: What's your view on that at the Migros Museum für Gegenwartskunst? Why should everyone be interested in art (or the particular art that we show here and now)? Aren't economic considerations and political progress equally important?

AN   I absolutely agree with you. We're in the midst of a discussion that is shifting between ideological demands and economic parameters. It's a fact that almost all museums need to increase visitor numbers. That can only happen if people that don't normally attend a museum are brought to it. Besides economic considerations, there are also questions about the relevance a museum should have in society—which, again, often shows up in the numbers. I also see the question in a broader context: I see educational offerings and public programs as a sort of opening of the "sacred temple" of the museum. We're trying to follow this path at the Migros Museum für Gegenwartskunst. But there's still a lot to do.

ZB   It depends on which institution you're talking about. That said, the arts, in general, have a class problem—especially in New York City. It's nearly impossible to live and work in the city as an artist or lower-level museum employee without having money coming from family. This leads to a system that's incestuous, employing only the wealthiest. One has only to look at where young curators and young artists with solo museum shows went to college to start to see a disheartening pattern. Many people who end up with senior administrative or creative roles at museums have had the luxury of taking many unpaid internships, where they make connections with people (often family friends) who help them into important positions. The sameness in this culture of museums will only lead to an echo chamber, repeating back to itself exactly what it expects to hear. The more diverse the staff and the audience, the more interesting and relevant the institution will remain.

A great program to commend for working to change this in New York City is the ARTS Intern program developed by Studio in a School. This program places students from low-income families, who can't afford to take an unpaid internship at a museum, in paid internships at many renowned institutions in the city, subsidized by Studio in a School. Participants in this program are often the most impressive of all the employees I've hired.

SA   You can't ignore the high tower from which art speaks. It's clear that the art world is not a democratic one. But these questions of openness, transparency, power, inequality—these are questions that many artists have challenged in various ways. However, I have to question this idea of being "open." What might it mean? Does it mean that art is something that's meant to be locked up, hidden, or closed? When I first started going to galleries in East London, it always used to amaze me how intimidating the whole visit could be. Galleries would be hidden on some back street, with a dubious-looking entrance and a small bell with the name of the gallery. It was as though only those who were meant to know could know.

It's a world that manufactures mystery and intimidation. Museums and public galleries find ways of doing this architecturally. For some, the giant entrance of the Turbine Hall says that it's not for them but for somebody else. How many museums must we enter by ascending an impressive staircase and passing under towering Athenian-looking pillars? I'm sure many educators would agree with me when I say a lot of time is spent demystifying the institution. It's like tearing down the curtain to reveal the Wizard of Oz. Once you get over all the pomp and ceremony, then you can get down to the real business of looking at and talking about art.

AN   What do you think the major points of discussion will be in art education in the coming decades? How will it position itself in the art field and in the hierarchy of museums? Will educators be equal to curators, or what do you see as their specific role?

BS   We will still be having the same discussions! The hierarchies in art institutions have not yet been destroyed, and many function in a precarious and impermanent way, but it's gradually coming to be understood that it makes sense to curate art education as well, and to involve the education department in the activities of a museum or art space from the beginning, or even first of all. I think small alternative spaces like Les Complices* in Zurich set standards in the way they work with their specific environment, establish bonds with partners, and create outreach. Bigger institutions have to create different types of structures, and that also has to do with questions of funding for culture and public education. Personally, I wish debates on advanced political critiques and educational questions were taken seriously in art education and the arts in general. And I think there should be more contributions from art educators in catalogues.

ZB   In an ideal future, educators and curators would work alongside each other. Curators should remain responsible for selecting works and laying them out in a specific way to tell the story they're interested in. Educators should be there to help the curator find the best methods of telling that story so that the widest array of people will comprehend it.

I don't see shifting hierarchies ever being fully resolved. The nature of museums is dynamic. They change alongside culture to reflect and preserve it. To do so, they need to shift priorities and hierarchies. The focus does need to be defined, as much as possible, by artists, with the assistance of civic leaders and donors.

I hope the biggest shift or point of discussion will be with regard to artists' relationship with education. We now have many artists growing up in an era of great museum education programs for children and teens.

Many future artists will have been inspired to create work because they were involved in these programs, and I expect we'll see an element of education inherent in their practice. Already, many artists are considering interpretation and access as part of their process, and I hope this trend will continue.

SA   I think we're already seeing the roles of curator and educator dissolving. In the United Kingdom, I've noticed that the pendulum is swinging toward understanding everything as a "program," whether it's education, exhibition, or public programming. So whether you're a curator, an educator, or a public programmer, you should always be considering whom you're speaking to. It's not just the responsibility of educators to "deal with the public." For the visitors, the distinction between programs is not so important. In my current project, "an education for documenta 14," you also see education projects—or at least their form—originating not just from the curators but from the artists themselves, whether for the exhibition or the public program.

I think the most important shifts will be the professionalization of the profession and an increase in criticality in the field—both of which I believe are needed. However, I do think it would be good not to specialize just in education. I think it's important that curating and educating be considered together—mostly because the needs of the artist and the work should not be separated from the needs of the public.

In terms of finding ways of critiquing educational practices, "What happened?" should be given the same weight as "What are you planning to do?" Education is an internal process. Can you measure how I see the world today as opposed to how I saw it yesterday, and did that guided tour have anything to do with it? Well, who knows? But I hope education allows for a lasting relationship with its public. Education programs are often seen as responsive strands that can only speak in response to curatorial programming. In my understanding, where a dialogue has been long established with various communities and publics, they might also be the first to speak, and it would be interesting to see how a curatorial team or artist would respond to that.

I think more education teams should work directly with artists. Many educators/mediators are better positioned to work with artists, and the power dynamic is different. Of course it still remains the fact that not all artists see education as a necessary part of their role. I've heard artists say, "yeah, I can work with that"—they misunderstand education teams as casting agents for their artistic production. This line will continue to blur. However, I think it's important for artists not just to use the public, but to find social ways of producing meaning in which the levels of mutual exchange, respect, and cultural value are shared and not merely mediated.

Lastly, museums, biennials, and public galleries have an immense ability to bring people together. Why should they not become cultural parliaments for the public, artists, educators, and curators alike? Art and artists have made a tremendous contribution to my life; they've transformed my view of the world and opened up new ways of thinking about how we relate to one another. I hope we continue to value this voice in the world—sometimes courageous, sometimes fleeting, sometimes misunderstood, sometimes challenging, and definitely always making things more complicated.

The conversation was realized via e-mail in June 2016.

Ethics
Accompanying the concluding conversation on "The Age of Ethics," the works featured in this image series spotlight various ethical questions from the standpoint of art and offer a critical take on the museum and the art system.

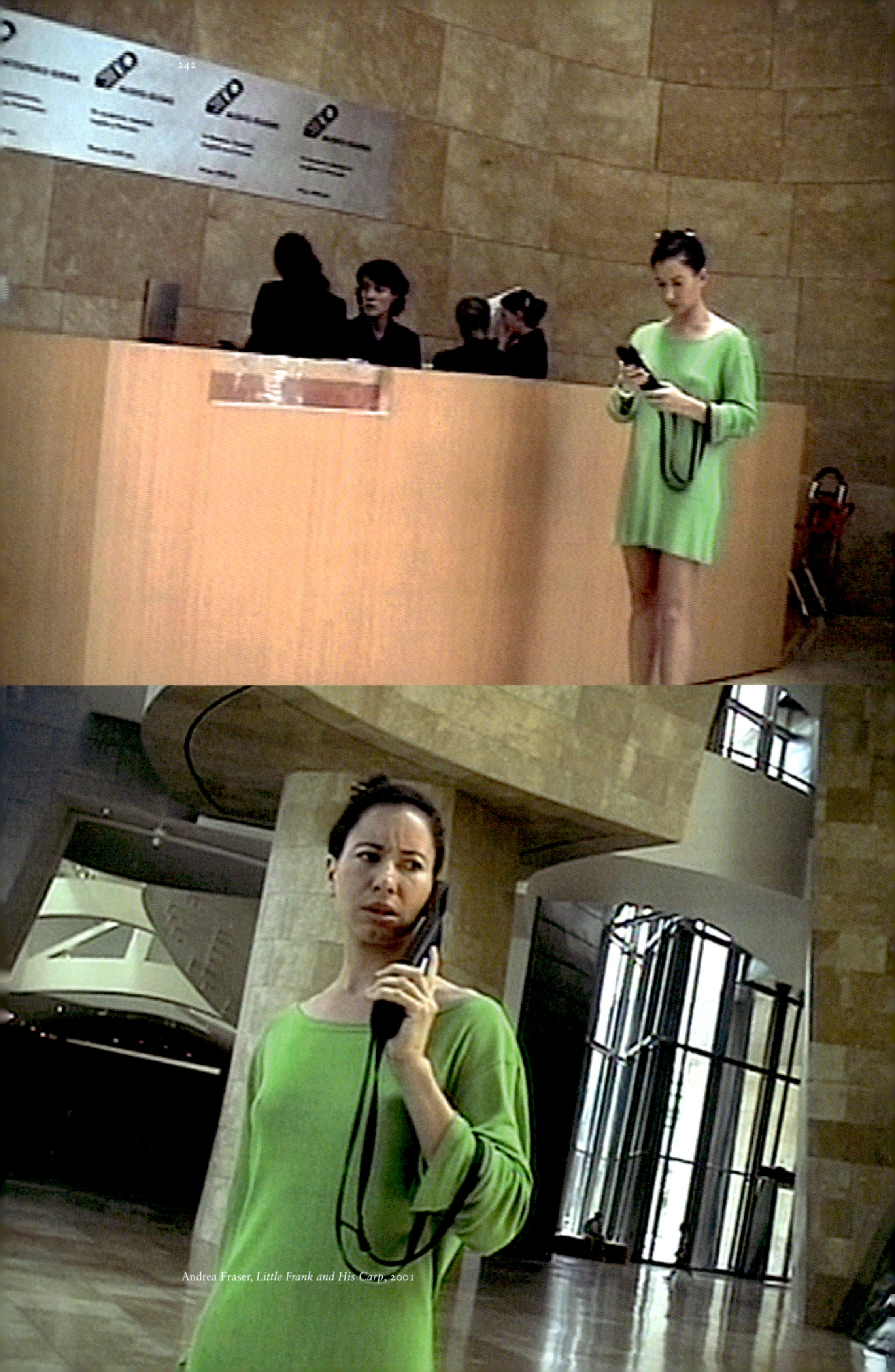

Andrea Fraser, *Little Frank and His Carp*, 2001

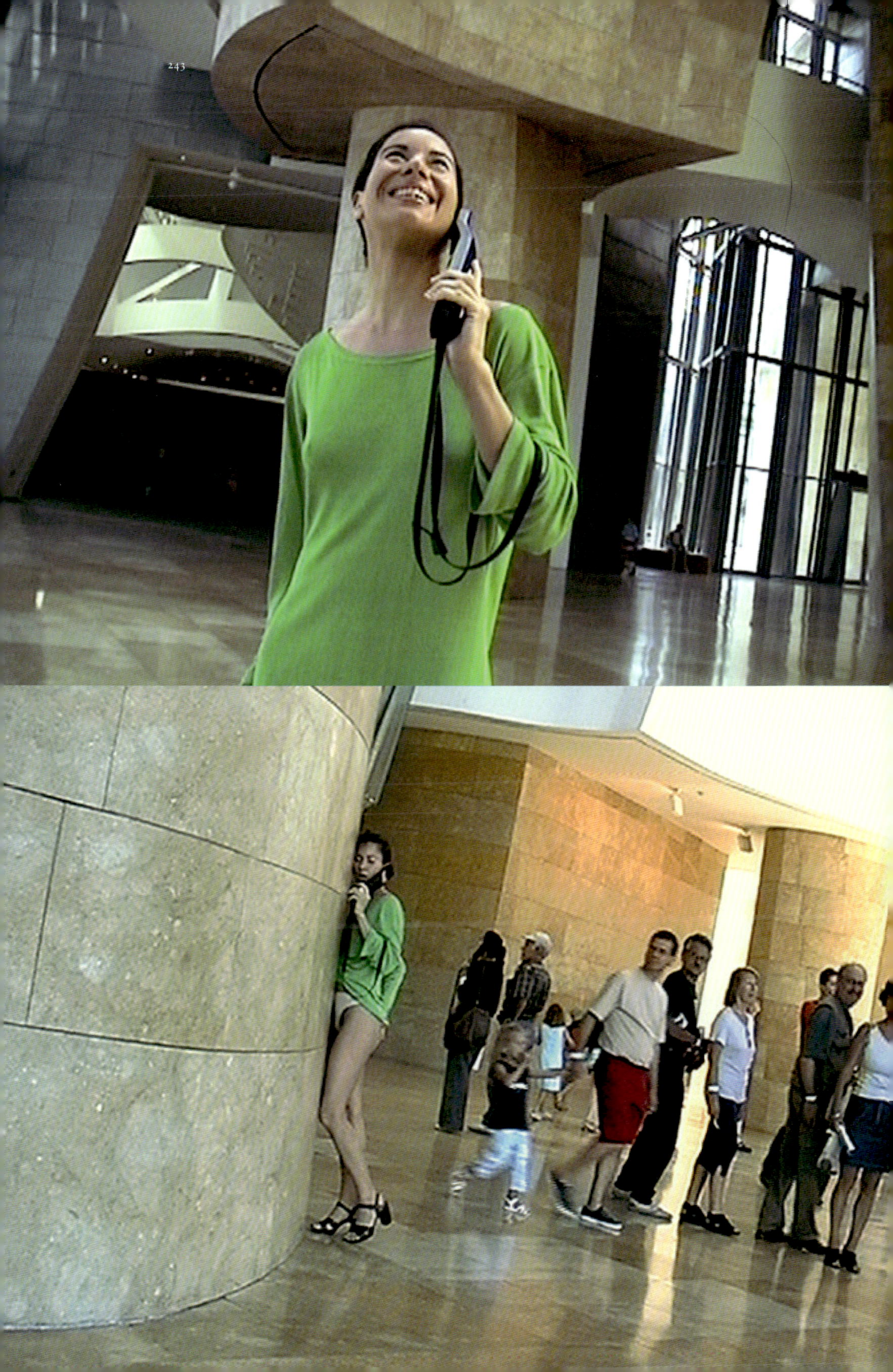

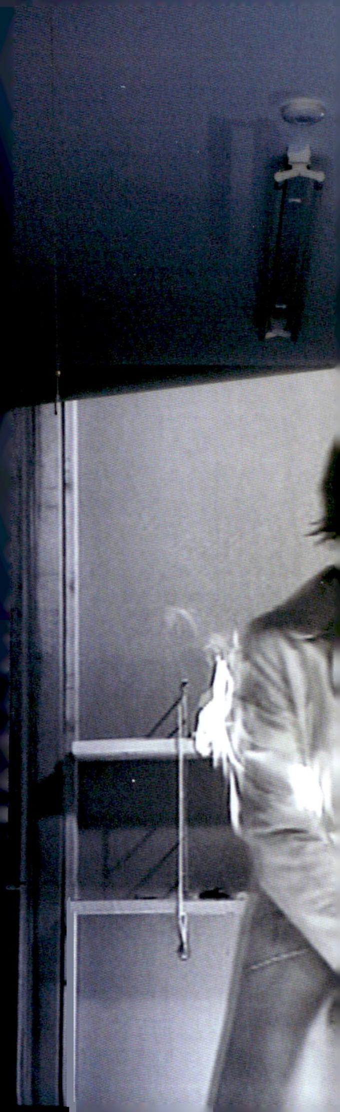

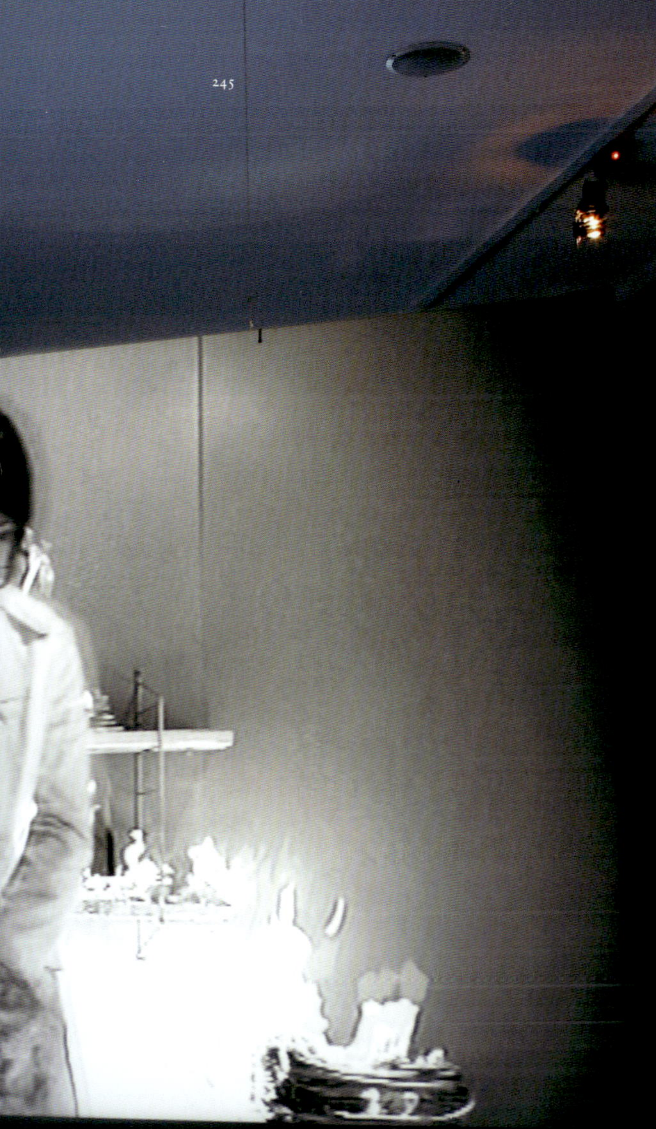

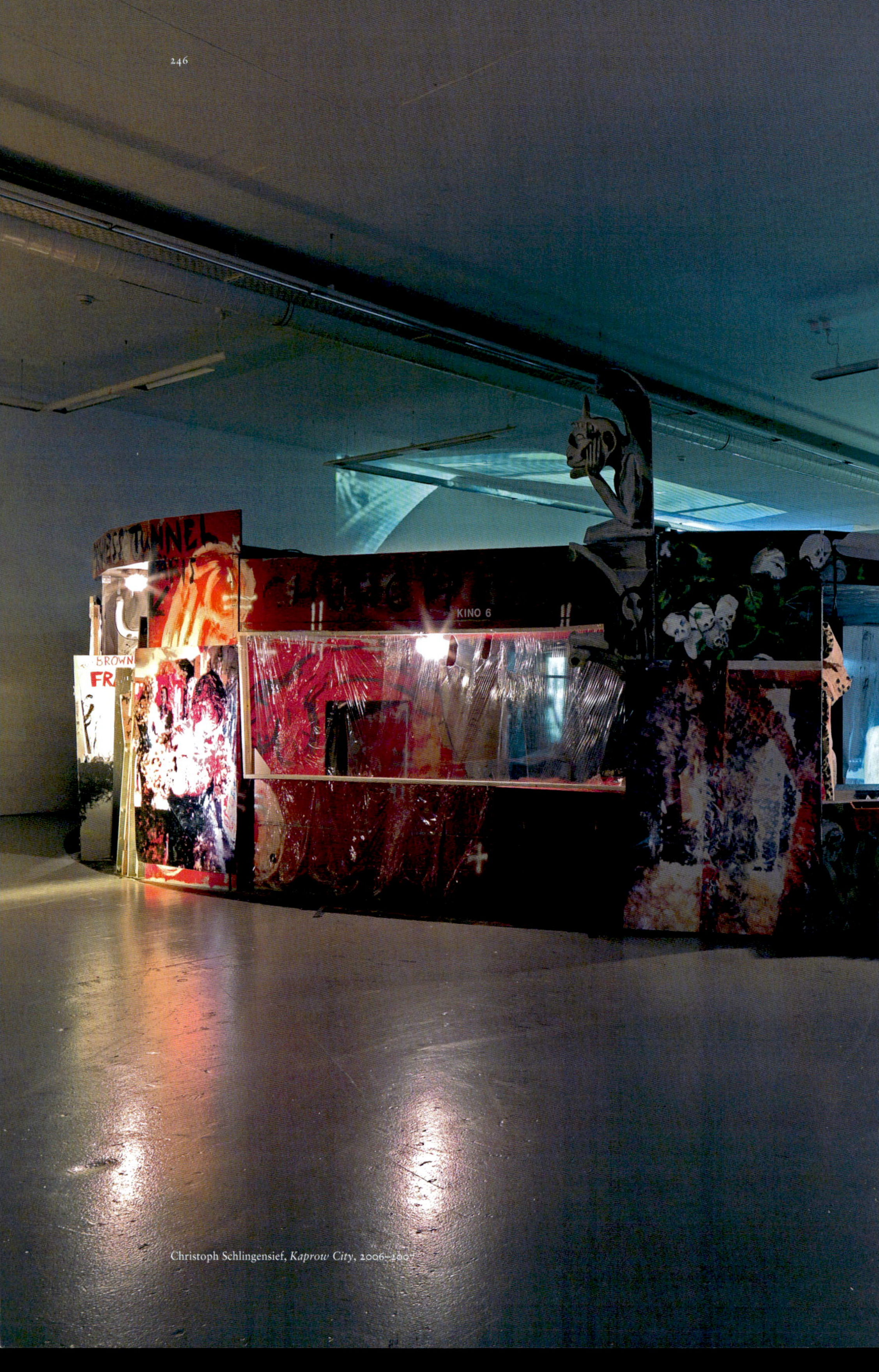

Christoph Schlingensief, *Kaprow City*, 2006–2007

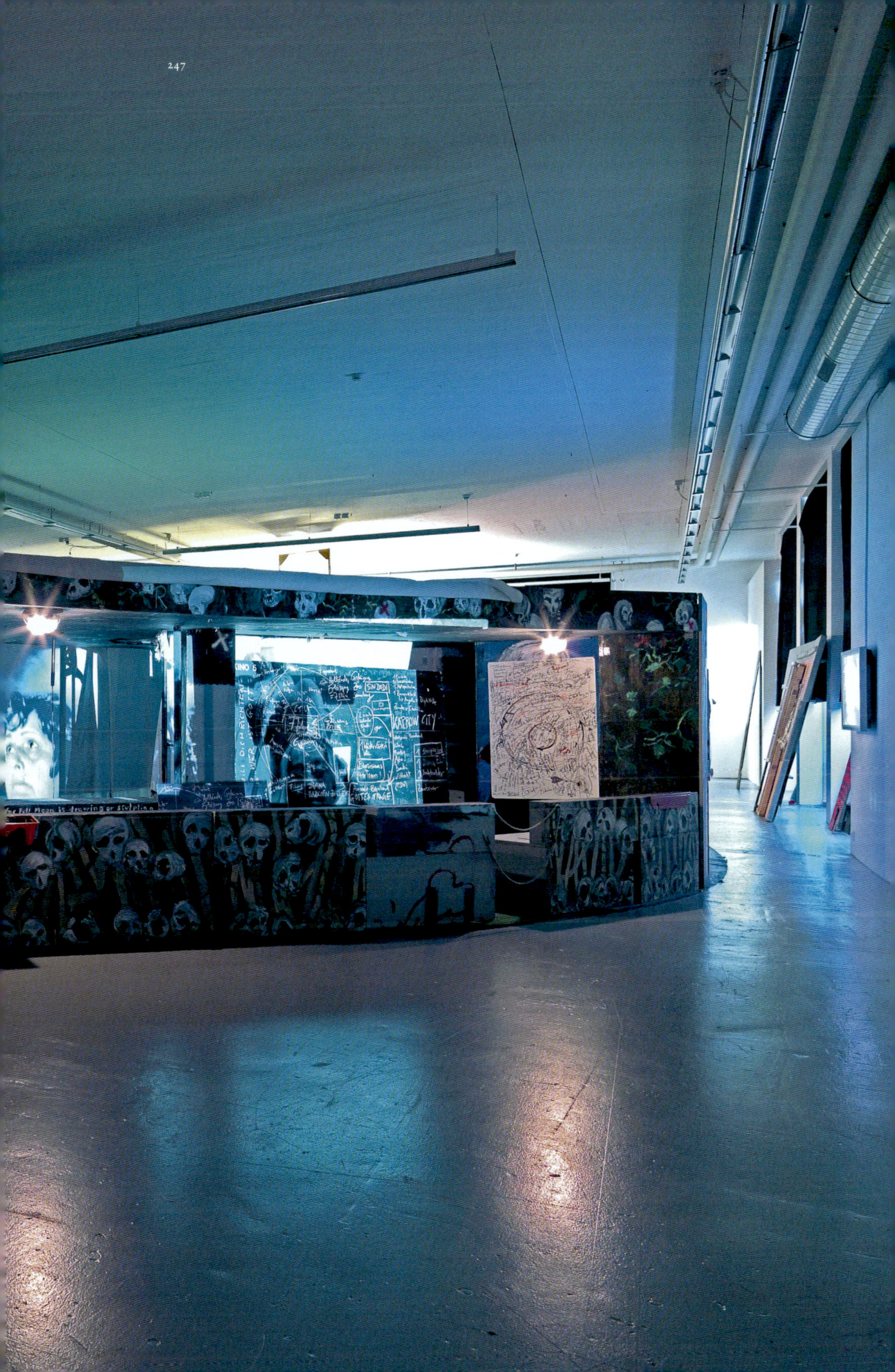

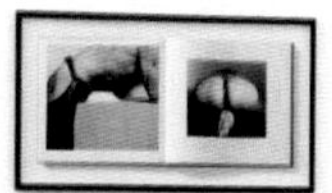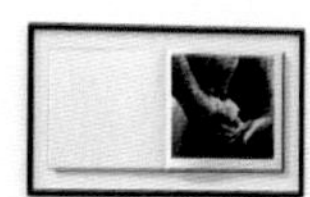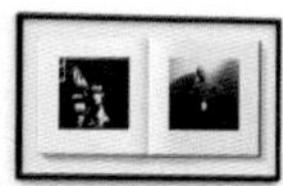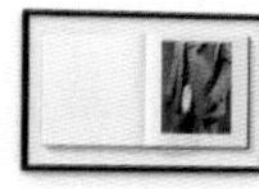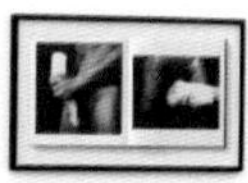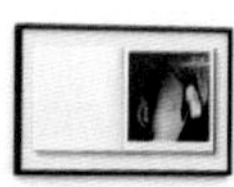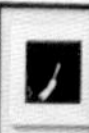

Maria Eichhorn, *Prohibited Imports*, 2003–2008

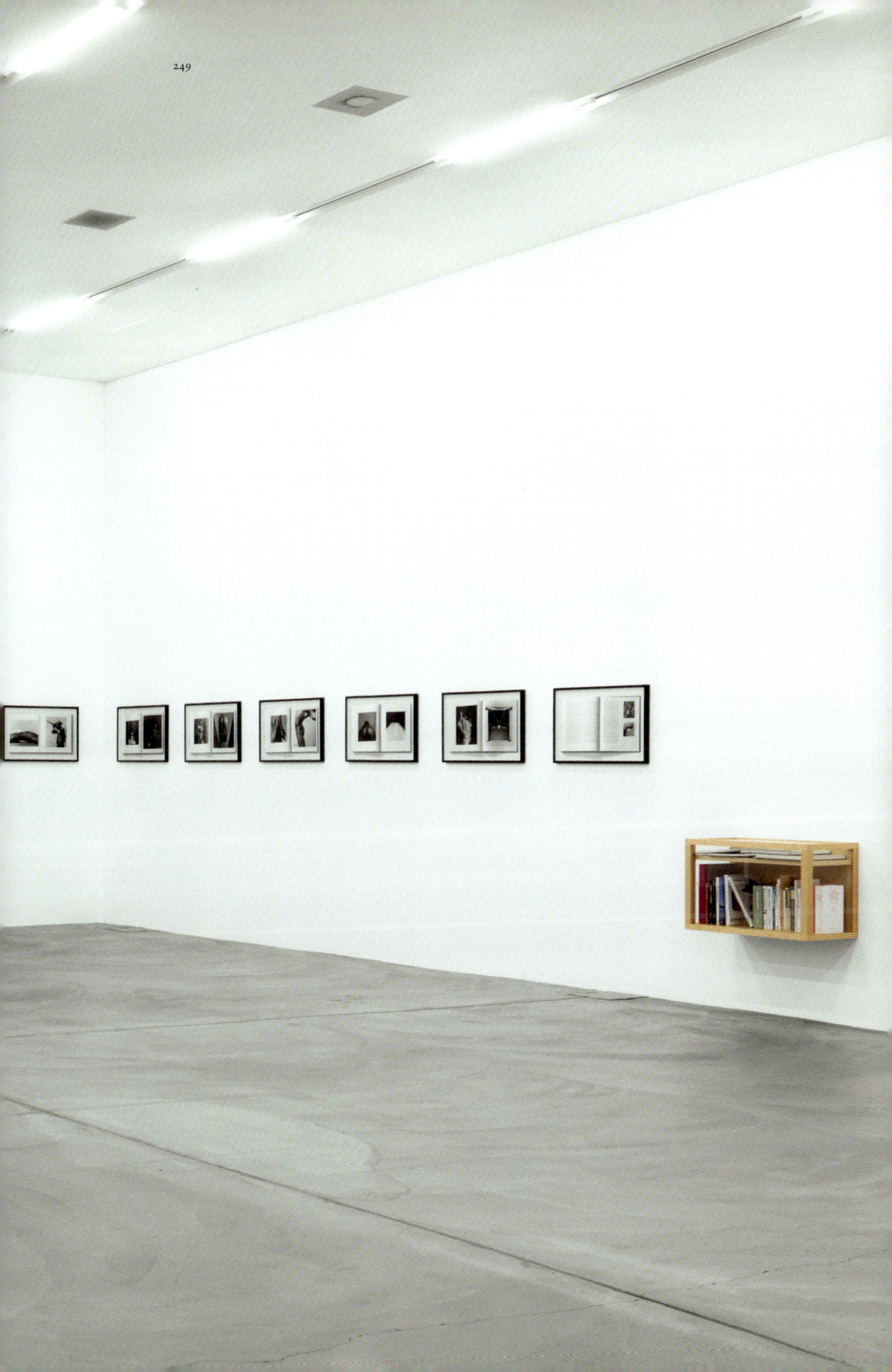

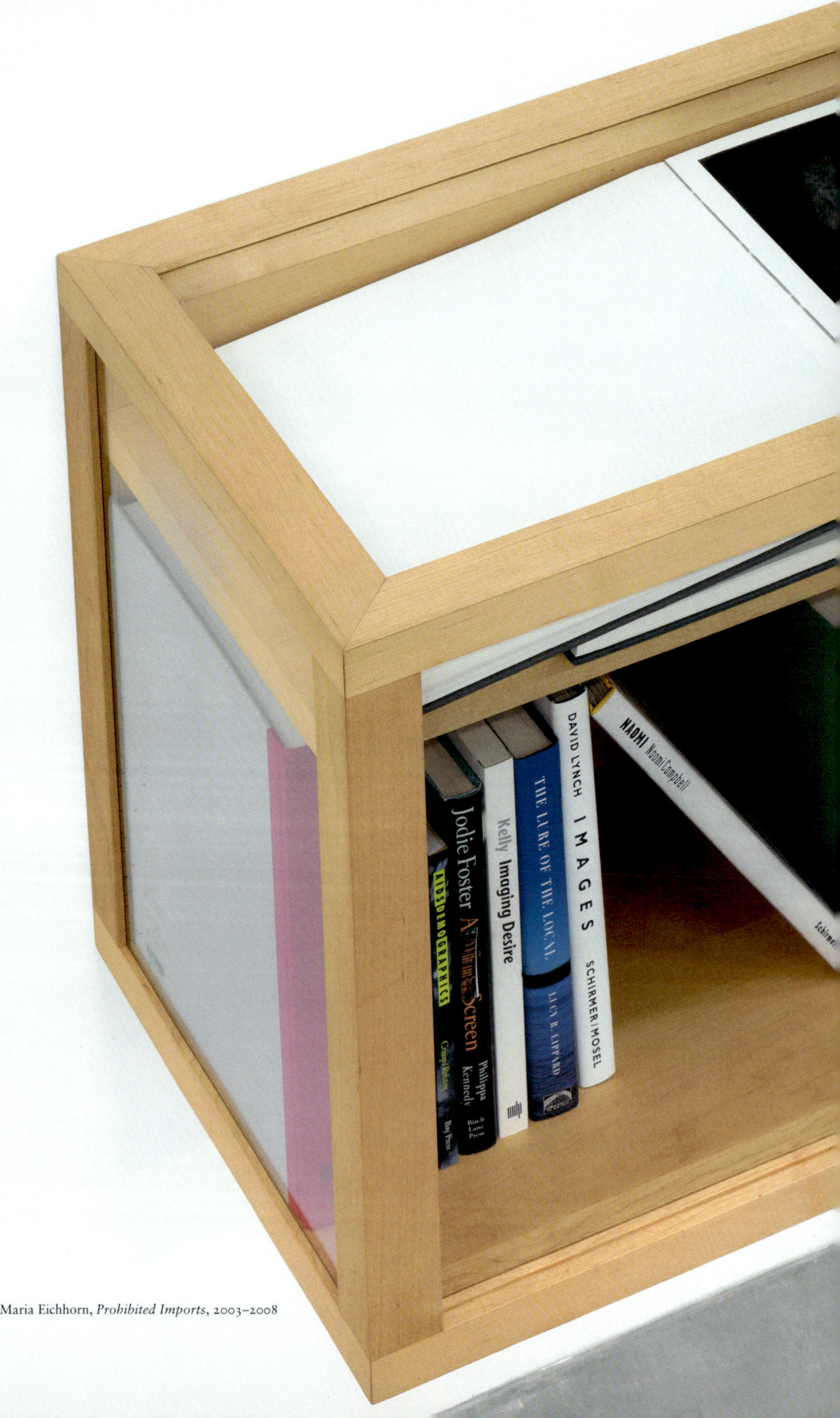

Maria Eichhorn, *Prohibited Imports*, 2003–2008

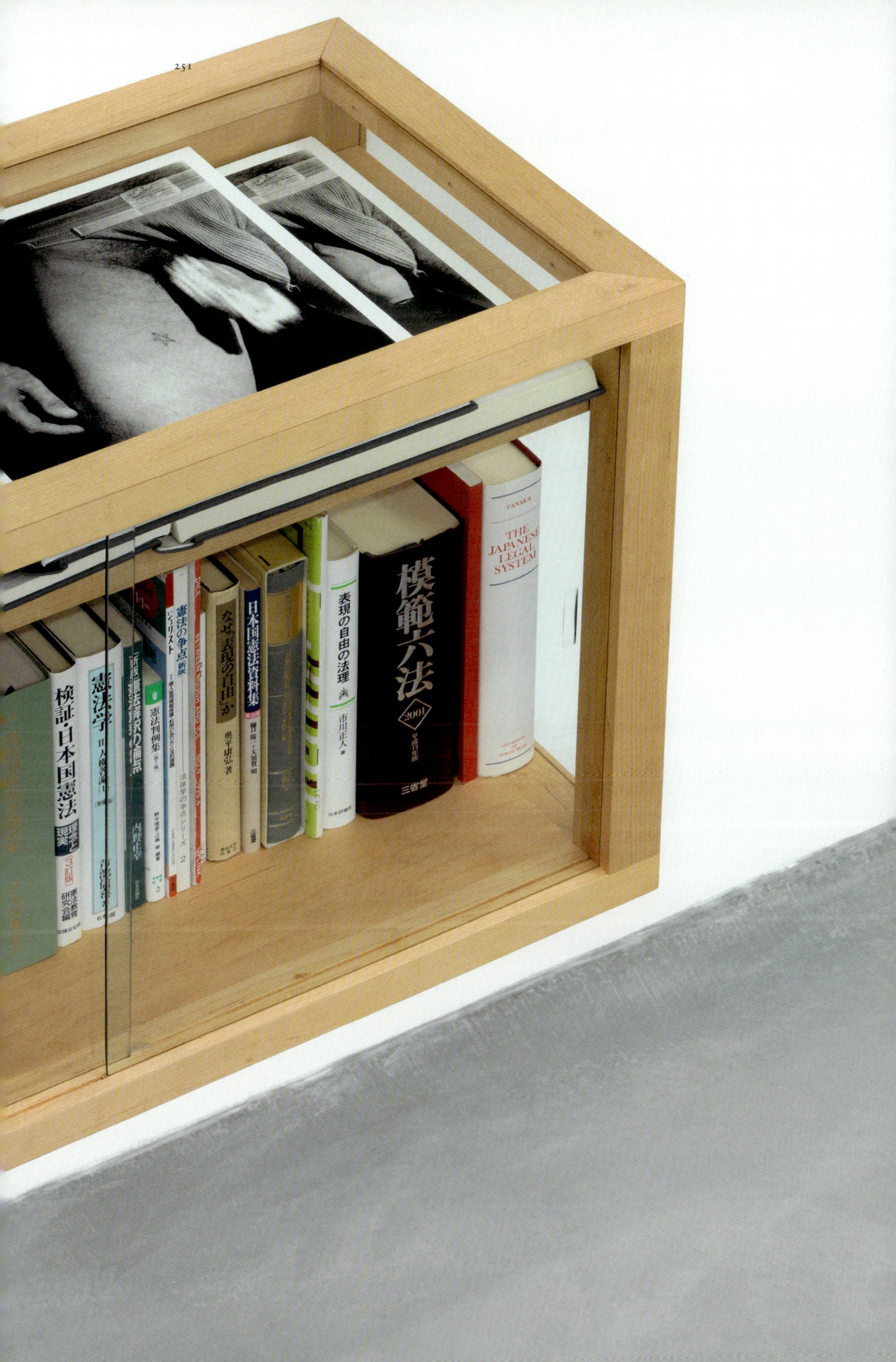

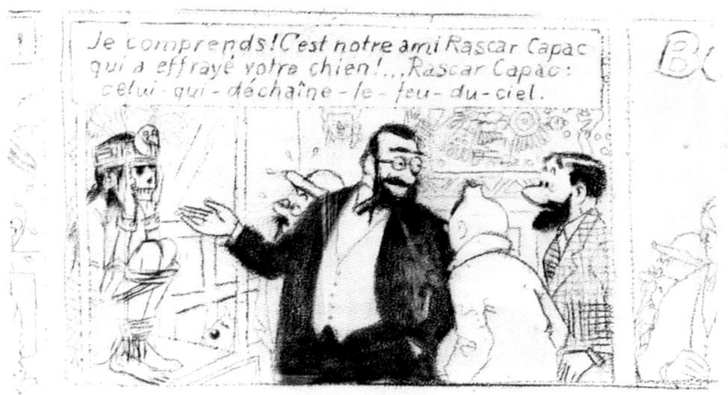

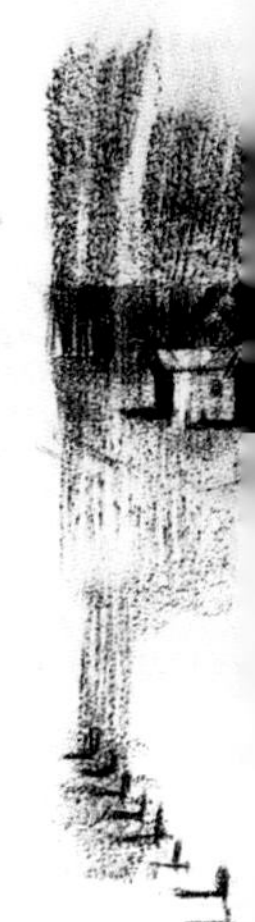

Marc Bauer, *Der Sammler (Tintin und die Baracke)*, 2012

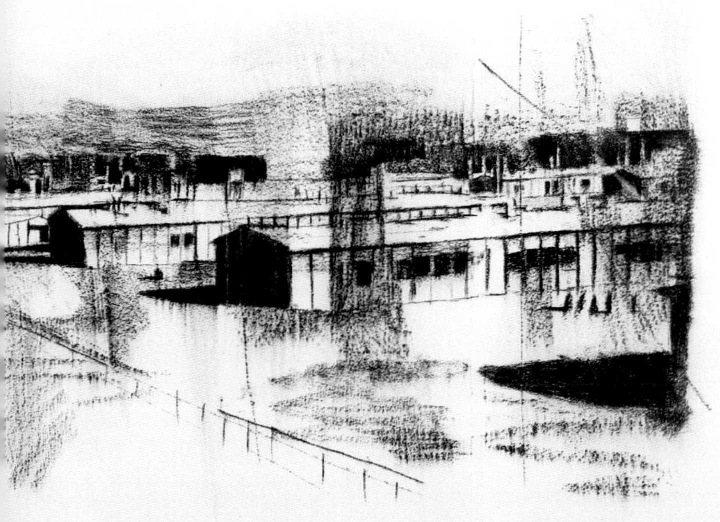

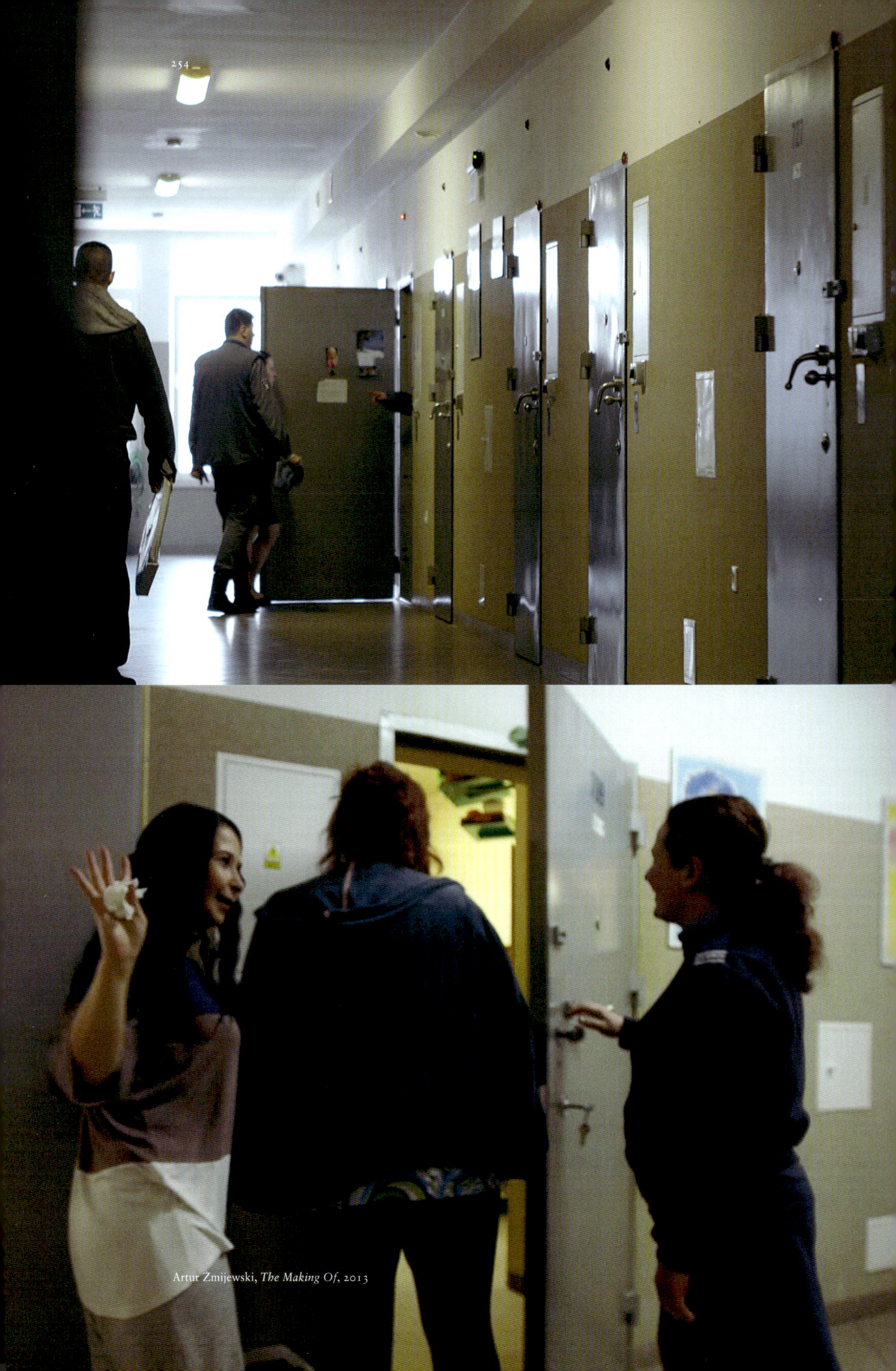

Artur Żmijewski, *The Making Of*, 2013

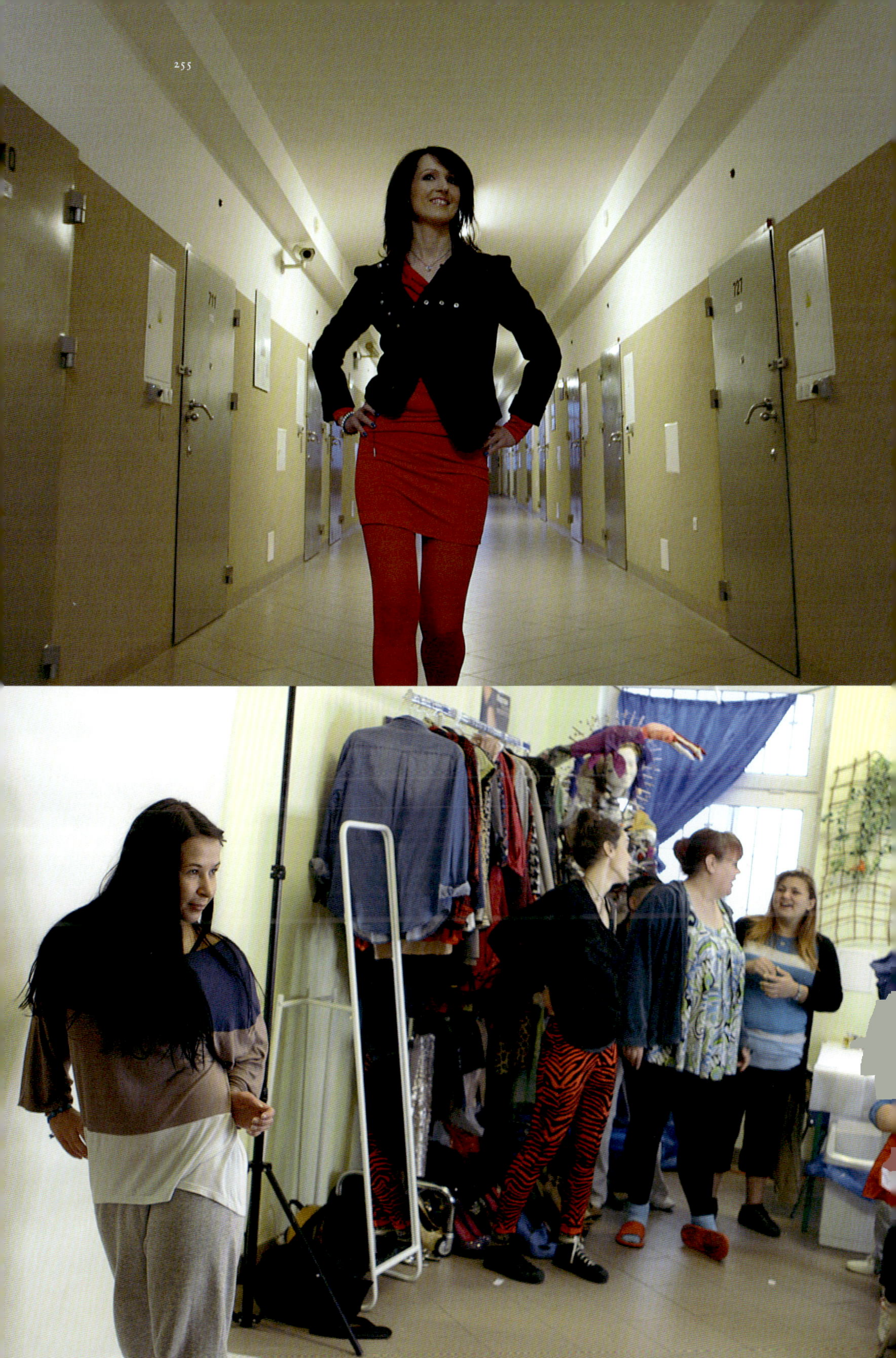

The Age of Ethics?!—Ethics and the Contemporary Art Museum
Raphael Gygax in conversation with Kate Fowle,
Andrea Fraser, and Philipp Kaiser

RAPHAEL GYGAX   Ethical criteria always reflect society's social values and norms—and show, of course, how these are in flux. Very often questions of ethics in the art world receive little attention until a "scandal" breaches the public eye.

Have you experienced a change in ethics in the last twenty years with regard to the "cultural globalization" and "corporatization" of contemporary art museums? Personally, I have the feeling that—at least in European museums—on the one hand, there's a certain developing sensibility toward a "code of ethics." On the other, we have seen some highly problematic developments, for example in connection with the display of private collections in public institutions, especially in Europe where—at least still at the moment—a different funding model exists for the visual arts. As a visitor, I often experience a lack of transparency about the financial background of such shows or curatorial approaches and liberties—and have the suspicion that ethical guidelines get ignored.

PHILIPP KAISER   Having worked in museums in three different countries (Switzerland, Germany, United States), I am aware that the above described issues are being handled very differently. Although it is difficult to generalize, I am convinced that American institutions are more aware of potential conflicts. One of the reasons might be that American museums are not rooted in nineteenth-century positivism and institutional structure. With all their advantages and disadvantages, American museums are mostly funded with private money and run as somewhat corporate enterprises. My experience is—as problematic and exceptional as the developments at MOCA Los Angeles were after 2008—that museums in the United States are less captive to the political agenda of local politicians and run more professionally and pragmatically. Pragmatically also in the sense that there is an awareness that exhibitions cost money. What you described, Raphael— that collectors take taxpayer-funded public museums hostage in order to feature their collections without making a permanent commitment—is highly problematic and, as far as I know, is not something that is allowed to happen in the United States. I believe that using the museum to avoid storage costs and to increase the value of personal assets without an actual donation cannot be an option. We all know the museums are (still) involved in generating long-term value and therefore are not detached from the art market. There have been a couple of bad examples of so-called permanent loans by individuals that later got flipped at auction after the museum was forced to return them. It would be easy to name a few of these incidents that have happened especially in Germany. There needs to be an awareness for this issue and regulation might be a solution.

KATE FOWLE   To ensure we are on the same page, I just want to outline what I understand "ethics" to constitute in the context of contemporary museum work: it is a code of conduct through which are established the preservation and display of collections; the presentation of exhibitions; the research and furthering of knowledge of contemporary art; the building of community around a museum; and related legal, financial, and profes- sional interests.

The International Council of Museums (ICOM) established a contemporary Code of Ethics in 1986, and it is what all member museums (and individuals such as myself) are expected to abide by. What is interest- ing in relation to what you call the "cultural gloabalization" of the art world is that ICOM currently does not accept into its council any of the recently established museums—those which are privately funded in coun- tries that have little or no state support for contemporary art, such as the Jumex in Mexico City, Ullens Center in Beijing, Garage in Moscow, and Mori Art Museum in Tokyo, to name a few—and so there is no established framework which these new institutions are expected to comply with or aim toward in terms of international standards. Of course they do, because

individuals within the institutions are professional, but as the landscape of
contemporary art institutions keeps expanding beyond traditional centers,
it is ironic that even the governing bodies that help to establish a common
ground for ethics currently just evade the issue. It seems to me that this
is an urgent situation to focus on if we want museums to thrive on shared
ethical values.

More specifically you seem to be focused on the issue of ethics in
relation to funding in the case of European—i.e. traditionally state-
funded—institutions, which are increasingly turning to the private sector
for support. This is indeed one of the big changes I have witnessed over the
last twenty years, but I am really not sure that this shift per se is a question
of ethics.

In other words, needing to diversify funding and the private sector
being a solution is a fact. As I mentioned above, there is a very large
proportion of the world where contemporary culture does not benefit from
state support in the first place. Furthermore, the United States has been
developing the model of privately funded, publicly minded cultural institutions for around one hundred years in lieu of state support—indeed
organizations that are recognized as public institutions (and key members
of ICOM) are actually philanthropic institutions.

So, it's not where the money comes from that is the issue, it seems to
me, as much as the terms on which funds are accepted. When new funders
and corporations are not interested in remaining "behind the scenes," but
instead define conditions that impact programming, curatorial direction,
and staffing structures, we have a responsibility to develop parameters that
create institutional models that we want to see thrive in the future. It seems
that we really need to look again at what philanthropy was, is, and could
be, and work toward a broader understanding of what that could look like,
within the new landscape of the contemporary museum world.

ANDREA FRASER   Your question presents some of the difficulties in
addressing ethics in relation to specific institutions and fields. Are we talking
about codified guidelines or generalized criteria? If the latter, on what are
those criteria based? In fact, many codes of ethics are full of references to
non-specified criteria. Codes developed by supra-organizations like ICOM
and AAM specify that museums must have written codes of ethics and
abide by these codes, but individual articles often refer only to "accepted
professional standards," "integrity," "ethical conduct," and conformity
with local or international law. What seems to underlie these references are

the logics of professional ethics and of public (or nonprofit) sector ethics. Both are rooted in limits on the individual exploitation of collective resources, following from the fact that authority in relation to those resources, whether professional or organizational, cognitive or material, is always given by a group on behalf of a group and is never an individual possession. However, professional ethics developed largely as a legitimizing framework serving to justify professional self-regulation and establish the trust necessary for client relationships. This can be seen, for example, in the emphasis one often finds on "the appearance" of conflict of interest over the fact of conflict itself. Transparency may also serve legitimacy above all: a clear view on the workings of an organization leaves open the question of how one judges what one sees and according to what "accepted standards" of conduct and conflict. Transparency may serve only to normalize conduct, while conflict can be difficult to determine much less prosecute.

Museum codes of ethics may be more specific about the duties and responsibilities of cultural trusteeship, but public and nonprofit sector ethics often break down around the definition of the communities or groups an institution is supposed to serve. The world? The nation? The city? A specialized community? Members, "friends," or other supporters? Of course, the interests of these groups are often themselves in conflict— if they can be determined at all beyond the projections of specialists and professional representatives.

I believe that conflicts of interest and investment are fundamentally constitutive of both psychological and social structures. All social fields are sites of contestation over the valuation and distribution of resources and, in the art field, between material and symbolic resources and the material and symbolic, private and public, individual and collective consumption of those resources. The field of art developed as a privileged site for such contestation through two different and conflicting logics: the logic of collective ownership of cultural heritage, and the logic of what Bourdieu called the "interest in disinterestedness" that motivated cultural as well as economic elites to sacrifice material rewards for the symbolic benefits of prestige, renown, and legitimacy. While the former was institutionalized in the European model of public museums created on the heels of bourgeois revolutions, the latter was institutionalized with the US model of private nonprofit museums. Both of these logics have weakened significantly in the past thirty years. The public museum model, like the rest of the public sector, has seen the neoliberal assault of austerity and privatization, resulting in a push toward the US model. At the same time, however, the

principle of disinterestedness that underlay the US model has lost most of
its legitimacy, due not only to the rise of financial interests but also to the
critique of the forms of legitimacy it produced.

I doubt either professional ethics or public and nonprofit sector
ethics can ever effectively manage the conflicts that structure art institutions
and the artistic field, if that is even their aim. More often they seem to
serve the aim of universalizing specific interests and historically specific
structures. It would be more ethical, from my perspective, to recognize the
political nature of these conflicts and be explicit about our stakes in them.

RG   Could the digitization of our society also be read as a positive
change with respect to transparency within the field of art? For a long time,
the art market has felt less controlled than, say, the financial system. Could
transparency also introduce a new visibility for ethics?

PK   The art market has always been a micro prototype for other
(deregulated) markets. I am not sure if there is a need for more transparency.
Transparency—why a Picasso costs $100 million? Transparency—why a
museum only features artists represented by so and so gallery? One of the
great things of the microcosm art system is that there is a multitude of
participants, players, and institutions that to a certain extent regulate each
other. Most artists and dealers know without the Internet who is a flipper,
who is ethical, who is serious and committed...

KF   I'm not sure I fully understand your reasoning, insofar as the art
market is still such a small part of the whole explosion of digital media and
its impact on art. I immediately think more about the impact of social
media and the use of phone cameras in museums for example, and the
repercussions on artists, who increasingly cannot control the way that their
work is disseminated digitally, or how their work could be used for others'
commercial gain. On the one hand, this mass circulation of "unofficial"
images has contributed to the mass popularization of, and commentary on
contemporary art, and on the other hand it has shifted the whole relationship of meaning that an artist may want to ascribe to a work and how this
becomes untethered from the immediacy of the image.

In Moscow, at Garage, however, it is a really important aspect of
the museum—that people can "use" art for their own interpretation and
communication—because access is a key aspect of what the museum
wants to give, and if people want to photograph works (and if we have

permission from the artist or estate to do so), then they are free to circulate images as they please. As yet we have not seen the rise of "bootleg" copies of art or merchandise, which would really concern me, but I guess it is a potential issue. I think that the speed of consumption in our society now means that very few people are actually thinking like this though.

From another perspective, the whole digitization of collections to make them available online seems to me to be a very important process. I think it is really essential to be able to access art, even if you don't live in the cities that great museums or art centers exist in. While again, of course, it has repercussions on the whole issue of the "aura" of an object insofar as you may never stand in front of a work of art and feel its materiality, it at least means that it is possible to access up-to-the-minute artworks, debates, and events no matter where you are (Internet access permitting). With the cost of books, and the problems of circulation, this has to be something that is good both for education and inspiration way beyond what has been possible before.

AF   I'm generally suspicious of technological determinism and I don't believe that transparency alone can protect against conflicts of interest or root out corrupt practices—although websites enabling the reporting of corruption do seem to have some impact in political and corporate spheres. If the art field and especially the art market is largely unregulated, as you note, part of the reason is that the stakes don't seem very high to those outside of what is still a pretty small number of professionally and financially invested participants. One would hope that exposing the role of the art market in money laundering and tax evasion by oligarchs and kleptocrats might spur some regulation. Unfortunately, I don't think this will happen unless the field itself fights for it—which seems unlikely, given how much it benefits from the lack of regulation and the wealth flowing into it as a result.

RG   In most museums' ethics codes, the main paragraphs concern the collection—responsibility, conservation, etc. How could these ethics codes be extended to acquisition politics? On one hand, there's the question of artist "diversity" on key points, like gender, race, sexual equality. But this also concerns materiality. Many institutions are still focused on acquiring very traditional art forms—mostly painting and sculpture. Often complex installations and even video get excluded. At the moment, many museums have—though they do not communicate it openly—

a "moratorium" on time-based art, as they simply do not know how to
take care of it.

PK   When it comes to acquisition criteria, it might make sense to
differentiate between the United States and Continental Europe again.
In Southern California diversity is a fact of life. Does the museum exactly
represent the racial, sexual, and gender ratio? Very likely not, but there is
definitely a much higher awareness of difference in California than in
Germany or Switzerland. This is partly based on a different history but also
on the incarnation of postmodern theory. When it comes to traditional art
forms, the US museum system is mostly conservative. Their advanced
system to accept donations that are tax deductible brings in many great
works but also many domestic pieces that would be better staying in
private homes. On a sad note, the American museum's corporate pragma-
tism turns away many fantastic installation works that seem financially
threatening for storage expenses.

KF   That's an interesting question, which perhaps I can respond to with
a specific example: At Garage we do not have a collection of contemporary
art. Instead, at the heart of the institution is the largest archive of Russian
contemporary art from the 1950s on. By this I mean it is currently the only
place in the country that you can access materials that give you the story
of the unofficial, or underground, artists of the Soviet Union as well as
a growing archive of practices, groups, and movements operating in Russia
since it was reestablished in 1991. Considering most of the works during
the Soviet period were destroyed or left the country, and there was very
little written about the work at the time, without an archive there would be
few ways to establish the detailed activities of the artists involved.

AF   Well, if I, as an artist working in video, were to propose, as an
ethical principle, that museums collect more video, that would be unethical
from my perspective. There is a blatant conflict of interest there to the
extent that I would stand to benefit financially from such a policy. Codes of
ethics should preclude that sort of thing. Most museum codes of ethics
define the museum's ethical conduct above all in relationship to its mission,
which really only begs the question of how that mission itself is defined,
including the art, culture, heritage, communities and constituencies, etc.,
that museums are established to serve. Again, I would say that these are
political rather than ethical issues, above all.

RG   Andrea, in regard to selling your work, could you elaborate the key points that are important for you? Do you have a blacklist of institutions and collectors that are "taboo" for you?

AF   I started out in the 1980s rejecting commercial galleries and unique, limited-edition art commodities, embracing the model of unlimited-edition videos coming out of the 1970s. Then, in the early 1990s, I worked with galleries and made some limited-edition works. Then I mostly stopped working with galleries again in the mid-90s to pursue the "services" model, working exclusively for fees and mostly with institutions (the model also included working directly with corporate art programs and individual "clients"—this was the period when I looked into the history of professional ethics). Then I started working with galleries again around 2001. Then I mostly stopped working with galleries again around 2012, although I maintain a relationship with the gallery I had my very first show with in 1990. The logic of all this? I can claim there is an artistic logic: my turns to commercial galleries always started with site-specific works. But these vacillations were driven by a whole range of conditions, from financial need to social relationships. My aversion to the speculative art market has been pretty consistent: I just hate the idea of my work being exploited for financial profit by others. But I'm too aware of the psychological compulsions underlying that aversion to describe it only as an ethical or political position. However, in the past ten years, with the intimate relationship between the art boom and the massive concentration of wealth that has impoverished millions of people globally, that aversion developed into a revulsion that I think does extend beyond my specific interests and conflicts. This was central to my decision to leave my New York gallery in 2012. At that time I also made the decision not to sell my work to individuals but only to public and nonprofit institutions. After the gallery sold my work to Charles Saatchi without asking me (I was able to buy it back, at a loss), I tried to control sales, but realized there there was a simpler solution. I would also be reluctant to sell my work to what are sometimes referred to as private museums—ostensibly nonprofit institutions that are founded and controlled by individual collectors, often as tax write-offs for collections—and to corporations, although it hasn't come up. I felt tremendous relief when I made that decision.

RG   Philipp, did you get into conflict with ethical codes at some point?

PK   No, I haven't so far. It is interesting that American institutions are asking curators to sign a kind of ethical agreement that stipulates that you are not allowed to accept gifts from artists you are working with, among other things. I have never encountered this in Europe but of course this is also a matter of personal ethics and a different legal system.

RG   Andrea, could you tell me more about your personal ethical guidelines in regard to your work and your collaboration with galleries and institutions? How do you apply ethics in your own career?

AF   Not very consistently, I'm afraid. While this may have something to do with my own ethical failings, I think it also has to do with the conflicting forces that converge on the art field and the absence of any standards of practice for artists at all. One thing that ethical codes—such as professional ethics—do is to limit the forms and stakes of competition and to socialize the loss of foregoing conduct that may provide benefit, so such loss is not an elective individual sacrifice but a mandated collective sacrifice. In the case of professional ethics, sacrificing the unregulated exploitation of authority and competence was the price of professional autonomy and self-regulation as well as public trust. Artistic autonomy developed by a much more complex and contradictory route, according to Bourdieu, through the negation of dominant economic and political criteria, which also entailed the sacrifice of financial benefits and "temporal power," as he put it. While this may never have been more than a relative and conditional structure, a half-century of negations of negations have demonstrated how adept artists are at rationalizing any conduct and form of ambition in terms of art's legitimizing discourse of negation. There are basically no internal artistic, critical, or institutional sanctions on "unethical" artistic conduct, only occasional external sanctions in the form of political backlash or copyright infringement suits. But the contradictions and conflicts of the art field are not only institutionalized in museums with their weak codes of ethics. They are also internalized by participants in the field and perhaps artists above all. To make matters worse, the highly individualizing character of artistic positioning basically precludes explicit collective mandates, rendering an ethical sacrifice no more than an individual loss, unless it can be turned to symbolic profit through artistic positioning, which not only renders it contradictory but also weakens its potential to have a collective impact.

Is all that rationalization? Perhaps. My "personal" ethic comes down to a commitment to the reflexive examination of conflicts of interest and investment, recognizing that these are both social and psychological and most will never be resolved—certainly not by an individual decision about where to show or what to sell or to whom. But I see the reflexive awareness of conflict as the basis of ethics rather than the outcome or even the means of ethical conduct. We all occupy positions of relative privilege as well as relative privation in distributions of power and resources. Politics is what we pursue from our positions of privation in efforts to improve our individual or collective share. Ethics apply to our positions of privilege as individual or collective efforts to mitigate the destructiveness of our own power and, fundamentally, of envy and greed. While politics may engage conflicts as only external, ethics deal with conflicts that are always also internal: to an individual who loves and hates the same object (whether person, thing, or aim), or to a group that must protect itself from its own competitive structures, or to a society with the capacity to destroy itself. Psychologically, ethics are born of the anxiety of loss consequent to our own destructiveness and are only sustained to the extent that we resist externalizing conflict by locating that destructiveness outside ourselves.

RG   Philipp, as an institutional curator you worked in Europe—as director of the Museum Ludwig and curator at the Museum für Gegenwartskunst in Basel—and in the United States. With regard to ethics and following "ethical codes," where do you see the biggest differences? Which continent has in your opinion a higher level of awareness in this area?

PK   Definitely the United States, no question. I think many Europeans assume that the United States represents a hegemonic culture but we have to ask ourselves if an American who grew up in the South with Caribbean or Latin American roots is any less diverse that someone who grew up in Spain or Eastern Europe. The United States might have one language but are not culturally homogeneous at all.

RG   Kate, you were the first international curator at the Ullens Center for Contemporary Art, a private institution in Beijing's 798 Art District. Before that you chaired the Master's Program in Curatorial Practice at the California College of the Arts in San Francisco. Two very different institutional contexts in two different regions: Could you tell us about the differences between curating an exhibition in China and Western institutions?

KF   Well, the main difference is context. To curate a show in the United States or Europe is to be able to assume a certain amount of knowledge, or at least access to knowledge, on the part of the viewer. To do the same thing in China, or in Russia, is to recognize that this is not the case. In places where there have been political restrictions and Western art history is not the abiding given, the premises for a show need establishing, particularly if it is going to introduce international and local works together, historical or otherwise. Actually, in my experiences of curating outside the Western art centers, I think there is both a potential freedom and care that could be more closely considered in terms of curatorial processes in the West.

RG   How did you handle censorship in China? I heard from colleagues working in China that there's a certain protocol to follow. Could you tell us how that worked?

KF   When I worked there it changed frequently, and in the decade since I started at the Ullens Center I am sure that protocols have changed numerous times. What's important to understand though is that there isn't a protocol for censorship as such. It's a process of application that you need to make to the government, whereby you inform them of what you will be showing, why, and how. It's about how you describe what you are doing and the frame that you are presenting ideas in a lot of the time. At least that's what I learned.

RG   Philipp, in your programming as the director of an institution, i.e. as curator, how did you treat topics like equal representation: gender, nationality, Eurocentric/non-Eurocentric positions? Are these questions discussed in museum boards?

PK   Absolutely. In many institutions they now have special curators and specialists who try to cover various aspects of history and the community, although I am sure many great artists are still overlooked in any gender, nationality, or race. Frankly, I don't know how many times I have heard in board and committee meetings that we are not allowed to show another elderly white male conceptual artist. It is crucial that museums reflect our cultural, historical, and political reality but they also need to stick to the best and most timely artists working today.

RG   Kate, how did you bring your "Western" curatorial ethical guidelines together with Communist China's culture politics? Is there already an awareness for such issues?

KF   Of course! I have never considered the people I am working with to be "behind," whether in China or Russia or anywhere else outside the West. I really don't think that issues of curatorial ethics are a case of people willingly wanting to do something wrong or bad. If there is any question it is almost always a case of it being a lack of information and training in terms of international standards in museum practices. With access to information, I don't think that there is a difference in the ethics of people working in Africa, Asia, Europe, America, or anywhere else. I would say however that in the rise of popularity of curating as a profession there are a lot of ideas that curators have which really put the artist second, and this is not a geographic issue. This is one of assumed agency anywhere in the world, which I take issue with. To curate is not to invent ideas that compromise the way in which an artist's practice is shared with an audience.

RG   After China you took up the position as chief curator at the Garage Museum of Contemporary Art in Moscow. What were the differences between China and Russia?

KF   I would say they are as diverse as my experiences of working and living in Europe and then America, or working in Mexico and then Brazil, or Japan and then Poland. Every place, every institution, has its differences and similarities. What you find everywhere are like-minded people, frustrations of bureaucracy, the joy of discovery, and so many contexts through which to learn.

The conversation was realized via e-mail in June 2016.

Appendix

List of Works

Unless otherwise indicated, the works reproduced in the
image series are part of the Sammlung Migros Museum für
Gegenwartskunst.

Archives

p. 34
Graciela Carnevale, *Archivo Tucumán Arda*, 1968
Documents, photographs, posters, newspaper, archive box
Dimensions variable
Photo: Stefan Altenburger Photography, Zurich

p. 36
Babette Mangolte, *Touching II & Collage 2*, 2008–2010
Photographs/digital prints, table, single-channel video on
monitor (b/w, sound)
Dimensions variable
Photo: Stefan Altenburger Photography, Zurich

p. 38
Henrik Olesen, *Some Gay-Lesbian Artists and/or Artists
Relevant to Homo-Social Culture Born between c. 1300–1870*,
2007
4 collages (photographic paper on paper), wood,
2 taxidermized chickens, 1 taxidermized rooster
Dimensions variable
Photo: FBM Studio, Zürich

p. 40
Manfred Pernice, *Ohne Titel (Badonviller)*, 2010
Metal, found objects, ceramics, wood, paper, chip board,
acrylic paint
5 parts: 1 part 153 × 97 cm; 1 part 136 × 103 cm ;
1 part 80 × 175 cm; 2 parts 72 × 85 cm each
Photo: Stefan Altenburger Photography, Zurich

p. 42
Art & Language, *Homes from Homes II*, 2000–2001
Various materials
Dimensions variable
Photo: Stefan Altenburger Photography, Zurich

p. 44
Eva Kot'átková, *Collection of Suppressed Voices*, 2014
Steel, fired clay, prints on paper, cardboard, chalk, baskets, wood
Dimensions variable
Photo: Stefan Altenburger Photography, Zurich

p. 46
Dani Gal, *The Record Archive*, 2005–2015
246 vinyl records
Dimensions variable
Photo: Stefan Altenburger Photography, Zurich

Productions

p. 90
Robert Kusmirowski, *Swimming Pool*, 2006
Various materials
Dimensions variable
Courtesy of the artist
Photo: Stefan Altenburger Photography, Zurich

p. 92
Rachel Harrison, *Trees for the Forest*, 2007
Various materials
Dimensions variable
Photo: Stefan Altenburger Photography, Zurich

p. 94
Florian Germann, *The Poltergeist Experimental Group (PEG)
Applied Spirituality and Physical Spirit Manifestation*, 2011
Various materials
Dimensions variable
Photo: Stefan Altenburger Photography, Zurich

p. 96
Ragnar Kjartansson, *The Visitors*, 2012
Nine channel video projection, duration: 64 min.
Photo: Stefan Altenburger Photography, Zurich

p. 98
Stephen G. Rhodes, *The Law of the Unknown Neighbor:
Inferno Romanticized*, 2013
3-channel video installation (color, sound); hospital curtains,
rubber snakes, ceiling fans, aluminum lightning bolts, books,
bookshelves, assorted institutional supplies.
Dimension variable
Photo: Stefan Altenburger Photography, Zurich

p. 100
Laura Lima, *Bar Restaurant*, 2010/13
Various materials
245 × 702 × 860 cm
Photo: Stefan Altenburger Photography, Zurich

p. 102
Teresa Margolles, *La búsqueda*, 2014
Sound installation, intervention with sound frequency on glass
panels transported from the historical center of Ciudad Juárez.
The audio was recorded from the train that divides the city,
and transformed into low frequencies.
8 parts: dimensions variable
2 parts in the collection: 1 part 285 × 150.5 × 120 cm,
1 part 285 × 103.5 × 120 cm
Photo: Stefan Altenburger Photography, Zurich

Conservation

p. 162
Gustav Metzger, *Liquid Crystal Environment*, 1965–66/1998
5 slide projectors, liquid crystals, glass slides,
mechanical control
Dimensions variable
Photo: FBM Studio, Zurich

p. 164
Heidi Bucher, *Hautraum (Ricks Kinderzimmer, Lindgut
Winterthur)*, 1987
Latex, gossamer tendrils, bamboo construction, wire
Ca. 350 × 500 × 500 cm
Photo: Stefan Altenburger Photography, Zurich

p. 166
Cory Arcangel, *Super Landscape 1*, 2005
4 projections on walls, 3 monitors (reprogrammed Nintendo
Famicom cassettes [Super Mario, Bros,, F1 Race],
Nintendo Entertainment System and Hyperkin RetroN)
Dimensions variable
Photo: Stefan Altenburger Photography, Zurich

p. 168
Rirkrit Tiravanija, *Untitled 1995 (Bon voyage, Monsieur
Ackermann)*, 1995
Opel Commodore GS coach (year of construction 1969,
converted) with an on-board kitchen in the trunk, iron stand
with 3 video cameras, 3-channel video installation on
3 monitors, 75 video tapes
Dimensions variable
Photo: Stefan Altenburger Photography, Zurich

p. 170
Marvin Gaye Chetwynd, *The Fall of Man, A Puppet
Extravaganza*, 2006
Cardboard, glue, paper, plastic tubes, sand bags, spotlights
Dimensions variable
Photo: Stefan Altenburger Photography, Zurich

p. 172
Karla Black, *Principles of Admitting*, 2009
Plaster powder, powder paint, sugar paper, spray tan, chalk,
concealer stick
20 × 2770 × 1025 cm
Photo: Migros Museum für Gegenwartskunst

p. 174
Alex Bag and Patterson Beckwith, *Cash from Chaos/
Unicorns & Rainbows*, 1994–1997
11-channel video projection on 11 monitors (color, sound)
each 30 min.
Photo: Stefan Altenburger Photography, Zurich

Ethics

p. 242
Andrea Fraser, *Little Frank and His Carp*, 2001
Single-channel video on monitor (color, sound)
6 min. (Loop)
Video stills

p. 244
Mathilde ter Heijne, *Small Things End, Great Things
Endure*, 2002
Single-channel video projection on 1 rear-projection screen
(b/w, dolby surround sound)
Photo: Christian Redtenbacher

p. 246
Christoph Schlingensief, *Kaprow City*, 2006–2007
Various materials
350 × 1800 × 1500 cm
Photo: Stefan Altenburger Photography, Zurich

p. 248/250
Maria Eichhorn, *Prohibited Imports*, 2003–2008
Inkjet prints framed, wall-mounted vitrine (wood, glass),
books, magazines
14 parts: 43.5 × 69.8 × 3 cm each; 1 part 47.5 × 76.5 × 38 cm
Photo: Stefan Altenburger Photography, Zurich

p. 252
Marc Bauer, *Der Sammler (Tintin und die Baracke)*, 2012
Lithographic crayon on wall
Dimensions variable
Photo: Daniele Kaehr

p. 254
Artur Żmijewski, *The Making Of*, 2013
Single-channel video on monitor or projection (color, sound)
11:45 min.
Video stills

Authors

Sepake Angiama
Is an educator and curator and currently the head of education for documenta 14. Her interest lies within critical, discursive education practices and the "social framework." Previously she was the head of education for Manifesta 10 in St Petersburg, Russia, and curator of public programmes at Turner Contemporary, Margate. She has also devised education programs for a number of leading international institutions including Hayward Gallery, London, and Frieze. Sepake Angiama received her MA in curating contemporary art at the Royal College of Art, London.

Claire Bishop
Is a professor in the PhD Program in Art History at the Graduate Center, City University of New York. Her books include *Installation Art: A Critical History* (2005) and *Artificial Hells: Participatory Art and the Politics of Spectatorship* (2012), for which she won the 2013 Frank Jewett Mather award, and *Radical Museology, or, What's Contemporary in Museums of Contemporary Art?* (2013). She is a regular contributor to *Artforum*, and her essays and books have been translated into eighteen languages. Her current research concerns the impact of digital technology on contemporary art and performance since 1989.

Beatrice von Bismarck
Is a professor of art history and visual culture at the Academy of Visual Arts Leipzig. She was co-founder and co-director of the project space "Kunstraum der Universität Lüneburg," program director of the Leipzig Academy's gallery and co-founder of the project space "/D/O/C/K-Projektbereich." Current research areas are: the curatorial; the effects of neo-liberalism and globalization on the cultural field; postmodern concepts of the "artist." Among other titles, she is author of *Hospitality: Hosting Relations in Exhibitions*, together with Benjamin Meyer-Krahmer (2016, in press); *Timing: On the Temporal Dimension of Exhibiting*, with Rike Frank, Benjamin Meyer-Krahmer, Jörn Schafaff, and Thomas Weski (2014); *Cultures of the Curatorial*, with Jörn Schafaff and Thomas Weski (2012).

Karla Black
Is a Glasgow-based artist who is regarded as one of her generation's pioneering contemporary artists. She creates abstract sculptures using a combination of everyday materials including polyethylene, powder, cosmetics, and soaps alongside traditional media such as plaster, chalk, paint, and paper. Her work has been featured in numerous international exhibitions such as at the Irish Museum of Modern Art, Dublin (2015); Kestnergesellschaft, Hannover (2013); Gallery of Modern Art, Glasgow, and Dallas Museum of Art (both 2011); and Migros Museum für Gegenwartskunst (2007). In 2011, she was nominated for the Turner Prize and represented Scotland at the 54th Venice Biennale. Her work is in several institutional collections, including the Hammer Museum, Los Angeles; Migros Museum für Gegenwartskunst, Zurich; Scottish National Gallery of Modern Art, Edinburgh; Solomon R. Guggenheim Museum, New York; and Tate Gallery, London.

Zachary Bowman
Is currently the manager of education and visitor experience at the Samuel Dorsky Museum of Art on the SUNY New Paltz campus. Previously, he worked at MoMA PS1 for five years, where he was the senior manager of visitor engagement and school programs. Prior to his work at MoMA PS1, Zachary was employed by the Solomon R. Guggenheim Museum as an admissions supervisor and museum educator.

Büro trafo.K
Is an office based in Vienna working in the fields of art, education, and critical knowledge production. Since 1999, Büro trafo.K has realized projects and initiated processes that question things perceived as simply given and that disrupt existing relations, more often than not using unexpected strategies. Their primary approaches consist in reflecting and intervening in the structures of institutions and media and in creating publics for alternative histories and images. Members are Renate Höllwart, Elke Smodics, Nora Sternfeld, and Ines Garnitschnig.

Martha Buskirk
Is a professor of art history and criticism at Montserrat College
of Art in Beverly, Massachusetts, since 1994. Her most recent
book, *Creative Enterprise: Contemporary Art between Museum
and Marketplace* (2012) investigates the institutional and
economic interests that shape both the reception of art and its
creation. She is author of *The Contingent Object of Contemporary
Art* (2003), and published numerous catalogue essays and articles
that have appeared in *Artforum, October, Art in America,*
and other venues.

Bruna Casagrande
Studied history at the University of Bern and restoration at the
Bern University of the Arts with specialization in conservation
of modern materials and media, where she developed a new
documentation method for performance art. After positions as
conservator at the Museum für Kommunikation, the Berner
Design Stiftung, and the Swiss Dance Archive, she currently
works as assistant at the Bern University of the Arts and focuses
on developing and establishing new approaches of documentation in research and teaching.

Beatriz Colomina
Is a professor of architecture and founding director of the Program
in Media and Modernity at Princeton University. She has written
extensively on questions of architecture, art, sexuality, and media.
Her books include *Manifesto Architecture: The Ghost of Mies*
(2014), *Clip/Stamp/Fold: The Radical Architecture of Little
Magazines 196X-197X* (2010), *Domesticity at War* (2007),
Privacy and Publicity: Modern Architecture as Mass Media (1994),
and *Sexuality and Space* (1992).

Yilmaz Dziewior
Studied art history and archeology in Bonn and London and
wrote his PhD dissertation on the subject of Mies van der Rohe.
He took leadership of Cologne's Museum Ludwig in 2015,
after serving as director of the Kunsthaus Bregenz since 2009.
From 2001 to 2008, he headed the Kunstverein Hamburg and,
at the same time, held a chair in art theory at the Hamburger
Hochschule der Bildenden Künste. He is a regular contributor
to publications and art magazines such as *Artforum, Camera
Austria,* and *Texte zur Kunst.*

Kate Fowle
Is the chief curator for the Garage Museum of Contemporary
Art in Moscow and director-at-large at Independent Curators
International (ICI) in New York, where she was executive
director from 2009 to 2013. Prior to this she was the inaugural
international curator at the Ullens Center for Contemporary
Art in Beijing. From 2002 to 2007, Fowle chaired the Master's
Program in Curatorial Practice at California College of the Arts
in San Francisco, which she co-founded in 2001. Before moving
to the United States, she was co-director of Smith + Fowle in
London (1996–2001) and curator at the Towner Art Gallery in
Eastbourne (1993–1996).

Andrea Fraser
Is an artist known mainly for her work in the areas of performance
and institutional critique. Fraser is based in Los Angeles and is
a professor of new genres in the Art Department at the University
of California, Los Angeles.

Bettina Funcke
Is a writer and editor based in New York City, where she
teaches in the Critical Theory & the Arts Masters Program at
the School of Visual Arts. From 2009 to 2012, Funcke was head
of publications for dOCUMENTA (13). She is author of *Pop
or Populus: Art between High and Low* (2009) and her writings
on contemporary art have been widely published, both in
monographic artist catalogues and in magazines like *Mousse,
Afterall, Bookforum, Parkett, Public Speculations,* and *Texte
zur Kunst.* She also hosts the *Artists Space Dialogue* program,
a series of public conversations with artists and visual thinkers.

Raphael Gygax
Studied art history, film, and drama studies at the universities
of Bern and Zurich, and holds a PhD in art history on the subject
of the "extra body" in contemporary art. He is a curator at the
Migros Museum für Gegenwartskunst in Zurich, where he has
curated numerous exhibitions including *Ian Cheng* (2016),
Xanti Schawinsky (2015), *Teresa Margolles* (2014), *Christoph
Schlingensief* (2007), *Marvin Gaye Chetwynd* (2007), and
Cory Arcangel (2005). He assumes frequent teaching positions
at the University of the Arts in Zurich and other institutions of
higher learning. He writes regularly for art magazines and
publications. From 2013 to 2015, he served as curatorial advisor
for the section Focus / Frame at Frieze art fair, London/New York,
and in 2015, he was appointed as Frieze projects curator
in London.

Francesca von Habsburg
Is an art collector. In 2002 she founded Thyssen-Bornemisza Art
Contemporary (TBA21) in Vienna and hosts one of the biggest
private collections for contemporary art in Europe. She was
educated at Le Rosey in Switzerland and subsequently attended
the art and design school Central Saint Martins in London.

Philipp Kaiser
Is currently an independent curator based in Los Angeles working
on various exhibition projects, amongst others at the newly
opened Broad and at the Getty. He was curator for modern and
contemporary art at the Museum für Gegenwartskunst in Basel
from 2001 to 2007, when he joined the Museum of Contemporary
Art Los Angeles as senior curator. In 2011, he was named
director of the Museum Ludwig, a position he held from fall
2012 to March 2014. In 2017, he will curate the Swiss pavilion
at the Venice Biennale.

Christian Kravagna
Is a professor of postcolonial studies at the Academy of Fine Arts
Vienna. He is the editor of the books *Privileg Blick: Kritik der
visuellen Kultur* (1997); *Agenda: Perspektiven kritischer Kunst*
(2000); *The Museum as Arena: Artists on Institutional Critique*
(2001), and co-editor of *Transcultural Modernisms* (2013).
He curated the exhibitions *Ghosts of the Civil Dead* (tranzit/sk
Bratislava, 2016); *Living Across: Spaces of Migration* (Academy
of Fine Arts Vienna, 2010); *Planetary Consciousness* (Kunstraum
of Leuphana University Luneburg, 2008), and *Routes: Imaging
Travel and Migration* (Grazer Kunstverein, 2002). From 2005
to 2014, he was artistic director (with Hedwig Saxenhuber)
of Kunstraum Lakeside in Klagenfurt.

Oliver Marchart
Is a professor of political theory at the University of Vienna.
His research has focused on theory of society, political theory,
sociology of art and culture, political sociology, and social
movement research. He is author of *Die politische Differenz:
Zum Denken des Politischen bei Nancy, Lefort, Badiou,
Laclau und Agamben* (2010) and *Hegemonie im Kunstfeld:
Die documenta-Ausstellungen dX, D11, d12 und die
Politik der Biennalisierung* (2008).

Heike Munder
Studied cultural sciences at the Leuphana University of Lüneburg.
She has been the director of the Migros Museum für
Gegenwartskunst in Zurich since 2001. She co-founded the Halle
für Kunst Lüneburg e.V., which she co-directed from 1995 to
2001. Previously curated exhibitions include *Resistance Performed*
(2015), *Dorothy Iannone* (2014), *Geoffrey Farmer* (2013),
Ragnar Kjartansson (2012), *Tatiana Trouvé* (2009), *Tadeusz
Kantor* (2008), *Rachel Harrison* (2007), *It's Time for Action—
There's No Option* (2006), *Marc Camille Chaimowicz* (2006),
Yoko Ono (2005), and *Mark Leckey* (2003). She teaches
regularly, including at the University of Lüneburg, Goldsmiths
College, London, the University of Bern, the Zurich University of
the Arts, and the Jan van Eyck Academy, Maastricht. Since 1995,
she has written extensively on art in catalogues and art
magazines. In 2012, she was on the jury of the Turner Prize.

Alena Nawrotzki
Studied cultural sciences at the Leuphana University of Lüneburg
and at the Università degli Studi di Milano with a special focus
on the art and bourgeoisie and literature of the twentieth and
twenty-first centuries. Since 2012 she has been working as a
scientific researcher for the public programs at Migros Museum
für Gegenwartskunst in Zurich. Prior to that, she worked at Kunstverein Hamburg and was co-founder of several project spaces.

Lars Nittve
Is a Swedish-born writer, curator, and museum director. For almost
thirty years has he been leading museums in Europe and beyond.
Among them are the Moderna Museet, Stockholm, the Louisiana
Museum of Modern Art, Humlebaek, Tate Modern, London,
and most recently M+ in Hong Kong, scheduled to open in 2019.
As of the spring of 2016, he is an independent advisor and writer,
based in Sweden.

Donald Preziosi
Is an emeritus professor of art history and critical theory at UCLA
and (from 2015) a distinguished research professor. He is the
author, editor, and co-editor of fourteen books on art and architectural history, theory, and criticism, archaeology, and the
interdependence of philosophy, theology, politics, museology, and
semiology, plus numerous published essays and lectures. Among
his recent books are *Art, Religion, Amnesia: The Enchantments
of Credulity* (2014); *Art Is Not What You Think It Is*, with
Claire Farago (2012); and *The Art of Art History* (2009), now
widely used as an introduction to that field. He earned his PhD
from Harvard University and has held professorships at Yale,
MIT, and Oxford.

Sophia Prinz
Is a postdoctoral research fellow at the Department of
Comparative Cultural Sociology at the European University
Viadrina, Frankfurt an der Oder, and head of research at the
Johann Jacobs Museum, Zurich. Her research focuses on practice
theory, poststructuralism, visual and material culture studies,
aesthetics, and transculturality. She is the author of *Die Praxis
des Sehens. Über das Zusammenspiel von Körpern, Artefakten
und visueller Ordnung* (2014).

Peter J. Schneemann
Is a professor of art history and has been chair of Contemporary
Art at the Institute of Art History, University of Bern, since
2001. For twelve years he served as administrative secretary and
treasurer of the Comité International d'Histoire de l'Art (CIHA).
His research interests include discourse analysis, paradigms of
art appreciation, art education, archival processes, and display.
His most recent publication is *Paradigmen der Kunstbetrachtung:
Aktuelle Positionen der Rezeptionsästhetik und Museums-
pädagogik* (2015).

Nadia Schneider Willen
Is collection curator at Migros Museum für Gegenwartskunst
in Zurich since 2015. Prior to this she was a freelance curator
and curator for modern and contemporary art at the Musée d'art
et d'histoire in Geneva (2008–2010). From 2001 to 2007, she
was the director of Kunsthaus Glarus, where she curated numerous
exhibitions by contemporary Swiss and international artists.
In 2005, she curated a section of the Prague Biennale at the
National Gallery. In the 1990s, she initiated the project space
Kombirama together with a group of artists, as well as co-curating
the space Kleines Helmhaus in Zurich. She has been president
of the Swiss Federal Art Commission since 2012.

Bernadett Settele
Is a Zurich-based art mediator and art theorist. She is a researcher
at the Hochschule Luzern—Design & Kunst in Lucerne, with
a focus on politically engaged art since the 1960s. Her work
theoreticizes the public(s) that are created in the context of art
and art education, positing these as collective aesthetic situations.

Wolfgang Ullrich
Studied philosophy, art history, and German literature at
Ludwig-Maximilians-University Munich. His MA (1991) focused
on Richard Rorty, while his PhD dissertation (1994) analyzed the
"Ereignis-Denken" of Martin Heidegger. From 1997 to 2003, he
was an assistant professor at the Akademie der bildenden Künste
in Munich. From 2006 to 2015, he was a professor of art science
and media theory at the University of Arts and Design Karlsruhe.
Since 2015, he has been based in Leipzig where he works as an
independent art theorist and author. In his publications he deals
with the history and critique of the concept of art, art sociology,
and consumer theory.

Judith Welter
Studied art history, Spanish literature, and religion at the
University of Bern, earning her PhD in art history on the subject
of the effect, function, and presentation of rumors and anecdotes
in contemporary art. From 2007 to 2015, she was collection
curator of the Migros Museum für Gegenwartskunst. In 2015,
she became the director of Kunsthaus Glarus. Additionally,
she is co-editor of the magazine for art criticism *Brand-New-Life*.

Beat Wyss
Is a professor of art research and media theory at the University
of Arts and Design Karlsruhe. He has held visiting professorships
at Cornell University in the US and Aarhus Universitet, Denmark.
In 2001, he won the Lucerne city art award. He is a member of
the Heidelberg Akademie der Wissenschaften and the Association
Internationale des Critiques d'Art (AICA). Some of his recent
publications are *Renaissance als Kulturtechnik* (2013); *Bilder
von der Globalisierung* (2010); and *Hegel's Art History and the
Critique of Modernity* (1999/2008).

Artur Żmijewski
Is an artist who lives and works in Warsaw. He studied sculpture
under Grzegorz Kowalski at the Warsaw Academy of Fine Arts
from 1990 to 1995. He frequently examines mechanisms of
power and oppression within the existing social order—as well
as social conflicts bordering on violence—while exposing the
instinctive human inclination toward evil. His work has been
displayed in numerous international solo and group exhibitions.
In 2005, he represented Poland at the 51st Venice Biennale.
Additionally, Żmijewski curated the 7th Berlin Biennale in 2012.

Colophon

This anthology is published by the Migros Museum für Gegenwartskunst, Zurich, on the occasion of its twentieth anniversary, in collaboration with the Institute of Art History, University of Bern, and the Academy of Visual Arts Leipzig.

Editors
Beatrice von Bismarck, Heike Munder, Peter J. Schneemann

Associate Editors
Raphael Gygax, Judith Welter

Editorial Coordination
Barbara Biedermann, Raphael Gygax

Translation
Gerrit Jackson

Copyediting
Anne O'Connor

Graphic Design
Nicolas Eigenheer, Nicolas Leuba

Typeface
Sabon LT

Cover
Marc Camille Chaimowicz
Celebration? Realife Revisited, 1972–2000
Mixed media
Dimensions variable
Photo: Stefan Altenburger Photography, Zurich

Photocredits
p. 36: Copyright © 2008–2010 Babette Mangolte. All Rights of Reproduction Reserved; p. 90: Courtesy of the Migros Museum für Gegenwartskunst and the artist; p. 164: © The Estate of Heidi Bucher; p. 246: © Nachlass Christoph Schlingensief; p. 248, 250: © 2016, Pro Litteris, Zurich

Color Separation and Print
Musumeci S.p.A., Quart (Aosta)

Published by

JRP|Ringier
Limmatstrasse 270
CH-8005 Zurich
T +41 (0) 43 311 27 50
F +41 (0) 43 311 27 51
E info@jrp-ringier.com
www.jrp-ringier.com

ISBN 978-3-03764-367-9

JRP|Ringier books are available internationally at selected bookstores and from the following distribution partners:

Switzerland
AVA Verlagsauslieferung AG
Centralweg 16
CH–8910 Affoltern a.A.
verlagsservice@ava.ch
www.ava.ch

France
Les presses du réel
35 rue Colson
F–21000 Dijon
info@lespressesdureel.com
www.lespressesdureel.com

Germany and Austria
Vice Versa Distribution GmbH
Immanuelkirchstrasse 12
D–10405 Berlin
info@vice-versa-distribution.com
www.vice-versa-distribution.com

UK and other European countries
Cornerhouse Publications
HOME, 2 Tony Wilson Place
UK–Manchester M15 4FN
publications@cornerhouse.org
www.cornerhousepublications.org

USA, Canada, Asia, and Australia
ARTBOOK|D.A.P.
155 Sixth Avenue, 2nd Floor
USA–New York, NY 10013
orders@dapinc.com
www.artbook.com

For a list of our partner bookshops or for any general questions, please contact JRP|Ringier directly at info@jrp-ringier.com, or visit our homepage www.jrp-ringier.com for further information about our program.

**Migros Museum
für Gegenwartskunst**

Director
Heike Munder

Curator
Raphael Gygax

Head of Administration
Catherine Reymond

Collection Curator
Nadia Schneider Willen

Registrar/Scientific Researcher, Collection
Anna-Lena Gugger

Registrar, Exhibitions/Scientific
Researcher, Collection
Cornelia Huth

Head of Press and Public Relations
René Müller

Administration Assistant
Katja Jaisli

Scientific Researcher, Public Programs
Alena Nawrotzki

Art Educator
Cynthia Gavranic

Interns
Barbara Biedermann, Angela Walti

Head of Technical Services, Exhibitions
Monika Schori

Technical Services, Exhibitions & Events
Markus Bösch

Technical Services, Collection
Muriel Gutherz, Barbara Lenherr

Coordinator Media Archive
Gabi Deutsch

Coordinator Visitor Services
Robin Bhattacharya

Visitor Services
Franziska Bigger, Yuko Edelmann, Niria
Frey, Simone Fröbel, Michèle Graf, Max
Heinrich, Daniel Keller, Céline Matter,
Nico Meyer, Christa Michel

Technical Services
Christian Eberhard, Cristina Golland,
Steffen Kuhn, Konstantinos Manolakis,
Monika Stalder, Oli Wahmann, Fabienne
Bodmer, Nicolas Duc, Wanda Nay,
Magdalena Bajani, Emanuel Masera,
Roman Gysin, Nina Weber

Migros Museum für Gegenwartskunst
Limmatstrasse 270
P.O. Box 1766
8031 Zurich
Switzerland
T +41 (0) 44 277 20 50
F +41 (0) 44 277 62 86
info@migrosmuseum.ch
www.migrosmuseum.ch

**MIGROSMUSEUM
für Gegenwartskunst**

An institution of the Migros Culture
Percentage. migros-kulturprozent.ch